Programmed Learning Aid for
PRINCIPLES OF MANAGEMENT

Programmed Learning Aid for

PRINCIPLES OF MANAGEMENT

GEORGE R. TERRY
Ball State University

Coordinating Editor
ROGER H. HERMANSON
Georgia State University

Third Edition

LEARNING SYSTEMS COMPANY

A division of
RICHARD D. IRWIN, INC.
Homewood, Illinois 60430

Also available through
IRWIN-DORSEY LIMITED   Georgetown, Ontario   L7G 4B3

© LEARNING SYSTEMS COMPANY, 1970, 1974, and 1978

All rights reserved. No part of this publication may be reproduced, stored in a retrieval system, or transmitted, in any form or by any means, electronic, mechanical, photocopying, recording, or otherwise, without the prior written permission of the publisher.

ISBN 0-256-02134-1

Printed in the United States of America

3 4 5 6 7 8 9 0 K 5 4 3 2 1 0

FOREWORD

Each of the books constituting the Programmed Learning Aid Series is in programmed learning format to provide the reader with a quick, efficient, and effective means of grasping the essential subject matter.

The specific benefits of the programmed method of presentation are as follows:

1. It keeps the reader *active* in the learning process and increases comprehension level.
2. Incorrect responses are *corrected immediately*.
3. Correct responses are *reinforced immediately*.
4. The method is *flexible*. Those who need more "tutoring" receive it, because they are encouraged to reread frames in which they have missed any of the questions asked.
5. The method makes learning seem like a game.

The method of programming used in this PLAID on principles of management and in most of the other PLAIDs is unique and simple to use. Begin by reading Frame 1[1] in Chapter 1. At the end of that frame answer the True-False questions given. To determine the correctness of your responses, merely turn the page and examine the answers given in Answer frame 1[1]. You are told *why* each statement is true or false. Performance on the questions given is used as a measure of your understanding of all the materials in Frame 1[1]. If any of the questions are missed, reread Frame 1[1] before continuing on to Frame 2[1]. This same procedure should be used throughout the book. Specific instructions are given throughout as to where to turn next to continue working the program.

You may desire to go through the PLAID a second time leaving out the programmed questions and answers, or to test your understanding by going through it a second time, answering all of the questions once again and rereading only those frames in which comprehension is unsatisfactory.

PLAIDs are continuously updated in new printings to provide readers with the latest subject content in the field.

The author of this PLAID is the author of leading texts on management and supervision. He has taught management for many years and is a nationally known business consultant.

Roger H. Hermanson
Coordinating Editor and Programmer

PREFACE

This edition of the *Programmed Learning Aid for Principles of Management* features an up-to-date, concise, and readable presentation of management fundamentals. It is designed to help you read and review the subject of management quickly and conveniently. The programmed learning format aids you in covering all the essentials of management in a manner encouraging self-study and self-testing.

The wide and enthusiastic acceptance given previous editions of this book, extending into the tens of thousands of readers, attest to its effectiveness in presenting management material that is easy-to-read, comprehensive, and informative.

Most people require about 25 minutes to work through a chapter. For further review, you may work the three examinations included near the back of this book. Each examination covers a different one third of the contents. The examination answers are included so that you can rate yourself on your understanding of the material. Each examination requires about 50 minutes to complete. Additional help can be obtained by reviewing the terms included in the Glossary-Index.

This PLAID covering the principles of management is designed to meet the special needs of the student entering a master's degree program, the participant in an executive development program, or the individual in business, government, or other employment aspiring to, or presently in, managerial work.

This volume is intended as a supplement to a text, not as a substitute for one. It can be used with any of the standard basic texts in the management area. The arrangement of the carefully selected topics follows a logical pattern. Although management books present the subject matter in different ways, the sequence followed here can be traced in most of the basic management texts by referring to the "Topical Outline of Course Content," which provides an alphabetical listing of major topics covered.

GEORGE R. TERRY

TOPICAL OUTLINE OF COURSE CONTENT

Appraising in management 115
Approaches to management study 1
Authority 69
Budgetary control 140
Communicating 103
Controlling 119
Controls, key 124
Controls, overall 131
Decision making 19
Departmentation and organizing 64
Developing managers 115
Directing 97
Environment and management 11
Forecasts and planning 35
Functions of management 5
Implementing plans 45
Leading 108
Management approaches 1
Management in foreign countries 145
Management functions 5
Management in the future 151
Motivating in management 91
Objectives 15
Organizing concepts 51
Organizing dynamics 85
Organization staffing 78
PERT 140
Planning, basic 30
Planning and premises 35
Plans, implementation of 45
Plans, types of 40
Quantitative methods 25
Social considerations of organizing 58
Staffing the organization 78
Values and management 11

CONTENTS

1. Approaches to management study 1
2. Managerial functions 5
3. Contemporary managerial values and environment 11
4. Objectives 15
5. Decision making in management 19
6. Quantitative methods in managerial decision making 25
7. The work of planning 30
8. Forecasts, premises, strategies, and planning 35
9. Types of plans 40
10. Putting plans into action 45
11. Organization concepts 51
12. Organization: Personal and social considerations 58
13. Departmentation 64
14. Authority 69
15. Staffing the organization 78
16. Organization dynamics 85
17. Motivation and modern managers 91
18. Directing 97
19. Communicating 103
20. Leadership in management 108
21. Appraising and developing managers 115
22. Controlling 119
23. Key controls of management 124
24. Overall controls 131
25. Budgetary and PERT control 140
26. Management in foreign countries 145
27. Management in the future 151

Examination 1: Chapters 1–10 157
Examination 2: Chapters 11–19 161
Examination 3: Chapters 20–27 165
Answers to examinations 169
Glossary-index of management terms 173

chapter 1

APPROACHES TO MANAGEMENT STUDY

Frame 1[1]

Management deals with goal achievement by individuals contributing their best efforts in accordance with predetermined actions. This implies knowing what they should do, determining how they should do it, understanding how to get them to do it, and measuring the effectiveness of their efforts. Furthermore, an environment must be established and maintained in which these individuals working together can perform well, a condition requiring a responsiveness of economical, psychological, social, political, and technical contributions and restraints.

Management is an activity, performing it is managing, and one who performs it is a manager. An individual who becomes a manager takes on new duties that are entirely managerial in character. Important among these is the relinquishment of a tendency to perform all things personally. The operating work tasks are accomplished through the efforts of the group members. Essentially, a manager's task is to utilize the group's efforts effectively. However, seldom do managers spend all their time managing; they normally perform some nonmanagement work.

The association of *management with a group* is the viewpoint adopted here. True, a person manages his or her personal affairs, but the important reference in management is to a group. Cooperative endeavor is the word of today. Vast material resources and technical skill are of small avail unless the managerial capacity to use these resources and skills through organized groups is encouraged and developed. Further, because of a person's individual limitations, it has been necessary to look to the group to achieve most personal goals.

Management is purposeful and intangible. It attempts to achieve specific results, commonly expressed in terms of objectives. The efforts of the group contribute to these specific accomplishments. Management may be described as intangible, since it cannot be seen, but is evidenced only by the results it brings about—adequate work output, human satisfactions, and better products and services.

Management is both a science and an art. There is an organized body of knowledge about management—a science—which explains management by reference to general truths. The causal relationships between management variables have been ascertained and are expressed as generalizations, but every generalization may be subjected to further research and modified with new knowledge. All science is dynamic, that of some fields more so than others. If this were not so, we would have no more accumulated knowledge today than did the early Egyptians or the citizens of the Roman Empire.

Art is the know-how to accomplish a desired result. It is the skill that comes with experience, observation, and study, and the ability to apply the management knowledge so acquired. The art of management requires creativity, based on and conditioned by an understanding of the science of management. Thus, the science and the art of management are complementary. As one improves, so should the other; a balance between the two is needed.

Indicate whether each of the following statements is true or false by writing "T" or "F" in the space provided.
_____ 1. Management is concerned solely with the establishment of goals.
_____ 2. Management is primarily concerned with one's handling of one's personal affairs.
_____ 3. Management is purposeful in the sense that it deals with the accomplishment of specific ends.
_____ 4. Management is an art rather than a science.
Now turn to Answer Frame 1[1], page 4, to check your responses.

Frame 2[1]

Management is as old as civilization. In ancient Greece and the Roman Empire, abundant evidence of management is found in the historical records of the government, the army, and the courts. By the first half of the nineteenth century, management had already made progress in keeping with the improving means of production. Incentives, cost determination, and work measurement were coming into use. Throughout the nineteenth and on into the twentieth century, more students, industrialists, and public officials became interested in management. Attention was given to organization, the effective use of time, and budgetary controls. Significant efforts were directed toward the development of a management theory and the building of a framework for future management thought.

About 1930, the idea that people were the most important consideration in management gained favor and caused many to turn to the study of human behavior. Several decades later, the computer became available, bringing with it increased emphasis on quantitative methods of analysis in management. The application of mathematics and statistics represented a new approach to management. More recently, other approaches, such as concentration on decision making and on systems, have entered the mainstream of management thought.

From these various developments, several major approaches to management have emerged. Frequently referred to as management theories or "schools of management thought," some have pioneered in brand-new areas, whereas others are modifications or a fusion of former concepts. A subject as vital as management, involving issues affecting people, values, wants, and technology will attract students and practitioners in different areas, such as economics, psychology, sociology, political science, and mathematics.

Indicate whether each of the following statements is true or false by writing "T" or "F" in the space provided.
_____ 1. Management was first utilized at the time of the Industrial Revolution.
_____ 2. Management theory has recognized the importance of the study of human behavior.
_____ 3. The study of management is free of quantitative analysis.
_____ 4. Management is an area of study only appealing to students of business.
Check your responses in Answer Frame 2[1], page 4.

Frame 3[1]

Acquaintance with each major approach is helpful in studying management and in assessing its development and usefulness. There are five main approaches:

1. The process or operational approach. Management is analyzed from the viewpoint of *what a manager does to qualify as a manager.* These activities or *fundamental functions of management make up a process called the management process,* which is operational and which also establishes a conceptual framework for the study of management. The process approach is widely used because it aids tremendously in developing management thought and helps identify management in readily understood terms. Any action for study by a manager can be classified in keeping with this basic process. Answers to the following questions can be found: (a) What is the purpose and nature of the activity? (b) What explains the structure and the operations of the activity? Followers of this approach regard *management as a universal process,* regardless of the type or level of enterprise; but they also recognize that both the internal and the external environments in which the management process is applied differ widely among enterprises and levels.

2. The human behavior approach. The core of this approach is *the behavior of the human being and of human beings.* It brings to management the methods and concepts of relevant social sciences, especially psychology and anthropology, from personality dynamics of individuals to the relation of cultures. *Emphasis is given inter- and intrapersonal relationships and their effect on management.* The individual is viewed as a sociopsychological being. *The art of management is stressed and the entire realm of human relations is seen in management terms.* Some consider the manager as the leader and treat all activities that are led as managerial situations. The influence of environment and its motivating effect on human behavior are given thorough study. Since there can be no question that managing involves human behavior and the interaction of human beings, the objectives of this school are without doubt appropriate, and its contributions beneficial to management study.

3. The social system approach. Advocates of this approach *look upon management as a social system,* or, in other words, as *a system of cultural interrelationships.* It is sociologically oriented, deals with various social groups and their cultural relationships, and attempts to integrate these groups into a social system. *An enterprise is considered a social organism,* subject to all the conflicts and interactions of its members. This approach takes into account the emergence, importance, and functioning of *"informal organization," which is seen as coming into being primarily as a result of social forces.* Also taken into account are ethical considerations, the influence of the community, trade unions, and government on the management of an enterprise. The net result of the social system approach is to bring the power of sociological understanding to management study and theory.

4. The systems approach. Systems are the focal parts around which this approach is developed. Its concepts, theory, and practice resemble those of the systems approach, so helpful in the physical sciences. *A system can be viewed as an aggregation or assemblage of two or more components that are in some definite relationship to each other, and between which an action in one brings about a reaction in another.* In other words, a system is an interrelated set of interacting components. *Systems are basic to most activities.* What is thought of as an activity may in reality be the result of many other subactivities, and these, in turn, of sub-subactivities. Thinking in terms of systems simplifies and unifies the conception of the many activities with which a manager works. A management plan, for example, can be thought of as a system with components of people, money, machines, materials, information, and authority. The adherent of the systems approach aims for the development of a systematic framework for describing relationships of activities. The systems approach provides a means to see clearly critical variables, constraints, and interactions. It has obvious importance.

5. The quantitative approach. Focus here is on the use of mathematical models and processes, relationships, and measurable data. This ap-

Answer frame 1[1]

1. False. Management is concerned with the *achievement* of goals. This includes the establishment of goals, determining how they should be achieved, understanding how to motivate individuals to achieve them, and determining the effectiveness of efforts made in achieving them.
2. False. The association of management with a *group* is the viewpoint adopted here A manager's task is to utilize the group's efforts effectively.
3. True. Management *is* purposeful because it is concerned with the achievement of specific objectives.
4. False. Management is *both* an art *and* a science.

An effort has been made to test the most important concepts in the questions concerning each frame, but this is not necessarily accomplished in each case. Therefore, you should use your performance on the questions answered as an indication of your comprehension of all the material in a particular frame. If you missed more than one of the above questions, you are advised to return to Frame 1[1] and reread the material. This same procedure should be used throughout this programmed learning aid.

When you are satisfied with your comprehension of Frame 1[1], turn to Frame 2[1], page 2, and continue reading.

Answer frame 2[1]

1. False. Evidence of the existence of management is found much earlier than that. In fact, management is as old as civilization.
2. True. The study of human behavior has been incorporated into the study of management. The idea that people were the most important consideration in management gained favor around 1930.
3. False. In recent years quantitative techniques have been employed in the study and implementation of management theory.
4. False. Management is a pervasive activity and attracts individuals from many disciplines.

Turn to page 3, and continue by reading Frame 3[1].

Frame 3[1] continued

proach has demonstrated its great managerial usefulness. *Management is viewed as a logical entity, which expressed and related in quantitative terms and processed by an accepted methodology, results in answers to carefully defined managerial problems.* This approach forces the user to precisely define the objectives, problems, and relationships in measurable data. Furthermore, the recognition of definite constraints and use of logical processing *supplies the manager with a powerful means or tool* for solving certain complex management problems. Primarily concerned with *decision making*, the approach is most effective when applied to physical attributes such as inventory, transportation distances, and product mixes.

Indicate whether each of the following statements is true or false by writing "T" or "F" in the space provided.

_____ 1. The *process* or *operational* approach to management stresses the similarities of each management situation.

_____ 2. The *social system* approach to management considers only the formal organization to be the social system.

_____ 3. The *systems* approach to management centers its attention on the action-reaction relationship between various components of the enterprise.

_____ 4. The *quantitative* approach to management is best applied to problems of human behavior.

Refer to Answer Frame 3[1], page 6, to check your responses.

chapter 2

MANAGERIAL FUNCTIONS

Frame 1[2]

As defined in the previous chapter, the process or operational approach identifies management by what a manager does to qualify as a manager. In turn, what the manager does is distinct; it is an activity made up of several fundamental functions that constitute a unique process —the management process. These fundamental functions are the subject of this chapter.

Belief in the management process is widespread and popular. It suffers, however, from *disagreement among management scholars and practitioners as to what the fundamental functions constituting the management process are.* To a degree, the problem is one of semantics and of failure to use terms with precision. Yet, there are real differences among scholars as to what functions should be emphasized in the management process.

Figure 1 illustrates the five most common combinations of fundamental functions leading to goal achievement. Reading from top to bottom, combination A consists of planning, organizing, actuating, and controlling; B is made up of planning, organizing, motivating, and controlling; C of planning, organizing, staffing, directing, and controlling; D of planning, organizing, staffing, directing, controlling, innovating, and representing; and E of planning, organizing, motivating, controlling, and coordinating. It is interesting to observe that in each case three functions are common: (*a*) planning, (*b*) organizing, and (*c*) controlling. Differences appear regarding the remaining function or functions. For example, should it be actuating or motivating, or should neither of these be included and the functions of staffing and directing inserted instead? Some say that staffing is really a part of organizing, and directing is akin to actuating or motivating; and, as the figure shows, others believe innovating, representing, and coordinating are fundamental functions.

Planning is the determination of what work must be done by the group to accomplish stated goals. It includes decision making, because it in-

Answer frame 3[1]

1. True. The *process* or *operational* approach to management does stress the *similarities* of management in varying situations. Management is viewed as a universal process.
2. False. Under the *social system* approach, the *informal organization* also is viewed as an important part of the social system.
3. True. The *systems* approach tries to identify and understand the interrelationships and interactions between components of the entity.
4. False. The *quantitative* approach is most effective when applied to physical attributes, such as inventories, transportation distances, and product mixes.

You have now completed Chapter 1. Begin Chapter 2 on page 5.

Frame 1[2] continued

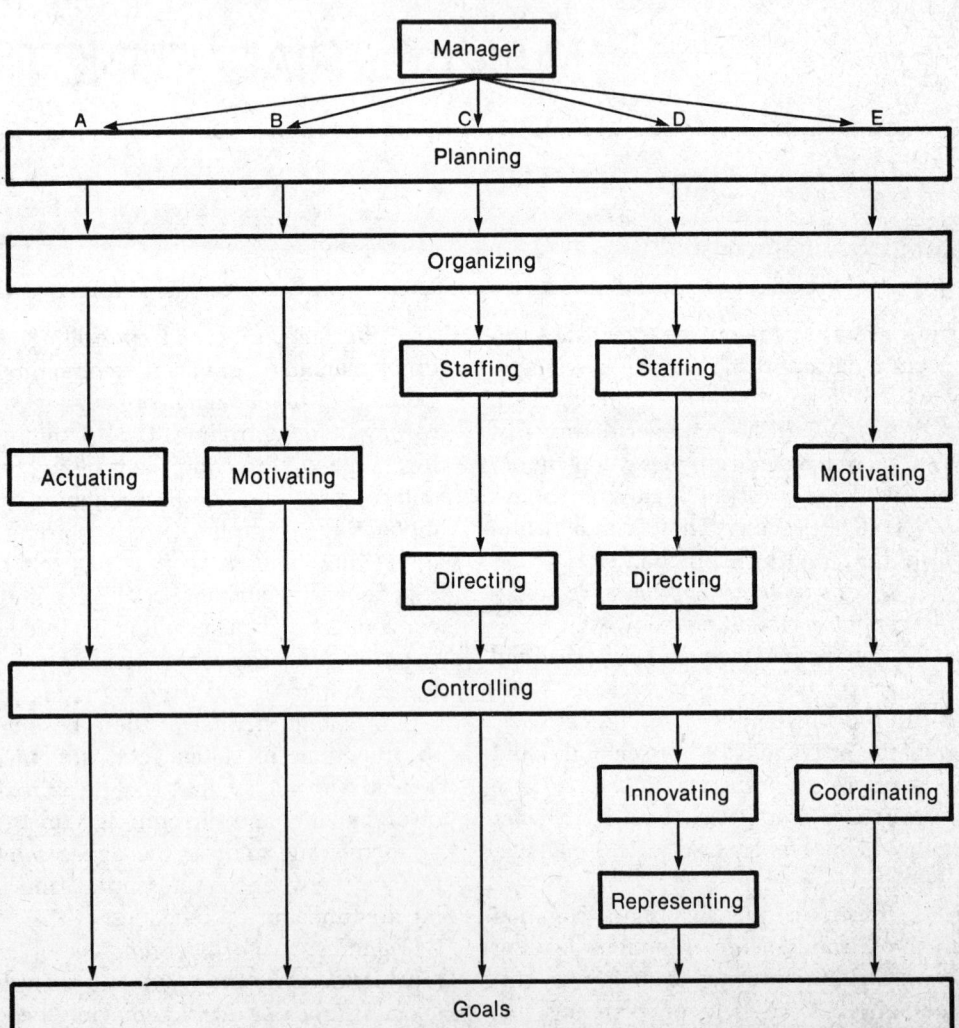

FIGURE 1

Fundamental Functions Making Up Management Process
(five combinations, A, B, C, D, E, are shown)

volves selecting among alternatives. Planning necessitates ability to visualize and purposefully look ahead to formulate *an integrated pattern of future actions.*

Organizing involves: (a) *dividing into groups the necessary component activities required to achieve the goals,* (b) *assigning such groupings to a manager,* and (c) *establishing authority relationships among the groupings or organization units.* Inasmuch as organizing is intimately concerned with people, many include the finding of members and their assignment to organization units as a part of organizing. Others disagree, and prefer to include staffing as a major function (discussed below). In any event, organizing results in a formal structuring of roles and is designed to make it possible for people to work together effectively to attain a common goal.

Indicate whether each of the following statements is true or false by writing "T" or "F" in the space provided.

_____ 1. Management scholars and practitioners disagree as to whether or not there is a management process.

_____ 2. The disagreement over identifying specific management functions is not merely one of semantics.

_____ 3. Planning, organizing, and controlling are generally accepted as basic management functions.

_____ 4. Organizing is the determination of what work must be done by the group to accomplish stated goals.

Refer to Answer Frame 1[2], page 8, to check your answers.

Frame 2[2]

Actuating, or the "moving into action," includes those activities taken by a manager to start and continue actions set forth by the planning and organizing in order that the goals are achieved. It supplies the stimulative power to the group members, and the form it takes will vary with the individual members of the group. Actuating involves determining and satisfying the human wants of employees, personnel appraisal, leading, developing, and compensating.

Motivating is a word preferred by some to *actuating.* To some, their meanings are similar. To others, motivating connotes more a feeling of force from within by the human being than does actuating, i.e., the emotional and irrational connotations of the word motivating may be greater. *Actuating* is motivational in its makeup, and implies more formal and rational formulation.

Staffing includes *acquiring, placing, and maintaining members for the positions called for by the organizing work.* Personnel requirements are defined, candidates for positions are recruited and selected, and incumbents are appraised and developed. Emphasis is on the importance and quality of managers throughout the spectrum of management.

Directing is the *guiding of subordinates so that they will be knowledgeable employees, and will work effectively* toward stated goals of the enterprise. Directing also includes activities designed to orient employees, such as providing information about interdepartmental relationships and personalities and about the history, policies, and goals of the enterprise. In addition, assignments are clarified, aids to achieve improved performance are shared, and adequate channels of communication are created.

Controlling involves the familiar *follow-up to see that events conform to plans.* Performance is evaluated, and undesirable deviations are corrected to assure accomplishment of goals. The correction takes many forms, including a change in plans or even goals, reassignment of duties, or adjustment of authority; but, *in every case, the controlling is done through people.* The person responsible for the unwanted deviation must be located and steps taken to correct what is or is not being done.

Answer frame 1²

1. False. It is generally accepted that there is a management process; however, there is disagreement as to the component functions of this process.
2. True. There are some substantive disagreements in defining the nature and extent of management functions.
3. True. Planning, organizing, and controlling *are* generally included in any listing of management functions.
4. False. *Planning* is the determination of what work must be done by the group to accomplish stated goals. Organizing involves dividing into groups the necessary component activities required to achieve the goals, assigning such groupings to a manager, and establishing authority relationships among the groupings of organizational units.

Continue with Frame 2², page 7.

Frame 2² continued

Innovating implies *developing new ideas, combining new thoughts with old ones, acquiring ideas from other fields and adapting them, or simply stimulating associates to develop and apply new ideas in their work.* The manager's task is creative, as well as adaptive. Most management scholars agree that creativity is essential in management; to do no more than continue what's been done in the past would be to forgo progress. But they also contend that *innovating is included in planning*, which encompasses the task of trying to better what is currently being done and to utilize any available opportunities for improvement.

Representing includes *serving as the official member of an enterprise in its dealings with government, civil groups, banks, vendors, customers, and other outside groups.* Sometimes the representation requires carefully handled negotiations; yet, it can consist of merely being accessible and pleasant. Many believe that when representing involves delicate negotiation it logically can be considered a part of planning, and being amicable is a human characteristic which can be developed.

Coordinating is the orderly synchronization of individual efforts with respect to their amount, time, and direction, *so that unified action* toward a stated goal is taken. To achieve coordination, each member should be made to see how individual work contributes to the goals of the enterprise. Continuous interchange of information is essential, as well as a willingness to compromise and adjust for the benefit of the enterprise. Many view *coordinating as synonymous with the purpose of managing, and not as a part of it.*

Indicate whether each of the following statements is true or false by writing "T" or "F" in the space provided.

_____ 1. The terms *actuating* and *motivating* are often used interchangeably.
_____ 2. *Staffing* would include those duties carried out by the personnel department of an enterprise.
_____ 3. *Controlling* encompasses the monitoring of results.
_____ 4. There is universal agreement that coordinating is an essential part of managing.

Now see Answer Frame 2², page 10, to check your responses.

Frame 3[2]

Suggestions have been made to consider additional functions as fundamental in the management process, including authorizing, communicating, counseling, evaluating, integrating, measuring, and specifying. A manager performs these, but to include such functions would appear redundant, for they are already included in at least one of the various combinations shown in Figure 1. It should be emphasized that *the fundamental functions of management are interrelated.* Planning, for example, affects organizing; and organizing influences controlling. One function does not cease entirely, before another is started. *They are inextricably interwoven;* and, normally, they are *not performed in any particular sequence*, but as the individual need seems to require. For launching a new enterprise, planning usually is first, followed by other functions, shown in Figure 1; but for an established enterprise, controlling at a given time may be followed by planning and, in turn, followed by motivating.

The management process approach to management study offers distinct and exclusive advantages. By constructing the management theory around the fundamental management functions, the following four advantages are gained:

1. A broad, easy-to-understand, conceptual framework of management is won. The totality of management is included, and a practical meaning of management that can be applied to every type of enterprise and to every level within a given enterprise is provided. Both the science and the art of management are included, and the development of helpful principles of management are fostered. (A principle is a fundamental truth at a given time, useful as a guide for understanding the relationships between two or more sets of variables.)

2. Contributions from other approaches to management thought can be used to advantage in the process approach. The best-known approach for a particular problem at hand can be used and the framework supplied by the process approach can be retained. In this way, specialized thinking can be integrated into the basic theory.

3. Flexibility is provided. The managerial thinking need not follow a mechanistic format. Room is available for creativity and improvement. The process approach applies to a variety of situations, yet insures sufficient rigorousness and consistency for dependable management thinking.

4. Genuine assistance in implementing managerial action is featured. The process approach is serviceable to practitioners, helping them to utilize existing management knowledge. Further, it aids the manager in ferreting out and understanding the major problems to be confronted in any given case.

Indicate whether each of the following statements is true or false by writing "T" or "F" in the space provided.

_____ 1. The fundamental management functions are interrelated.

_____ 2. The *management process* approach ignores consideration of management functions.

_____ 3. The *management process* approach cannot be used in conjunction with other approaches to the study of management.

_____ 4. The *management process* approach is an inflexible approach to the study of management.

Now check your answers in Answer Frame 3[2], page 10.

Answer frame 2²

1. True. Some people prefer the term *motivating* to the term *actuating*. To some the meaning of each is similar; to others, it is not.
2. True. The personnel department of an enterprise would be primarily concerned with the *staffing* function.
3. True. *Controlling* involves the familiar *follow-up to see that events conform to plans*.
4. False. Some view coordinating as synonymous with the *purpose* of managing, rather than as an essential part of managing.

Now continue by reading Frame 3², page 9.

Answer frame 3²

1. True. It should be emphasized that *the fundamental functions of management are interrelated*. One function does not cease entirely before another is started.
2. False. The *management process* approach structures management theory around the fundamental management functions.
3. False. Contributions from other approaches to management thought can be used to advantage in the process approach.
4. False. The *management process* approach is flexible. There is room for creativity and improvement.

You have completed Chapter 2. Now begin Chapter 3, page 11.

chapter 3

CONTEMPORARY MANAGERIAL VALUES AND ENVIRONMENT

Frame 1[3]

In managing, one has either an implicit or explicit philosophy of management. A philosophy of management means a way of management thinking consisting of perceptions, concept understandings, and beliefs. Some system of thought prevails in a person's management efforts. A manager builds a pattern of judgments, acceptable criteria, social relations, and preferred economic atmosphere in the decisions reached and actions taken.

The manager, in formulating and making known a philosophy of management, enjoys three major advantages. First, such a manager is more likely to win enthusiastic support and followers. People know what the manager stands for and what managerial actions are likely to be taken. People tend to have more confidence in the manager because they know what actions probably will be taken in given situations and why they are taken. Second, a foundation for managerial thinking is supplied. This becomes especially important in handling changes, reaching basic decisions, and meeting new challenges for which no previous solutions or near solutions are available. Third, a framework is provided within which meaningful thinking by the manager takes place. Orientation is provided and progress toward a satisfactory answer is stimulated.

Over the years various philosophies of management have developed, flourished, and then given way to new philosophies. These changes take place primarily due to increased knowledge and experience, social development, and technological as well as environmental dynamics. To illustrate, the following changes are typical: managerial emphasis on results, not activities; asking *why* an objective is set rather than how it should be attained; fuller utilization of the computer; and harnessing the contributions of numerous technical break-throughs. Change is the order of the day. It is common to hear, "We don't do it that way anymore."

Values are the basis for a philosophy of management. They reveal what is personally meaningful to a manager. The relative esteem or estimated worth, attributed to a concept, preference, or belief represents a value of its holder. Commonly a value is considered as a "concept of desirability." A manager assimilates values to the degree that they appear to satisfy his or her needs.

The values held by a person are greatly influenced by the culture in which that person has lived and now lives. Culture can be thought of as a system of values and sanctions of society. Through its institutions (competition, marriage, education, customs) culture determines what is desirable and what actions are possible. The manager is influenced strongly by institutions which serve as equilibriating mechanisms between personal values and exterior environment. In short, cultures and institutions represent and influence a way of life, a way of managing.

People seek values, test them, and change them, but the process is relatively slow because most human beings continue lifestyles for ex-

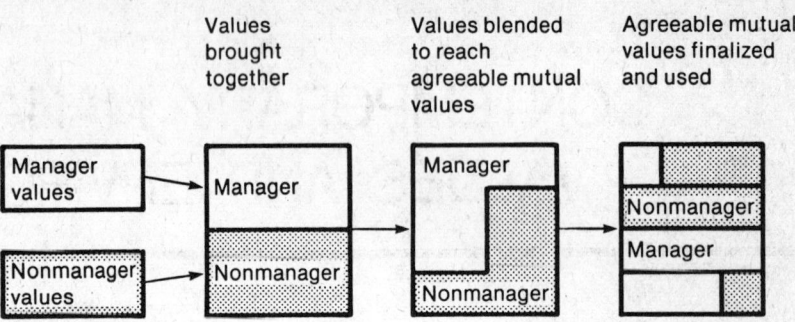

FIGURE 2

Values of Both Manager and Nonmanagers Are Brought Together and Blended. Ultimately Mutually Agreeable Values Are Finalized and Used

tended periods of time. Values tend to be tested every generation. Observe also that values, cultures, and institutions vary among people, committees, and nations. What is desirable and acceptable to one group may be rejected by another group. This fact may be of considerable importance to a manager.

Value systems are complex. What is considered vital to one person may be considered somewhat unimportant to another. Typically in any work population a number of different value systems exist. Commonly, several values must be accepted simultaneously in order to achieve the needed objective; otherwise, conflict may result. To avoid such conflict it is paramount that the manager keep two fundamentals in mind. First, he or she should have a ranking of respective values so that the dominant one will be satisfied and, if not, it may be sacrificed for the next in the hierarchy of values. The second fundamental is that the manager follow a means for accomplishing the goal in keeping with the value system prevalent among the employees performing the work. This means that the manager develops plans and acts jointly with the employees, who may have different values. In other words, the values of both manager and nonmanager should be considered in formulating plans and actions for goal accomplishment (see Figure 2). Complete conformity to a managerial prescribed set of values cannot be expected. Today's successful manager avoids the error of assuming all members of a work group have values close to those held by the manager.

Indicate whether each of the following statements is true or false by writing "T" or "F" in the space provided.

_____ 1. It is possible to manage without having a philosophy of management.

_____ 2. There are certain advantages which derive from a manager making known his or her management philosophy.

_____ 3. The values held by a person are determined entirely by his or her needs.

_____ 4. Employees should be expected to subordinate their personal values to those of the manager in achieving company goals.

Now turn to Answer Frame 1[3] on page 14 to check your responses.

Frame 2[3]

Significant in management is the environment or the general surroundings or conditions directly or indirectly affecting work efforts. Technically, environment neither governs nor is governed by management. For convenience, environment is commonly divided into (1) internal and (2) external components. The first includes the general working conditions brought about by forces internal to the enterprise. The second is the environment brought about by forces external to an enterprise. We will discuss internal environment and management in subsequent chapters. Our major interest now is external environment and the discussion of four crucial external factors: (1) social, (2) governmental, (3) economic, and (4) technological.

Social environmental considerations are becoming of increasing importance. The achievement of the oft-mentioned goal for society—economic abundance—does not make sense if our social environment is one of squandering natural resources, permitting racial tensions, defacing landscapes, and permitting pockets of poverty, product unreliability, and inadequate health care. Managers are challenged to solve a long list of social ills. These challenges are given to managers because they have the knowledge, skill, and power to solve them.

The social environment of management is changing because the expectations of society are changing. Most managers of businesses feel they have social obligations. However, for them to take decisive action presents difficulties including (1) how to maintain a healthy business operation and at the same time deploy personal energies to pressing social problems, and (2) how to operate in and among our total social environment which may have philosophies and values that are quite different from those existing in the area of business.

Governmental influence is a major factor in the external environment. Increasing legislative controls have pushed government to the foreground in any discussion of environment. Emphasis upon social needs and the government's guarantee of equality of opportunity have contributed significantly to the prominence of government in management considerations. With this increasing prominence of government has come both a big demand and a big increase in government programs. The prevailing attitude is that government is expected to fulfill not only public needs, but also what was once considered private wants. Government is destined to play an important role in shaping the future environment within which the manager will operate.

Economic forces influence the functioning of management as well as the manner in which it is practiced. Questions pertaining to credit, commercial banks' operations, international trade, wages paid, and generation of profits are illustrative. Worldwide economic issues are among the vital influences on much management practice. International monetary systems and worldwide inflation are in the spotlight of external environment formulation and influence affecting managerial actions. Further, economic forces focus on costs and revenues which are highly influential in the decisions and behaviors of the manager.

Technology greatly conditions the external environment in which a manager operates. Capable of bringing about numerous changes in the search for improvements and progress, technology is a force which must be reckoned with. The transfer of resources into products and services by means of the discovery of new materials, new methods, and new machines poses tremendous challenges. Managers are influenced by, and in turn influence, technology. Whether the uses made of technology are good or bad depend upon human beings. Technology can be our greatest servant in the future. The future will be influenced to a great extent by managers giving due recognition to technology as a powerful factor of the external environment.

Answer frame 1³

1. False. The philosophy might be implicit rather than explicit, but every manager has internalized some perceptions, concept understandings, and beliefs.
2. True. First, such a manager is more likely to win support for decisions made. Second, a foundation for management thinking is present. Third, a framework is provided for making future decisions.
3. False. Culture is also a strong determinant of values held by an individual. The culture of a society is expressed largely through its institutions.
4. False. The values of both the manager and employees should be considered in formulating plans and actions for accomplishing company goals.

If you missed any of the above, you should restudy Frame 1³ before turning to Frame 2³ on page 13.

Frame 2³ continued

Indicate whether each of the following statements is true or false by writing "T" or "F" in the space provided.

_____ 1. Economic abundance should be the sole goal of business.

_____ 2. Government influence on business is increasing dramatically.

_____ 3. The manager needs to consider worldwide economic developments in decision making.

_____ 4. Managers influence, and are influenced by, technology.

Now turn to Answer Frame 2³ on page 16 to check your responses.

chapter 4

OBJECTIVES

Frame 1[4]

Objectives are of paramount importance in management, for they give purpose and direction to effort so that management can be meaningful. Objectives must be defined and made known in such a way that they can serve as a measure of success or failure. *Targets and goals* are commonly used interchangeably for the word *objectives*. To some, the word target connotes that a quantitative measurement is involved, but this definition is not universal.

Well-known and well-defined objectives, most managers would agree, *have motivating power in and of themselves. They lead to action,* guide managerial efforts effectively, and put an end to much of the energy wasted on unproductive tasks and interpersonal conflicts. Defining and making known the objective are major challenges. All concerned must know what the goal is, and all management members must work together toward it. It seems that this could be taken for granted; but, too frequently, the objective is vaguely stated, if at all, and it is ignored by the manager, who gets lost in immediate problems. If objectives are not precisely stated, chance rather than managerial direction may determine the course of the undertaking.

Objectives must be practical. The manager may well ask: What is the individual or group really capable of achieving? What is occurring in the industry? Should a conservative or an optimistic view be taken? If a conservative objective is set it may not spur employees toward greater achievement; yet if the objective is too optimistic it may not serve as a challenge because employees do not believe it to be attainable. The consensus is that objectives should be practical and attainable, but should require some stretching and reaching by employees.

Objectives must have precise meaning for the manager. To state objectives in vague terms, such as "to make constructive corporate citizens" or "to make profits," leaves much to be desired. The manager needs to know how many citizens with what characteristics within what period, or how much profit in which products for what period. Only *specific objectives,* pointing out definite ends toward which to strive, can give the manager an effective basis for action. What resources to use, what premises and risks to assume, what the probabilities of success are, and what to do are all more easily determined when the objectives are specific.

Quantified goals are preferable; for example, the goal is best defined as *a given profit percentage on sales dollars or a certain return on assets.* Many objectives can be quantified, and those not directly quantifiable usually can be indirectly quantified. For instance, management development, an objective not directly measurable, can be indirectly quantified by reporting the number of qualified promotions. Normally, several indicators which correlate and verify the answer are employed when indirect quantification is applied.

Many managers find *long-range objectives* (over five years) helpful in forecasting an enterprise's requirements for production facilities, sales, financing, and staffing against the probable environmental changes. With regard to specificity and timing, long-range objectives may differ

Answer frame 2³

1. False. Pursuing this goal does not make much sense if we squander natural resources, have racial tensions, deface landscapes, and tolerate pockets of poverty, product unreliability, and inadequate health care.
2. True. The government's push for the realizing of social needs and for equal opportunity have made government an increasingly prominent influence on business.
3. True. Worldwide inflationary trends and the relative worth of the dollar as compared to other currencies have effects on companies even if they do not engage in international trade (e.g., balance of payments problems affect the domestic rate of inflation, unemployment, interest rates).
4. True. For instance, managerial decisions influence the development of new materials, methods, and machines. Also, the availability of these influences production and marketing decisions which managers make.

If you missed any of the above, you should restudy Frame 2³ before turning to Chapter 4 on page 15.

Frame 1⁴ continued

from the purpose of an enterprise. The former (long-range objectives) usually refer to a stated time period; the latter (purpose) may extend over a considerable and indefinite period. They must be logically related, but this requirement can pose difficulties. If the enterprise's purpose is to triple its net capital worth within 10 years, an enterprise may achieve this by any or all of these long-range objectives: buying established firms, merging, or expanding internally. Which objectives should be pursued; if more than one, in what sequence; and how they should be coordinated are representative of the problems faced.

Indicate whether each of the following statements is true or false by writing "T" or "F" in the space provided.

_____ 1. Objectives should be stated in a general and unstructured manner, to permit a manager the maximum leeway in interpreting them.

_____ 2. Objectives should be set at a level that is unattainable, so that managers will continually be striving to reach them.

_____ 3. Wherever possible, goals should be reduced to quantitative terms.

_____ 4. All objectives should be logically related.

Check your responses in Answer Frame 1⁴, page 18.

Frame 2⁴

Differences of opinion exist regarding *who should establish major or top objectives*. Some take the view that such objectives should be formulated primarily by a board of directors, government, or social environmental factors. That is, in a sense, they should be handed to the management team to achieve. The majority, however, hold that top managers must decide top objectives. At any rate, regardless of their initiation, top objectives must be interpreted, refined, and expressed in terms understandable to the management members. Clearly it is best *to have the managers, who will perform the planning for the objectives, participate in defining the objectives*. This helps ensure that they will understand, trust, and be loyal to the goals.

Managers have multiobjectives, not a single objective. Ideally, a manager makes progress simultaneously toward several objectives; but, in practice, this does not always happen. The reasons are: (a) the objectives may be quite diverse, (b) managers are most attentive to objectives in which they or their superiors have the greatest interest, and (c) unanticipated circumstances may arise to unbalance the accomplishment of multiobjectives. However, the competent manager strives to simultaneously move forward toward all assigned objectives, knowing that they are prerequisites to achieving long-range objectives.

Managerial objectives can be classified in many different ways, such as: (a) economic, social, political, and philanthropic; (b) basic and derivative; (c) general and verifiable; and (d) those pertaining to an enterprise, to its managers, and to its individual members. While each is important, the latter classification is especially helpful in management study.

Objectives of an enterprise deal with the purposes, created values, and actions taken by the enterprise. Broad in scope and typically not precisely defined, they are subject to wide interpretation. Objectives concerning managers frequently deal with quantity and quality levels to be achieved. "To increase the size of the enterprise" is illustrative, or for a production manager, the goal may be "to increase the acceptable parts to 99.6–100.0 percent." Or, the managerial objective may be to maintain the enterprise's present level, in terms of market position or profit. This type of objective is referred to as "satisficing," meaning that what is being derived from the current activities is good enough.

Objectives pertaining to individual members of an enterprise include economic, psychological, and social satisfactions made possible in the work environment. They are numerous and take a variety of forms, including the goal of: (a) getting a job and gaining economic security, (b) acquiring status, (c) becoming a recognized leader of a work group, or (d) being an employee of an enterprise offering a much needed product or service.

These three types of objectives—of the enterprise, of managers, and of individuals—are blended together; that is, they are *harmonized*. The objectives of the enterprise should be established within the limits consistent with the values and beliefs considered desirable in society. Each manager's objectives should be in keeping with those of the enterprise; no cross-purpose should exist. And a manager's goals should supplement the goals of colleagues. It is entirely possible for the same goals to be sought by more than one manager of an enterprise; in fact, this is a normal state of affairs. Further, objectives of each individual should be in harmony with those of the manager. This aids human relations, the accomplishment of greater team effort, and work satisfaction. Experienced managers claim that the placing of team goals (usually those of managers) before individual goals promotes high morale. Most individual goals will be surrendered if group goals are a sufficiently rewarding substitute.

Indicate whether each of the following statements is true or false by writing "T" or "F" in the space provided.

_____ 1. Ideally, the board of directors should define the objectives of an organization, and then hand them to the management team to achieve.

_____ 2. Ideally, a manager should strive for several objectives at a time.

_____ 3. The objectives of the individual should always displace the objectives of the enterprise.

_____ 4. A manager's goals should complement, rather than impede, the goals of another manager.

Check your responses in Answer Frame 2[4], page 18.

Answer frame 1[4]

1. False. Failure to precisely spell out objectives usually results in a hopeless undertaking, strongly influenced by chance. Specific objectives should be stated.
2. False. The consensus is that objectives should be practical and attainable, but should require some stretching and reaching by employees. If an objective is unattainable, it may fail to motivate employees to greater achievement.
3. True. Quantified goals are more specific and are, therefore, preferable.
4. True. Management must decide which objectives should be pursued, in what sequence, and how they should be coordinated.

Now continue by reading Frame 2[4], page 16.

Answer frame 2[4]

1. False. It is best to have the managers who will perform the planning for attaining the objectives participate in defining the objectives.
2. True. Ideally, a manager should make progress toward several objectives simultaneously; but, in practice, this does not always happen.
3. False. The objectives of the enterprise, of managers, and of individuals should be *harmonized.* Each manager's objective should be in keeping with those of the enterprise, and objectives of each individual should be in harmony with those of the manager.
4. True. Each manager's goals should supplement the goals of colleagues. Of course, this ideal is not always achieved in practice.

Now continue by reading Frame 3[4], immediately below.

Frame 3[4]

The harmonizing of objectives suggests *a hierarchy of objectives,* and such a hierarchy exists in every enterprise. At the top organizational level are the objectives of the enterprise, sometimes called *major objectives.* Subordinate, but directly related to these major objectives, are *departmental objectives* which identify the goals of a particular departmental or organizational segment. In turn, departmental objectives have subordinate *group objectives* for a specific organizational unit; and, in similar manner, group objectives are segregated into *unit objectives* and, finally, into *individual objectives.* Ideally, each subsidiary objective contributes to the accomplishment of its immediately superior objective, supplying a thoroughly *integrated pattern of objectives* to all members of the enterprise.

Laypersons state that profits are the objective of most enterprises; but this is highly controversial. In the case of many enterprises, profits are *not* the objective; for example, churches, schools, and government agencies. In some business enterprises, the emphasis is on growth, supplying a needed social service, or contributing to the well-being of humanity. When profits are stated as the objective, the profits are gained *indirectly* as a result of achieving other objectives. Profits are the final link of a long chain of events; they are the by-product of many other direct efforts. A manager cannot go out and directly secure profits. However, some form of support—profits, gifts, endowments, or tax receipts—is required "to keep the enterprise going."

Recognition of the tremendous importance of objectives in management has led to the practice of *management by objectives.* In this concept, each manager has predetermined results, usually measurable, that are expected to be achieved within a given period and for which the manager is fully responsible and is evaluated on the success in achieving the expected results. Objectives are set, in conference with the superior, by the manager immediately responsible for the work. The various objectives, from all the managers at all organizational levels, are consolidated and turned over to the chief executive, who may or may not make modifications in keeping with overall objectives of the enterprise. The approved objectives are then returned to the department heads and, subsequently, to the managers of the lower levels. Variations of this approach are used; but the emphasis is always on accomplishment of objectives. Also, the approach is used at the level between a manager and nonmanager.

Indicate whether each of the following statements is true or false by writing "T" or "F" in the space provided.

_____ 1. In structuring a *hierarchy of objectives,* the procedure used is to move from major objectives to objectives for succeedingly lower levels of the organization.

_____ 2. Profits are the only objective of all enterprises.

_____ 3. Profits are unimportant for all enterprises.

_____ 4. Under a *management by objectives* program, a manager has no control over setting the objectives he or she is expected to attain.

Now refer to Answer Frame 3[4], page 20.

chapter 5

DECISION MAKING IN MANAGEMENT

Frame 1[5]

The one universal mark of a manager is that he or she is a decision maker. To achieve objectives, the manager must decide what specific actions are necessary, what new means can be introduced, and what to do in order to maintain a satisfactory work output. Decision making takes place in every part of an enterprise.

Decision making is the selecting of an alternative, from two or more alternatives, to determine an opinion or a course of action. It is the psychic and creative event in which thought, feeling, and knowledge are brought together for action. It involves uncertainty. In decision making, a manager is dealing with future values which are to some degree unknown. Further, the selection of the alternative is always based on some criteria, such as to: reduce cost, save time, or develop managers. The criteria used influence the selec-

Answer frame 3[4]

1. True. The structuring of a hierarchy of objectives proceeds from the major objectives to integrated lower level objectives.
2. False. Although profits are important to profit-motivated enterprises, they often are not the sole objective of even these enterprises. And there are not-for-profit enterprises, such as churches, schools, and government agencies.
3. False. Profits are vital for long-run survival, unless an enterprise is supported by some other means, such as gifts, endowments, or tax receipts.
4. False. Under the *management by objectives* approach, the objectives *are* set, in conference with the superior, by the manager immediately responsible for attaining those objectives, subject to the review of the chief executive.

You have completed Chapter 4. Now go to Chapter 5, page 19.

Frame 1[5] continued

tion of the alternative. For decision making to exist, there must always be two or more alternatives. In many cases, there are just two; for example, the maximum-or-minimum type or the yes-or-no type.

For each alternative, the possible outcomes are predicted and then evaluated in terms of relative desirability. Normally, the most desirable is the one that will contribute best to the objective sought. This evaluation can pose real difficulties. It is influenced greatly by one's values, and conflict among these values is quite likely. Desirable and undesirable elements seem to exist in every alternative. These conflicting aspects must be reconciled in some way satisfactory to the decision maker, because *decision making* literally means "to cut off," or to come to a conclusion.

In these efforts, both *tangible and intangible factors* are considered. The former include profits, dollars, labor-hours, machine-hours, and other quantitative data that are assessed. These factors are interrelated. To illustrate: profit maximization usually depends, in part, on comparison of various physical factors. In production planning, the utilization of personnel and the loading of machines may be the limiting physical factors in measuring the production schedule programs. When the presence of the tangible factors is high and measurable and the intangible factors are relatively minor, the selection of the alternative on the basis of tangible factors is relatively simple. However, it must be remembered that the physical factors are based on estimates and forecasts that are rarely exact and accurate. A margin of error and uncertainty still exists.

Intangible factors are normally quite difficult to evaluate. They must first be recognized, then ranked in terms of their importance, and finally compared with respect to their probable effect upon the ultimate results. In other words, an attempt is made to weigh each intangible. These judgments are difficult and fallible. A manager may know that a new invention will someday make a product obsolete, but is unsure as to the timing. Or the manager is unsure as to the possibility of a strike in a vendor's plant.

Furthermore, in this evaluation, it is helpful to *concentrate on the really important or limiting factors, be they tangible or intangible*, that are critical to the goal attainment. Through this approach, the evaluating task becomes manageable. However, discovering the limiting factor or factors may not be easy, especially if the reactions are complex and the factors obscure. Some use the terminology *limiting factors and complementary factors* to designate, respectively, those that are critical or limiting and those that are not.

Indicate whether each of the following statements is true or false by writing "T" or "F" in the space provided.

_____ 1. All managers are responsible for some type of decision making.

_____ 2. Uncertainty in decision making refers to the existence of two or more alternatives, any one of which can be selected.

_____ 3. A manager is more likely to have a better understanding of the tangible factors surrounding a decision than the intangible factors.

_____ 4. In scheduling production, a manager would be faced with his plant's capacity as a *limiting factor*.

Check your responses in Answer Frame 1[5], page 22.

Frame 2[5]

The bases for evaluating alternatives are many. The pervasiveness of decision making has stimulated much thought as to which basis is best in given circumstances. The techniques run the gamut from what amounts to guesses to highly sophisticated mathematical analyses. There is no one best basis for all circumstances. The selection depends on the manager's background and knowledge. The following are among the most important:

1. Marginal analysis. This technique compares the extra cost and revenue resulting from the addition of one more unit. The profit maximizing point is that volume where, for the last unit added, the additional revenue equals the additional cost. At any lesser volume, the marginal revenue exceeds the marginal cost, and, at any greater volume, the marginal cost exceeds the marginal revenue.

2. Psychological theory. Many issues that a manager must decide are not economic. The decision concerning the size of a private office, for example, might well be influenced by psychological values. Other examples include: decisions based on the personal satisfaction of ego aggrandizement of a management member; adherence to an inherited set of traditions deeply revered by top managers; or desire for bigness just for bigness sake.

3. Intuition. Decision making, based on intuition, is characterized by the use of the "inner feelings" of the decider. It may be a sort of sixth sense, a deep feeling about the situation, or an inexplicable insight into a certain state of affairs. Sometimes the intuition is an almost instantaneous feeling that a certain action is bound to lead to certain stated results. The process of the decision making may be highly irrational, following no set pattern. Intuition probably is present, to some degree, in most decision making. It does not always give satisfactory results; but it quickly supplies a decision, and appears effective, in some instances.

4. Experience. Intimacy with and understanding of issues require experience. Experience supplies guides, helps to discriminate, and helps to generalize past situations. Practical knowledge is utilized, and acceptance of the decision by others usually follows. Some contend that reliance upon experience makes for excessive conservatism in decision making. Things change; past successful decision making does not necessarily ensure future success. Experience should be used, but a manager need not be bound to it.

5. Follow the leader. A considerable number of decisions are made by following and, in some instances, duplicating the decision that the leader has made. Usually, when this practice is followed, the major decisions have already been reached. *Patterned decisions* result from a follow-the-leader practice.

6. Experimentation. "Try out the alternative and see what happens" is effective in deciding which course to follow. This is the common decision-making basis in scientific inquiry and in new product design and development work. Testing sales acceptance in selected markets be-

Answer frame 1[5]

1. True. The one universal mark of a manager is that he or she is a decision maker.
2. False. Uncertainty in decision making refers to the lack of assurance as to the *outcome* of a specific alternative, rather than to the fact that there are two or more alternatives.
3. True. The intangible factors pertaining to a decision are normally more difficult to evaluate than are the tangible factors.
4. True. Plant capacity is a *limiting factor* on production.

Now go to Frame 2[5], page 21.

Frame 2[5] continued

fore going nationwide is illustrative. Experimentation is relatively expensive, and it is assumed the future will duplicate the past.

7. Analysis. What decision to reach, in a given case, can be aided by breaking the problem into its components, and studying each component by itself and also in relationship to the other components. Thus, the critical aspects of the decision making are brought to the fore, and causal relationships, as they affect objectives, are identified. In many cases, answers to questions are employed to assist in the analysis. This approach narrows the facts, believed essential for the decision, to the most important specifics. Ability to conceptualize the problem is an important step in making a decision about it.

Indicate whether each of the following statements is true or false by writing "T" or "F" in the space provided.

_____ 1. Marginal analysis applies only to situations where an enterprise is not maximizing profits due to underproduction, i.e., marginal revenue is greater than marginal cost.

_____ 2. *Intuition* has been eliminated as a factor that affects business decisions.

_____ 3. *Patterned decisions* arise from a manager's using previous decisions as a guide for making current decisions.

_____ 4. *Experimentation* may sometimes be rejected as a basis for evaluating alternatives because of its relatively high cost.

Check your responses in Answer Frame 2[5], page 24.

Frame 3[5]

Who should make particular managerial decisions? A given decision should be made by a person, at the lowest organizational level, who possesses the ability, desire, and access to the relevant information and who is in a position to impartially weigh the factors. It is not always easy to determine who this person is. Hence, it is common to define what types of issues a manager can decide.

Decision making is either on: (*a*) *an individual basis* or (*b*) *a group basis.* The former is common, when the decision is simple and all the alternatives are fully comprehended. Individual decision making fulfills the popular role of what a manager should do. Emergency situations are typically decided on an individual basis. Emergencies always arise but should not be permitted to justify emergency decision making as the accepted mode. Whether to make or defer an emergency decision is conditioned mainly by the consequences of not deciding.

The group basis for decision making has

gained tremendous acceptance. Through group decision making, those who will be affected by a decision are given the opportunity to participate in its formulation. Further, enthusiasm for the decision and assistance in management development are aided. It also makes it possible to incorporate the judgment of specialists and technicians who have specialized knowledge concerning the issue being decided. The contribution of individual members will vary. Some will have very little to say, and others, when they speak, will offer little or normally will accede to what already has been stated. There are many who believe decision making is essentially a lonesome task and a one-person job. They contend that even under the group basis, in the final analysis, one person must actually make the decision. The initial judgment may be modified by the group, but the individual must still make the final decision.

Indicate whether each of the following statements is true or false by writing "T" or "F" in the space provided.

_____ 1. The responsibility for decision making should be decentralized.
_____ 2. The responsibility for decision making always is delegated to a group.
_____ 3. Decisions dealing with an emergency usually are made by a group.
_____ 4. The group method of decision making has been discredited.

Now refer to Answer Frame 3[5], page 24, to check your responses.

Answer frame 2[5]

1. False. *Marginal analysis* is also used to determine if an enterprise is overproducing, i.e., marginal cost is greater than marginal revenue. It involves comparing the extra cost and extra revenue resulting from each additional unit produced. The optimum point at which to produce is at the volume where marginal cost and marginal revenue are equal.
2. False. Intuition probably is present in most decision making to some degree.
3. False. *Patterned decisions* arise from a manager's using *superiors'* decisions as a guide for making decisions. This is the follow-the-leader approach.
4. True. In a specific situation, the relatively high cost of *experimentation* may preclude its use.

Go to Frame 3[5], page 22, and continue reading.

Answer frame 3[5]

1. True. It generally is agreed that the responsibility for a specific type of decision should be delegated to the lowest organizational level at which there is an individual possessing the ability, desire, impartiality, and access to relevant information needed for these decisions.
2. False. The responsibility for decision making can be delegated to a specific individual, and, even when a group is involved, there are those who believe that one person usually makes the final decision.
3. False. Emergency decisions typically are decided by an individual because of the need for speedy action.
4. False. The group method for decision making is quite popular and has gained tremendous acceptance.

You have completed Chapter 5. Now begin Chapter 6, page 25.

chapter 6

QUANTITATIVE METHODS IN MANAGERIAL DECISION MAKING

Frame 1[6]

During recent years, there has been an increasing trend toward the use of quantitative methods for the purpose of managerial decision making. These methods feature: (1) a broad point of view, sometimes termed a systems-wide view; (2) identification and measurement of the objectives; (3) the quantification of all relevant variables; (4) the use of models, commonly mathematical abstractions, showing relationships quantitatively; (5) optimizing or minimizing a certain function, such as cost efficiency; and (6) orderly thinking and logical methodology.

The technique used in quantitative managerial decision making usually gives decisions applicable to the entire enterprise or a large portion of it, recognizes the impact of these decisions on the various components, and focuses managerial efforts on the vital issues. The objective itself is definite and measurable. Examples of objectives are to realize a specific rate of return on investment or to ensure that transportation costs do not exceed five cents a unit. Objectives should not be stated in general terms such as, "to better utilize the machines" or "to reduce transportation costs." The act of incorporating and quantifying most or all of the relevant variables characterizes the quantitative approach. Increased computer availability has helped make this possible. The use of models and the optimizing or minimizing of a particular function also are common characteristics in the quantitative decision-making approach.

Models are constructed after the goals have been set and the relevant variables have been identified and quantified. The pertinent relationships are studied and analyzed so that the proper background for constructing the model is gained. Then the model is built or created so that it accurately represents the relationship pattern existing among the variables and the objectives, all within the constraints or assumptions recognized in the solving of the problem. The model must fit the problem, i.e., it must be appropriate. Frequently, mathematical models are used—as exemplified by equations, formulas, charts, and diagrams—but they can also be of other types, such as replicas or miniature facsimilies of the entity itself.

By using models, different alternatives can be tried out and the results noted; or, especially in the case of a mathematical model, the model itself can be manipulated to reveal certain rational outcomes in keeping with the fundamental relationships of the variables included in the model. The mathematical model is an abstract concept. It shows the interrelatedness of quantifiable data. Use of different values for the variables will bring about different results. In brief, the model serves as an effective means toward determining the answers sought.

26 Programmed learning aid for principles of management

Indicate whether each of the following statements is true or false by writing "T" or "F" in the space provided.

_____ 1. The main output of any quantitative method is the identification of the relevant variables affecting a manager's decision.

_____ 2. Quantitative methods are used to identify objectives.

_____ 3. There is an increasing trend toward the use of quantitative methods by management in decision making.

_____ 4. Mathematical models are characterized by the use of qualitative data.

Refer to Answer Frame 1[6], page 28 to check your answers.

Frame 2[6]

Either optimization or minimization of the results can be calculated by utilizing a mathematical model. To illustrate, assume a model has been created and is $Y = 60X - 10X^2$, which shows the relationship between the values of Y, the efficiency achieved, and of X, the continuous hours worked. The equation shows that efficiency achieved, Y, is equal to 60 times the number of continuous hours worked, $60X$, less 10 times the continuous hours worked squared, $10X^2$. The efficiency, Y, is dependent upon the number of continuous hours worked, X, in the relationship represented by the equation.

Figure 3 shows the graphic representation of this equation. The chart is constructed by substituting values for X in the equation, starting with the value of zero and calculating the corresponding value of Y. The table of values is included in Figure 2. For example, when $X = 2$, $Y = 80$ ($Y = 60$ times 2 minus 10 times 2 squared, or $Y = 120$ minus 40). Plotting the values of the table gives the chart shown. From this chart it can be observed that the greatest, or optimum, efficiency is when $X = 3$, at which value the level of efficiency equals 90 percent. The same solution can be achieved quickly and directly from the equation by means of calculus.

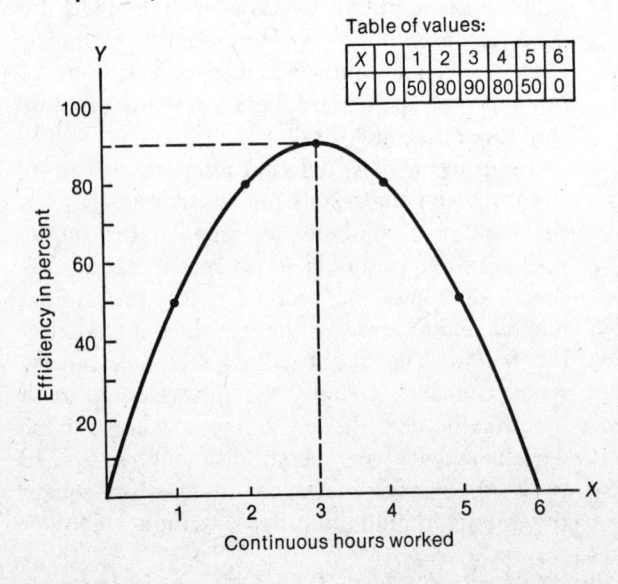

Observe from either the chart or the table of values that the value of Y with respect to X first increases and then decreases. The optimum point is where the *rate* of *change* for Y is zero. This zero rate of change is determined by calculus as follows:

The equation:
$$Y = 60X - 10X^2$$

The rate of change of Y with respect to X is:
$$dY/dX = 60 - 20X$$

When rate of change is zero:
$$0 = 60 - 20X$$

Value of X at point of optimization:
$$X = 3$$

The same mathematics is employed for minimization. In this case, the curve would be U-shaped, the minimum value being at the bottom, but the ideal point would still be where the rate of change for Y is zero. Determining the minimum cost, Y, in relation to the number of mar-

FIGURE 3
Graphic Representation of Equation, $Y = 60X - 10X^2$

Table of values:

X	0	1	2	3	4	5	6
Y	0	50	80	90	80	50	0

kets covered, X, would be illustrative of this relationship.

Simulation makes it possible to test various alternatives and combinations of variables to determine what results they would bring about, before actually implementing any of them. "Dry runs" are made to observe the effect that changes in variables have upon the results obtained. Simulation models are commonly empirical models or quantitative representations of the attributes being analyzed. Normally, they are not used to calculate optimization or minimization, but serve as a systematic trial-and-error approach to solving complex problems. Use of a model for simulation is not imperative, but it usually makes simulation more feasible. The computer is of great assistance in processing the voluminous amount of data. Distributions, from actual data and that believed logical, are assumed; and then, at random, artificial sequences of events are generated, against which the distributions are evaluated. Many random sequence generations help to disclose the behavior of the phenomenon. Many managers view simulation as a vital decision-making tool of the future. It promises to supply insight into a multicomponent concept of an extensive area.

Indicate whether each of the following statements is true or false by writing "T" or "F" in the space provided.

_____ 1. In the example depicted in Figure 3, X (continuous hours worked) is dependent on Y (percent of efficiency achieved) for its value.

_____ 2. The example in Figure 3 is one in which we are trying to maximize efficiency (Y).

_____ 3. Simulation models are used only when the objective is minimization.

_____ 4. Simulation models allow one to test the possible outcomes of various alternatives without actually implementing them.

Now refer to Answer Frame 2[6], page 28.

Frame 3[6]

Probability is also used in managerial decision making. Most decisions by managers involve some uncertainty but not total ignorance. To minimize the effects of uncertainty a manager can deal systematically with it by mathematically evaluating data considered representative of the events being decided. Certainty is 100 percent; a 70 percent probability expresses odds of 70 out of a 100 that the prediction as to the outcome of a decision will prove correct. Probability is based on the assumption that when an event is repeated sufficiently, a pattern of outcomes is usually established so that a measure of what causes bring about what events is possible. There is no guarantee that the predicted results will occur. For example, a 70 percent probability indication is impressive that the result will occur; but there is a 30 percent chance that it will not occur.

For decision making in management, a mathematical theorem developed by Thomas Bayes, called the *Bayesian formula,* can be used. (Consult a statistics book for details.) The decision maker estimates the probability of an event taking place, such as a 70 percent chance that sales will double over the forthcoming year, based on knowledge of the market, marketing research studies, and economic forecasts. The same situation is estimated by a second party with resultant different data on the probability of the event occurring. Substituting appropriate values in the formula supplies a conditioned probability figure which aids the decision maker to decide one way or another.

Closely related to probability and of assistance to the decision maker is the *decision tree.* This is a diagrammatic chart. The predicted outcomes of each decision are evaluated in measurable terms such as dollars or units of production; the outcome having the highest desirable end value is normally followed. Subsequently and in similar

Answer frame 1⁶

1. False. The identification of the relevant variables is a key *input* for any quantitative method, whereas the output is a recommended action or decision.
2. False. Objectives are not determined by a quantitative method, but rather are prerequisites for the use of such methods.
3. True. Quantitative methods are being used increasingly in managerial decision making.
4. False. Mathematical models are characterized by the use of *quantitative* data.

Now go to Frame 2⁶, page 26.

Answer frame 2⁶

1. False. In Figure 3, Y (percent of efficiency achieved) is the dependent variable and X (continuous hours worked) is the independent variable.
2. True. The example in Figure 3 *is* one in which we are trying to maximize efficiency (Y). The maximization point (of 90 percent efficiency) occurs when the value for continuous hours worked is three hours.
3. False. Simulation models normally are not used for optimization or minimization problems, but rather serve as a systematic trial-and-error approach to solving complex problems.
4. True. Simulation models *are* used to predict the results of choosing various alternatives before implementation of any of them.

Now continue with Frame 3⁶, page 27.

Frame 3⁶ continued

manner, the alternatives for this outcome are evaluated and the process is continued so that a chain of decision points and outcomes are developed from which the decision maker can decide what to do. The finished chart resembles a tree lying on its side and hence the name, decision tree. Normally, the chart is extended for three cycles or phases of decision making. To extend the chain further makes the analysis complex and cumbersome.

The *Monte Carlo* technique is used in predicting the timing or frequency of events occurring within a specific future period. Monte Carlo is actually a form of simulation using probability factors. It assumes that the particular spacing of events will occur in random fashion. It utilizes random samples of past events to predict future events. Its applications are many. For example, it can be used in determining the optimum personnel level to maintain over a given future period.

Queueing deals with waiting-line situations, such as those involved when several sales representatives must see one buyer of a company. A cost is involved in tolerating waiting lines. The problem is to balance the costs of bottlenecks against the costs of idle capacity. If the number of buyers is insufficient, the cost of waiting is high, whereas having too many buyers results in excessive idle-time cost. In other words, the decision making involves a balancing of expenditures for existing queues with the cost of supplying additional buyers. Monte Carlo technique can be utilized to determine the timing or frequency of arrivals, especially when the queue is not constant. Complex equations and a computer are commonly employed.

Gaming includes the study of situations in which two or more players or competitors seek to maximize gain and minimize loss. Players are given similar motivation and consider not only their own strategy but also that of their opponents. It is assumed that each player acts rationally. Frequently, to begin the game, each competitor is assumed to possess similar facilities as shown on identical balance sheets which are distributed. The decisions made by each affect individual future balance sheets. Utilizing these results, decisions again are made and new results calculated. Typically, each player is given certain selected data concerning the results of opponents' decisions. Several sequential "rounds of decisions" are made to make up the total game. A winning player or team often is determined at the conclusion of the game.

Linear programming is perhaps the best known of the quantitative decision-making techniques. Linear programming is useful when: (*a*) several variables related to attaining an objective exist; (*b*) the relationship between each variable and the objective is linear (or constant); (*c*) constraints on the overall relationships are present—the objective cannot be attained unencumbered; and (*d*) the problem is to find the best (e.g., least cost) combination of variables that will satisfy the objective. Linear programming often involves arranging the data in a matrix or row-column form, but graphic and algebraic methods also can be used in solving the problems. Intensive application of linear programming is found in problems of production, inventory, and transportation. Figure 4 shows, in matrix form, the data of a problem in which three factories, 1, 2, and 3, ship to three warehouses, A, B, and C, the unit cost of transportation indicated by the figure in the lower right of the appropriate square. Cost from factory 1 to warehouse A is $8, from factory 3 to warehouse B is $5, and so on. Total respective capacities of factories are indicated in the last column to the

FIGURE 4

Linear Programming Data in Matrix Format

Warehouses → Factories ↓	A	B	C	
1	8	(100) 4	7	100 units
2	(100) 5	(300) 6	7	400 units
3	(100) 3	5	(100) 4	200 units
	200 units	400 units	100 units	700 units

right, 100–400–200, capacities of warehouses on the bottom line or row, 200–400–100. The problem is to determine the amount each factory should ship to each warehouse to obtain *total minimum transportation costs*. The answer is shown by the circled numbers, the total costs for which are $3,400. The answer is obtained by any one of several methods. One is to start at the "northwest corner" and fill in the cells, working across and down. This distribution is then improved by evaluating each blank cell to determine if cost reduction would result by assigning an entry in any one of them. Another method is VAM (Vogel Approximation Method), which is less time consuming and simple to apply. You should consult a text for fuller explanations of these methods.

Indicate whether each of the following statements is true or false by writing "T" or "F" in the space provided.

_____ 1. Bayesian statistics may be used where subjective probabilities (rather than certainty) are indicated.
_____ 2. *Monte Carlo* analysis utilizes the results of a random sample of historical data to predict future events.
_____ 3. *Queueing* is the most elementary of all analytical techniques.
_____ 4. *Gaming* involves decision making under certainty.
_____ 5. *Linear programming* can only be applied to situations that are free from constraints.

Turn to Answer Frame 3[6], page 30, to check your answers.

Answer frame 3[6]

1. True. In some situations, persons may have different perceptions as to the probability that an event will occur. Bayesian statistics can be used to arrive at a conditioned probability figure which aids the manager in deciding between alternatives.
2. True. *Monte Carlo* analysis *does* utilize random samples of past occurrences to predict future events.
3. False. *Queueing* typically involves complex equations, and a computer usually is needed for the solution of these problems.
4. False. *Gaming* involves decision making under *uncertainty*. Each player is unaware of his or her competitors' decisions in the current round of decisions.
5. False. *Linear programming* is useful when there *are* constraints on the overall relationship i.e., the objective cannot be attained unencumbered.

You have completed Chapter 6. Now proceed to Chapter 7.

chapter 7

THE WORK OF PLANNING

Frame 1[7]

Present-day managers must operate in a highly dynamic economy where change is the rule, not the exception. Planning allows the manager to master change. The planner is the one with the greatest opportunity to bring together all the resources of an enterprise into a more effective entity. In short, planning is indispensable. It is the intellectual arm of our future growth.

It can be reasoned that planning is basic to the other management functions. A manager performs the managerial functions to realize wanted objectives, the means for achieving them being set up by planning efforts. In other words, planning is the foundation of management. No manager can manage successfully over a period of time unless planning has taken place.

Definition of planning. *Planning is the selecting and relating of facts, and the making and using of assumptions regarding the future in the visualization and formulation of proposed activities believed necessary to achieve desired results.* Some express planning as an organized approach to future problems and describe it as evolving the present design for future action. Planning bridges the gap between where you are and where you want to go. It answers, in advance, the who, what, when, where, why, and how of future actions.

Effective planning is based on facts and information, not on emotions or wishes. Facts relevant to the situation under consideration are related to the manager's experience and knowledge. Reflective thinking is required; imagination and foresight are extremely helpful. A planner must be able to visualize the proposed pattern of activities clearly. Planning is basically an intellectual process. By its use, managers try to look ahead, anticipate eventualities, prepare for contingencies, map out activities, and provide an orderly sequence for achieving the objective.

Adequate planning should take place before acting. To reverse this sequence means that action is being confused with accomplishment. In terms of effort, a person shuffling papers can be working as hard as one filing papers. The significant difference is the *usefulness of the achievement.* The need is to think before taking action. What a manager thinks greatly influences what actions are taken. This is why planning is so important.

Every manager has a planning function to perform. Planning is not concentrated among top-level managers only. Although it is true that top managers may devote more of their time to planning, and work with more vital issues than do managers of the middle and lower levels, the fact remains that every manager has planning to perform within a particular area of activities.

It follows then that planning exists in most enterprises, regardless of their size. In the larger enterprises its presence is more apparent, due to some managers giving all, or a good portion, of their time to planning efforts. In contrast, in small enterprises planning is commonly of a somewhat informal type; the general manager does most of it.

The planning effort is continuous; it is a never-ending activity. All plans are tentative and subject to revision and amendment, as new facts become known and as the variables are reevaluated. The common practice is to reexamine plans regularly and, if necessary, to modify them promptly in view of the new situations. Planning is just as important when things are going well, as when current troubles abound.

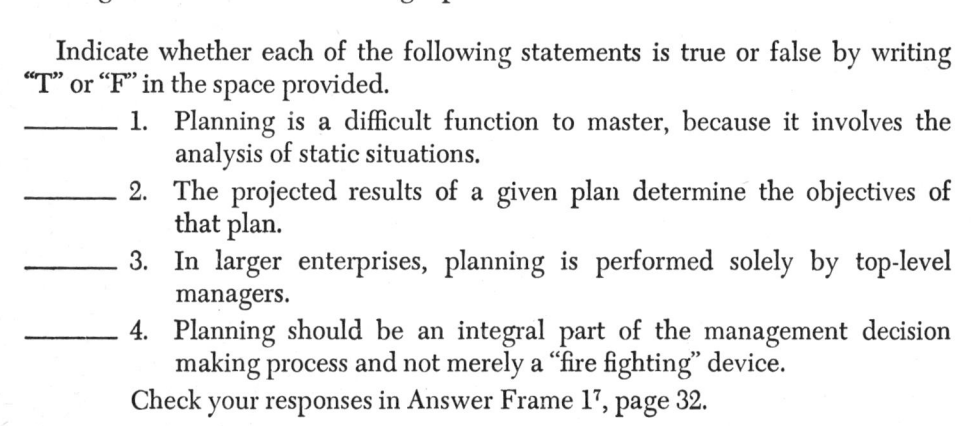

Indicate whether each of the following statements is true or false by writing "T" or "F" in the space provided.

_____ 1. Planning is a difficult function to master, because it involves the analysis of static situations.

_____ 2. The projected results of a given plan determine the objectives of that plan.

_____ 3. In larger enterprises, planning is performed solely by top-level managers.

_____ 4. Planning should be an integral part of the management decision making process and not merely a "fire fighting" device.

Check your responses in Answer Frame 1[7], page 32.

Frame 2[7]

The timing aspect of planning is also important. There is a proper time for most action. Help in recognizing this proper time is provided by planning. Most plans can be conveniently divided into phases, or successive time periods, for planned activities to take place. Thinking in terms of phases in planning helps to: (*a*) reduce the plan to a simple series of actions, (*b*) keep the planned efforts on schedule, (*c*) coordinate the separate activities within the plan, and (*d*) insure acceptance of the plan by all concerned or affected by it.

Assigning specific time periods to each component of a plan is also essential. When and within what time limits the activities must be accomplished are equally as important as the determination of what must be done. This assigning of time periods, or scheduling, gives vitality and practical meaning to a plan. But sufficient flexibility in the assigned due dates

Answer frame 1[7]

1. False. Planning is difficult because it deals with the analysis of *dynamic* situations.
2. False. Projected results do not determine objectives. Objectives guide the manager in the selection of a proper plan.
3. False. Every manager, regardless of position in the organization, has a planning function to perform.
4. True. Planning is just as important when things are going well as when current troubles abound.

Turn to Frame 2[7], page 31, and continue.

Frame 2[7] continued

should be provided, to permit adjustments as needed in the execution of the plan.

For any given case, the encompassing goal of management planning can usually be identified by any one of the following:

1. Maintain the status quo. Correct obvious deficiencies, but preserve the customary and current means of pursuing activities. Survival is vital; breaks with the past are minimized.

2. Adapt to major future changes. Utilize important modifications concerning trends, premises, or means of goal attainment. An element of opportunism is present. Changes are incorporated to improve overall facilities utilization, yet the general goals are maintained. Adaptive planning usually reduces the complexity of the planning.

3. Strive for maximum achievement. Emphasize optimization, i.e., to do as well as possible within known constraints of facilities and stated objectives. This utopia is achieved by using quantitative management techniques and ordinarily involves the use of a mathematical model. Seldom are inclusive optimum plans attained, but close approximations of them are.

For greatest practicality, plans should: (*a*) feature simplicity, be easy to understand, be profusely illustrated, and provide pertinent examples; (*b*) point out their advantages to each of the adopters; (*c*) fulfill a recognized need, and be within the capability of the management team; (*d*) pinpoint and contribute to the accomplishment of the objective; and (*e*) show clearly the respective responsibility and authority required for each group or individual, as well as the relationships among participants in the plan.

Indicate whether each of the following statements is true or false by writing "T" or "F" in the space provided.

_____ 1. Assigning specific time periods to each component of a plan is essential.

_____ 2. When management desires to maintain the status quo, the planning function is abandoned.

_____ 3. Management does not have to seek optimization in all plans.

_____ 4. Courses of action generated through planning cannot justifiably be criticized for being too complex or impractical.

Now see Answer Frame 2[7], page 34.

Frame 3[7]

Perhaps the outstanding argument for planning is that the act of putting thoughts down on paper and evolving a plan provides the planner with guidance and purposiveness. Ferreting out the facts; determining the course of action to follow; and estimating the time, energy, and materials needed are of themselves positive forces toward good management. Planning, by its very nature, helps to achieve goals. Planning reduces random activity and needless overlapping efforts.

Many managers point out that planning provides for effective utilization of available facilities of an enterprise. For any given period, the best use is made of what is available. This condition is envisioned, put together mentally, and offered in a communicative form by the planner. Guesswork by uninformed personnel is eliminated.

Furthermore, planning assists a manager in attaining confident and aggressive leadership. By means of planning, managers successfully cope with their affairs and problems, rather than allowing them to dilute and negate their efforts. Not to plan is to manage as a result of events rather than by use of foresight, influence, and action.

In addition, "what if" questions are answered by planning. Such answers permit a manager to see through a complexity of variables that affect what action should be taken. Typical questions are: "What would happen to our costs if we close plant No. 3?" "What would happen to our sales if we add a line of prepared foods to our product list?" Judgment, various "studies of the situation," and/or quantitative techniques and computers can be used to answer such questions.

Also, planning can point out the need for future change. It can reveal opportunities for new services. It guides management thinking to future desirable activities, and spells out how best to make the shift and what must be done to attain goals.

On the other hand, planning has practical limitations to its use. One such limitation is the accuracy of information and facts regarding the future. The usefulness of any plan is affected by the subsequent correctness of the assumptions, regarding the future, that were used in formulating the plan. No manager can completely and accurately predict future events.

Others contend that planning has limited value, because satisfactory results are obtained by a "muddling-through" type of operation in which each situation is tackled when and if it appears pertinent to the immediate problem. In this way, opportunism can be utilized to full advantage. Few plans, it is contended, are followed consistently to specific ends. However, to combat this contention, it can be stated that, in this day of many complexities, planning is the rule, not the exception, for work accomplishment.

Some feel that planning stifles employee initiative and forces managers to operate within rigid and limited constraints. These rigidities, it is contended, may tend to make the work of management more difficult than it need be. Instead of helping, they actually hinder. Such a viewpoint is not without justification; but as previously stated, the most effective, and preferred, plans provide some degree of elasticity and interpretation in their application.

There is also the psychological limitation to planning, exemplified by the propensity for people to have more regard for the present than for the future. The present has certainty and is more acceptable. The future is uncertain, unknown, and untried. Some also feel that planning tends to accelerate change and unrest.

In addition, it is believed by some that planning delays actions. Emergencies and the sudden occurrence of unusual situations demand immediate on-the-spot action. Undoubtedly, there are conditions where to permit postponement of action may result in chaos. Yet, it seems feasible to have outlines of plans to cover such emergencies, or at least to conduct affairs along uncharted courses only until adequate thought can be given to what the desired results should be, how best to achieve them with available facilities, and the probable consequence of the adopted course.

Answer frame 2⁷

1. True. Assigning specific time periods to each component of a plan *is* essential. But sufficient flexibility in the assigned due dates should be provided to permit adjustments as needed.
2. False. Maintenance of the status quo can be a goal of management and a guide for the planning function. A considerable amount of planning may be necessary to maintain things as they are.
3. True. Optimization is only one of the possible encompassing goals of the planning function.
4. False. Planning should result in the selection of courses of action that can be implemented by management.

Now continue with Frame 3⁷, page 33.

Frame 3⁷ continued

Indicate whether each of the following statements is true or false.

_____ 1. The fact that a plan is based on the future must be considered when the plan is translated into operating policies.

_____ 2. Some people support a "muddling-through" type of operation instead of one guided by formalized planning.

_____ 3. Planning does little to reduce random activity and overlapping of duties.

_____ 4. Some people criticize the planning function for dampening employee initiative and for complicating the work of management.

Check your answers in Answer Frame 3⁷, page 36.

chapter 8

FORECASTS, PREMISES, STRATEGIES, AND PLANNING

Frame 1[8]

Forecasting is the attempt to predict, through study and analysis of currently available pertinent data, future potential operations and conditions. It also tries to anticipate the future state of the social environment in which the enterprise will operate. Although all forecasts are subject to error and must rely to some extent on guesswork, forecasting is an essential prerequisite of management planning. To reduce the margin of error, managers must examine with great care all assumptions underlying their forecasts. Then, it is advisable to be reasonable about what is expected from the forecast, recognizing that it cannot achieve perfection.

Skill in forecasting is enhanced by: (a) using orderly procedures in the investigation of the available pertinent data on which the estimates are made, (b) enlisting the interest and participation of key managers in the preparation of the forecasting, (c) periodically checking actual results against forecasts and running down reasons for major differences, and (d) refining and improving the forecasting effort, as experience is gained and new forecasting tools become available.

Figure 5 shows the means for forecasting sales of an enterprise. Note that data from many sources are brought together into a unified corporate estimate.

To formulate the actual plan, a manager uses premises and constraints. Their use tends to reduce the uncertainty inherent in the future and to supply identifiable foundations on which planning can be based. *A premise is an assumption, providing a background against which estimated events affecting the planning are expected to take place.* Such assumptions must be made; otherwise planning would be impossible. For example, one could not draw up a master plan for an enterprise if one did not assume future markets, prices, taxes, and population growth.

Furthermore, constraints or boundaries, within which the planning efforts are confined, characterize the work of the planner. To illustrate: The basic resources at the disposal of the manager, the managerial philosophy followed, and attitudes toward society, in general, and toward associates condition and constrain the manager's planning efforts. Constraints tend to confine the planning within areas considered appropriate and feasible by the planner.

Both premises and constraints create boundaries within which the planning takes place; but constraints condition the planner's thinking, and supply a foundation on which plans are built, to a greater degree than do premises. Constraints are established more by intuition, judgment, attitude, and belief, than are premises.

Observe that premises and constraints do not generate specific plans. They provide the means for determining and assessing the future environment. Also note that *all planning premises are based on predictions.* However, some premises involve relatively little uncertainty, whereas

Answer frame 3[7]

1. True. Because no manager can completely and accurately predict the future, the potential error of a plan must be considered in the formulation of the operating policies.
2. True. The fact that satisfactory results have been obtained is used as an argument against the use of formal planning.
3. False. The reduction in random activity and in overlapping efforts is one of the strongest arguments for the planning function.
4. True. Some people do view planning as being responsible for the loss of employee initiative and for complicating the work of management.

You have completed Chapter 7. Now proceed to Chapter 8, page 35.

Frame 1[8] continued

others have great uncertainty. When the premises have this high degree of uncertainty, planning is looked on by some as a great guessing game.

Prediction is used to establish premises, not plans. Planning has a much broader connotation, and serves a different purpose from predicting. It is possible to predict without planning and, likewise, to plan without predicting. To recognize this fact helps to distinguish the controllable from the noncontrollable elements in planning efforts.

Within an enterprise, several different planning premises may be used, but these must be correlated, in order to achieve integration of the overall planning. Furthermore, as time advances the extent of the validity of the premises unfolds and subsequent adjustments in the premises are made. Frequently, additional premises are added. This process of review of premises is continuous. Actually, because of the interrelatedness of plans and their dependence on one another, every major plan adopted by an enterprise tends to become a planning premise.

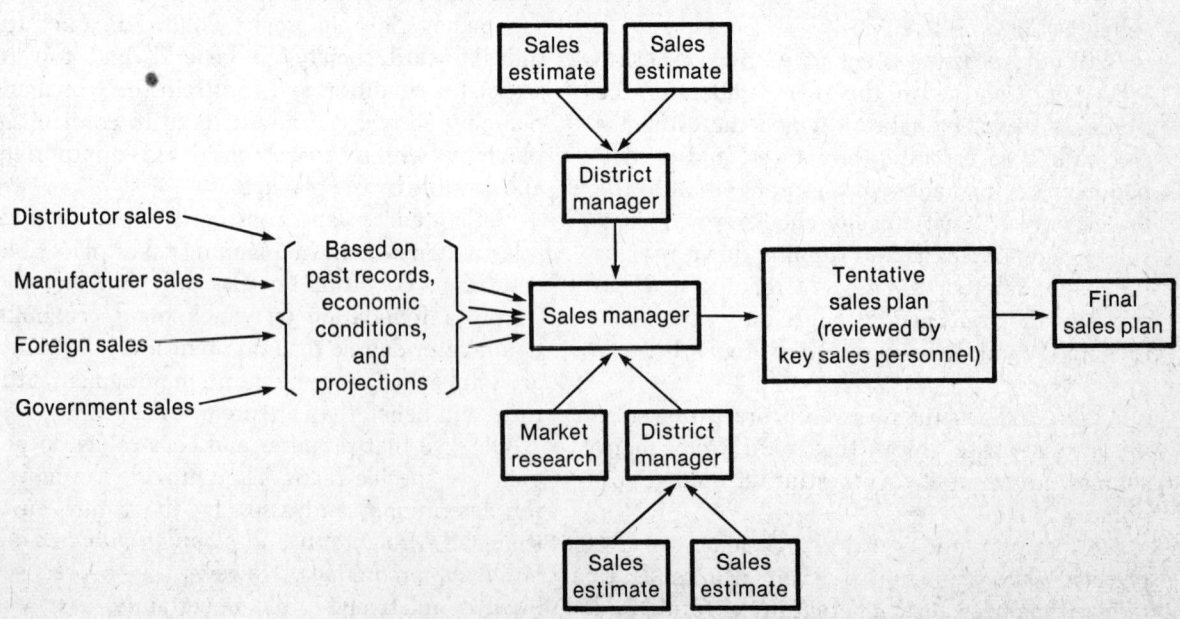

FIGURE 5

Developing Sales Forecast

Indicate whether each of the following statements is true or false by writing "T" or "F" in the space provided.

_____ 1. Since forecasts result from the analysis of pertinent data, they are free from errors due to guesswork or individual opinion.

_____ 2. The contribution of most managers in the forecasting process is the analyses of variances of the actual results from the forecast.

_____ 3. A manager's individual biases are more likely to influence definition of the constraints than definition of the premises.

_____ 4. Premises and constraints provide the means for determining and assessing the future environment.

Check your responses in Answer Frame 1[8], page 38.

Frame 2[8]

To perform planning intelligently, the manager must have information relating to the following:

1. Environment. Data on economic, political, and social factors influencing the climate in which the enterprise must operate.

2. Competition. Information on: (*a*) the industry, and (*b*) the accomplishments and activities of member firms within that industry.

3. Individual enterprise. Identification of the enterprise's strengths, weaknesses, characteristics, accomplishments, and ambitions.

Not all information is useful. From the information available, the planner must select what appears relevant to the task at hand. Too much or too little information can hamper planning. One must guard against hastily assuming that no facts are available about a certain activity, when adequate research would reveal that pertinent data can be found.

Facts contribute to the establishing of premises and the formulating of plans. To a lesser degree, they help shape the planning constraints that are adopted. But, it should also be remembered that intuition, judgment, and guesswork play a part in most plans. The manager does more than find facts and tie them together into a neat package.

Planning premises are numerous. Some are tangible, others intangible; some external to the enterprise, others internal; and some are vital, whereas others are of minor importance. The following premises, applicable to nearly every enterprise, serve to indicate the types used in planning:

1. Government controls. The activities of an enterprise are prohibited, regulated, or promoted by various laws and regulatory measures of government. The manager must anticipate the immediate future and long-range effect of such governmental regulation.

2. Government fiscal policy. The role of government in income distribution, taxation, and investment exercises important influences that the manager must take into account in making premises and plans.

3. General business environment. Premises about employment, national income, and productivity are representative. Data and well-considered estimates for such activities are available, and the planner can tap numerous sources to obtain realistic projections.

4. Price levels. The course of future price levels affects economic activity, inventories, consumers' confidence, and market development. Will prices rise, stabilize, or decline, and at what rate? Price is the universal regulator of economic activity.

5. Public attitudes and behavior. These are representative of a somewhat intangible, yet important, area in which premises must be drawn. How producers, consumers, groups, and individuals view and react to bigness in business, freedom of choice in the marketplace, and a "fair" profit, for example, are important considerations in planning.

Answer frame 1[8]

1. False. Forecasts are not free from error, because the analysis of data is subject to an individual's opinion.
2. False. As indicated in Figure 5, managers actively participate in the formulation of the forecast, and are not limited merely to the review of the variances of the actual results from the forecast.
3. True. Constraints are established more by intuition, judgment, attitude, and belief than are premises.
4. True. Premises and constraints provide means for determining and assessing the future environment within which specific plans are to be formulated.

Proceed to Frame 2[8], page 37.

Frame 2[8] continued

Strategic planning and tactical planning are two concepts widely used in today's management. Stated succinctly, strategic planning answers the question, "Where should we be going?" In contrast, tactical planning answers, "How will we get there?"

Strategic planning begins by asking questions with reference to the purpose and operations of an enterprise. What products and services are we trying to provide? Should we be doing everything we now are? What is happening socially, politically, and technologically that could have serious impact on us? Answers to questions such as these aid in determining whether what is now being done should be done, deciding what actions should be retained, what added, and putting these ideas into plans.

Common topics of strategic planning are the purpose of the enterprise, major environmental influences, the demand for the product or service, and competitive practices. Several advantages occur from strategies planning such as: (1) present mistakes and weak areas can be corrected; (2) assistance in arriving at decisions about the right things at the right time is provided; (3) aid in coping with future contingencies is gained; and (4) future actions to take in order to shape the future as desired are identified and highlighted.

The goal of strategic planning is to develop several strategic alternatives from which the strategic choice is made. Some alternatives may be expressed as: the size of the enterprise should reflect sales of $25 million; the amount of earnings before taxes should be 20 percent on sales; or the minimum return on investment should be 15 percent. Selection of the strategic choice is not entirely rational, since usually emotion, trade-offs, and judgment influence the choice. Actually, the choice is personal since to some degree it is influenced by the personal beliefs and values of the decider. In addition, timing is usually critical and a willingness to assume risk is paramount.

The term *strategy* connotes choosing how an enterprise's resources may be used most effectively to reach a stated goal. The strategy is planned to adjust to both internal and external environments. Expressed another way, the strategy states which factors will be emphasized in reaching the objective.

Several types of strategies are:

1. Strike while the iron is hot. Take prompt action while the situation is propitious; tomorrow may bring opposition and difficulties. Be prepared and act when a favorable situation develops.

2. Time is a great healer. Many problems disappear or take care of themselves if given sufficient time. Do not hurry or insist that certain actions take place; wait until they dilute themselves or begin moving toward the actions included in the plan.

3. Bore from within. Find out those members sympathetic to a specific course of action, and use them to spread this desired point of view. Give indirect assistance to this dedicated group. When a sufficient number of followers is obtained, proceed with the implementation of the plan.

4. Divide and rule. Keep group members separated into different factions to make it possible for one individual to maintain overall rule and control. Of questionable value in the long run, from the point of view of human development, it is highly effective in solving immediate problems of control. Some contend that it stifles management development and, in the long run, creates more problems than it solves. Nevertheless, it is used, and it thrives because of ignorance, strong differences of opinion among people and lust for power by some leaders.

Turning now from strategic planning to tactical planning, the latter consists of determining the tasks to be done, establishing who is responsible for what, allocating resources, setting quantitative measurements for each task, and implementing the planned actions with adequate exercise of controls to evaluate progress. Tactical planning is supportive to strategic planning. The combination of strategic and tactical planning makes it feasible for employees to have an understanding of the various activities of an enterprise and of why these activities will be performed.

Indicate whether each of the following statements is true or false by writing "T" or "F" in the space provided.

_____ 1. It is virtually impossible to attempt to use too much information in planning.
_____ 2. To be useful, information must be capable of being reduced to quantitative terms.
_____ 3. Planning premises all have equal importance in formulating plans.
_____ 4. Strategic planning answers the question, "How will we get there?"

Now see Answer Frame 2[8], page 40.

Answer frame 2[8]

1. False. Not all information is useful. From the available information, the planner must select only that which is relevant to the task at hand. Too much (or too little) information can hamper planning.
2. False. Useful information can be qualitative as well as quantitative.
3. False. Some premises are vital, whereas others are of minor importance.
4. False. Tactical planning answers that question. Strategic planning answers the question, "Where should we be going?"

You have completed Chapter 8. Now begin Chapter 9.

chapter 9

TYPES OF PLANS

Frame 1[9]

Because planning has been applied to all types of activities, there are numerous types of plans. Some plans deal with broad areas, some with narrow ones; some concern space considerations, whereas others emphasize performance, cost, quality, or another major attribute.

In the opinion of some managers, plans can be conveniently classified into the following:

1. Growth plans. These plans chart the direction in which the enterprise is going, its goals, and the rate of expansion sought. The rational way to ensure desirable growth is by the commitment of competent management members to growth, and by planning for that growth. In turn, this requires knowing where the enterprise is, where it is going, and where it should go; what major problems now stand or will stand in the way of achieving its goals; the time phasing for implementing the growth plans; and what specific activities are required to fulfill them.

2. Profit plans. Commonly, this type of plan is focused on profit per product or group of products. Headed by a profit planner, the entire plan points toward minimum effort and expenditure, in order to realize maximum profits. The normal time span for profit plans is one to three years.

3. User plans. How to market a selected product, or to serve a selected market better, is answered by user plans. Commonly called product planning or market planning, this type of plan is popular. Most people understand the subject being planned for, and user plans are widely used to illustrate planning techniques. The period covered by user plans is generally one year.

4. Personnel-management plans. Plans formulated to attract, develop, and retain management members are growing in importance. It is being recognized that managerial personnel cannot be left to chance; planning is essential.

Specific courses of action, tailored to the individual's needs and the company's requirements, are necessary for adequate leadership and for the development of management members to take place.

Indicate whether each of the following statements is true or false by writing "T" or "F" in the space provided.

_____ 1. Growth plans focus on the minimum effort and expenditure necessary to realize maximum profits.

_____ 2. User plans answer questions concerning the direction in which the enterprising is going.

_____ 3. Management-personnel plans deal with bringing about the availability of management members.

_____ 4. Profit plans commonly focus on profit per product or product line.

Now check your answers in Answer Frame 1[9], page 42.

Frame 2[9]

The classification of plans according to the period of time they cover is common. This leads to designating plans as *long range*—those dealing with five or more years, and *short range*—those involving two years or less. Plans covering from two to five years are termed long or short depending on the enterprise; some use the term *intermediate plans*, but this is not in wide usage.

Most managers like to use a time period sufficient to justify the dollar expenditure required by the plan. That is, they want the plan to include the time needed to recover their total dollar commitments. This is frequently expressed in terms of recovery costs. Acceptance of the commitment concept means that planning periods will vary considerably, depending on such things as the enterprise, the subject area planned for, and the beliefs of the top managers.

Further identifications of plans are orientational and operational plans. Usually, they are a particular type of either a long- or short-range plan. An orientational plan seeks to reveal the enterprise's current goals, activities, strengths, personnel, and relationship with customers. With these types of data as a background, a projection is made of what the future expectancies might be. In turn, this leads to an evaluation of whether this is where the managers want the enterprise to be. In contrast, an operational plan deals with current activities. It answers: Who is going to do what? The activation of physical resources—facilities, materials, and personnel—is dealt with. The planning is tangible, definite, and specific.

Indicate whether each of the following statements is true or false by writing "T" or "F" in the space provided.

_____ 1. Managers usually take a "recovery cost" approach to the analysis of potential expenditures.

_____ 2. A plan dealing with a three-year period is undoubtedly a short-range plan.

_____ 3. An operational plan relates the current environment to future expectancies.

_____ 4. An operational plan deals with activating the physical resources.

Check your responses in Answer Frame 2[9], page 42.

Answer frame 1[9]

1. False. Growth plans deal with the direction in which the enterprise is going, its goals, and the rate of expansion sought. Profit plans focus on the minimum effort and expenditure necessary to generate maximum profits.
2. False. User plans try to determine the best method to market a selected product or serve a market segment. Growth plans deal with the direction in which the enterprise is going.
3. True. Management personnel plans concern the attraction, development, and retention of management members.
4. True. Profit plans point toward minimum effort and expenditure, to realize maximum profit on specific products or groups of products.

If you missed any of the above, reread Frame 1[9] before beginning Frame 2[9] on page 41.

Answer frame 2[9]

1. True. In planning for an expenditure, most managers like to use a time period sufficient to justify the dollar expenditure required by the plan.
2. False. A plan dealing with a three-year period can either be regarded as a short-range or long-range plan, depending on the enterprise. The classification in this area is not standardized. Some would classify it as an *intermediate plan*.
3. False. An *orientational* plan relates the current environment to future expectancies. An *operational* plan coordinates current activities.
4. True. It answers "Who is going to do what?"

Continue with Frame 3[9], below.

Frame 3[9]

The following classification of plans is especially helpful in the study of management:

1. Objective. Although not always thought of as a plan, an objective is a basic type. It deals with future activities, requires foresight to formulate, and necessitates at least a modicum of planning for its determination. Some do not consider objectives and their identification as a part of managerial planning. They well justify their viewpoint, but the question is more academic than practical in the basic study of management and its application. What managers are trying to accomplish deserves special attention in management. Objectives are vital; they provide the targets for all managerial efforts, and they should focus all efforts of a manager.

2. Policy. An extremely important type of plan, a policy provides elastic and comprehensive boundaries or limitations within which managerial action will take place. For any given subject, a statement of policies reveals the manager's future intentions by defining the areas within which decisions will be made, but the decision itself, in keeping with the stated policy, is a prerogative of the manager. Judgment by the manager is required to interpret a policy; in fact, good policies tend to be broad, in order to leave room for judgment. In essence, policies give predetermined boundaries, but the manager has freedom to make decisions within these stated limits. Every enterprise needs enough policies to supply the basic guides for each major classification of its activities. Such policies should be individualistic and reflect the unique characteristics of the operating management members, yet should also be integrated within the enterprise, as discussed at the end of this chapter.

Policies help the manager to make decisions and yet stay within limits that are believed desirable. Their use: (*a*) enhances the confidence of the management member, (*b*) assists communication, (*c*) implements the effective utilization of authority, and (*d*) helps develop managerial skill.

3. Procedure. A procedure is a plan prescribing the exact chronological sequence of specific tasks required to perform designated work. It features the identification of the specific tasks, when each will take place, and by whom it is to be performed. Total expenditures of time, money, and effort are emphasized. Procedures find their greatest use for repetitive work; most procedures are employed over and over again, thus exemplifying what is known as "repetitive use plans."

Procedures tend to remain long after their usefulness has passed. Eliminating obsolete procedures and updating those proven necessary constitute one of the big challenges of modern management. Periodically, all procedures within an enterprise should be evaluated and subjected to the test of usefulness under current operating conditions.

4. Method. Basic to every action is a method—a prescribed plan for performing a specific task. Normally, a method is confined to the work of an employee while he is engaged in some specific task. A method details how the work is to be done, and is far more limited in scope than a procedure.

A manager's experience, knowledge, and ability to innovate determine, for the most part, what method is planned. "Motion study" is widely used today to determine the best means of performing a given task. Efforts to find a better way are codified in an approach called "work simplification," which is made up of these major steps:

1. Select the work to be simplified.
2. Analyze the selected work in detail.
3. Question each segment of the work.
4. Seek improvements by means of eliminating, combining, arranging, or simplifying the present work components.
5. Put improvements into effect.

5. Program. A comprehensive type of plan, the program brings together in an integrated format various plans for the future use of different resources of an enterprise. Its makeup is variable; for example, it might include any or all of the following: long- or short-range plans, orientational plans, operational plans, objectives, policies, and procedures. Unfortunately, the term program is used in many different ways in management planning literature. But, in practically all instances, a program involves large segments of an enterprise, especially those related to the work of accomplishing specific basic goals.

6. Standard. Plans that set forth norms or expectancies used in management are termed *standards*. To evaluate performance, a manager must have a reference or norm so that meaningful comparison can be made between what is accomplished and what is expected. A standard serves as a model for comparison. A standard does not represent perfection. Standards are essential in: (*a*) planning schedules, (*b*) achieving proper balance among resources available to a manager, and (*c*) ascertaining requirements.

7. Budget. This is a vital plan in many enterprises. A budget comes into being by means of planning that logically arranges data to represent expectancies for a stated period. Money, personnel, or any other entity, for which it is believed a future course of action will help management, can be budgeted. Characteristically, a budget; (*a*) is comprehensive—covers a large segment or all of an enterprise, (*b*) always applies to a specific period, (*c*) deals with activities that are to happen, and (*d*) increases in accuracy and usefulness, with experience in its preparation.

8. Techno-factor. This is a relatively new type of plan. It utilizes a technical approach with respect to time, cost, or material flow. Frequently, the planning–controlling functions of management are brought into clear focus by a techno-factor. No doubt in the future we will see more of this type of plan designed to assist the manager in specific critical managerial areas. Illustrative of techno-factor is PERT (Program Evaluation Review Technique), full discussion of which is included later in this book (Chapter 25) since its use places great emphasis upon controlling.

Integration of all plans within an enterprise is a cardinal consideration of management. Each plan used must, in effect, support every other plan and contribute to the major goal of the total managerial effort. Within a given enterprise, plans are interdependent. The policies followed are in keeping with the objectives. The long-range plans must be compatible with the operational plans, also with the growth plan, and with the user plans. Likewise, procedures are related to other procedures, and also to policies, methods, standards, and budgets. Serious trouble can arise when this interdependence is ignored.

Finally, plans tend to beget plans. The human tendency is to add or to modify existent plans; few are done away with completely. This means that current plans serve as guides in developing new plans, but more specifically, that the integration of plans can be elusive. The need for integration is paramount.

Indicate whether each of the following statements is true or false by writing "T" or "F" in the space provided.

_____ 1. Policies are vital; they provide the targets for all managerial efforts, and they should permeate all efforts of a manager.

_____ 2. A method is far more limited in scope than is a procedure.

_____ 3. Both standards and budgets are based on the assumption of maximum efficiency or perfection.

_____ 4. Due to the interdependence of all types of plans, integration of plans must be considered to properly implement the results of the planning function.

Compare your answers with those given in Answer Frame 3[9], page 46.

chapter 10

PUTTING PLANS INTO ACTION

Frame 1[10]

Frequently, the approach used in planning is to ask questions, the answers to which suggest not only material that should be included in the plan, but areas for further study to make the plan complete. Many different lists of questions have been prepared to help the planner, but all such aids tend to cluster around the "Five W's and the How" questions. These always should be asked in the following sequence:

1. Why must it be done? This highlights the real need for the work and the essentials of it.

2. What is necessary? The types and amounts of activities called for, as well as the machine and equipment requirements, are disclosed by the answers to this question.

3. Where will it take place? This stresses space considerations. In an office, in the field, in a branch office—at what location must the work be done?

4. When will it take place? This stresses time considerations. When should each segment of the work start and stop? Scheduling and simultaneous operations are discovered by answering this question.

5. Who will do it? This question is designed to reveal the type and availability of skill and experience needed to perform the planned work satisfactorily.

6. How will it be done? This question directs attention to the proposed manner of work accomplishment. Actually, it serves as a check on the entire plan and as a test of the thoroughness with which the first five questions have been answered.

Indicate whether each of the following statements is true or false by writing "T" or "F" in the space provided.

_____ 1. In utilizing the checklist of questions for the planner, the first question to be answered is "Why must it be done?"

_____ 2. The answer to the question "What is necessary?" indicates the factors of production that will be necessary.

_____ 3. The answer to the question "How will it be done?" deals with the thoroughness of the entire plan.

_____ 4. The answer to the question "Who will do it?" refers to the skill and qualities of the individuals needed to carry out the plan.

Now check your responses by referring to Answer Frame 1[10], page 46.

Answer frame 3⁹

1. False. *Objectives* provide the targets for all managerial efforts, and they should permeate all efforts of a manager. Policies provide elastic and comprehensive boundaries or limitations within which managerial action will take place.
2. True. Methods *are* more limited in scope than are procedures. Procedures prescribe the exact chronological sequence of specific tasks required to perform designated work; normally, a method is confined to the work of an individual employee while engaged in a specific task.
3. False. Both standards and budgets are based on expectancies, rather than maximum efficiency or perfection.
4. True. All plans of an enterprise are interdependent. Difficulty and serious trouble arise when this interdependence is ignored. Integration of all plans within an enterprise is a cardinal consideration of management.

You have completed Chapter 9. Now begin Chapter 10, page 45.

Answer frame 1¹⁰

1. True. The question "Why must it be done?" is the first question to be answered, because it highlights the real need for the work and the essentials of that work.
2. True. The answer to the question "What is necessary?" requires the determination of the types and amounts of activities called for, as well as the machine and equipment requirements.
3. True. The answer to the question "How will it be done?" serves as a check upon the entire plan, and indicates the thoroughness in answering the other questions.
4. True. "Who will do it?" deals with the type of skill and experience that will be needed to satisfactorily perform the planned work, and with the availability of individuals possessing these traits.

Begin Frame 2¹⁰, below.

Frame 2¹⁰

Most planning is characterized by key steps that serve as a common thread in this basic managerial effort, as follows:

1. Visualize and state the problem which the planning is intended to help solve. It is vital that the planners be able to vividly see what they are trying to accomplish, what major hurdles or present conditions appear to require modification or elimination, and what additions seem desirable. Seeing the problem clearly is fundamental to good planning.

2. Obtain and classify usable information about the proposed activities. Ideas and concepts of what the plan should include are obtained from records, observations, interviews, experience, practices of other enterprises, magazine articles, research reports, and selected books. However, what has been done in the past should not necessarily be continued. To render information useful, it must be classified. This, in turn, requires careful examination of the information to reveal its relevancy to the planning at hand and also the pertinent relationships among the various bits of information.

3. Select planning premises. The planner's beliefs, the purpose of the plan, and the information assembled will suggest what premises to assume. Premises, always present in a plan, supply the needed assumptions against which it is believed future actions of the plan will take place. They should be identified, so that the plan can be completely understood.

4. Draw up several plans and from these choose the plan to follow. There are several means of achieving every goal. The various possibilities are revealed in this step. Much creativeness may be required to do so, but unless more than one means is evolved, the planning will be incomplete. From the array of possible plans, a choice is made. Cost, adaptability, efficiency, custom, and personal preference are given top priority in making the final choice.

5. Determine details and timing of the selected plan and arrange for proper follow-up.

The precise sequence of activities—who does what and when, instructions, paper forms, and needed supplies—are now worked out. Results obtained are the true measure of the appropriateness of the plan. To ensure satisfactory results, provisions for adequate follow-up are developed.

Indicate whether each of the following statements is true or false by writing "T" or "F" in the space provided.

_____ 1. If the premises of the planner are not specifically stated, individuals reviewing the plan may have trouble in understanding the plan.

_____ 2. A planner should concentrate on the formulation of just one way of achieving the goal; i.e., only one plan should be generated from a particular planning process.

_____ 3. The last point to be investigated is identifying and understanding the problem that the resultant plan is designed to solve.

_____ 4. Follow-up is an essential feature of putting plans into action.

Compare your answers with those in Answer Frame 2[10], page 48.

Frame 3[10]

Dynamic programming (*DP*) is a term being used more and more in management planning. DP's aim is the achievement of the best decision at each stage of a multistage planning project. Figure 6 shows three sequential stages with four alternates at stage No. 1, two alternates at stage No. 2, and two alternates at stage No. 3. The initial planning sets forth the pathway B–1A2–2A2–3A2–R as the most desirable. However, we really don't know whether 2A2 is the best alternate at stage No. 2 until after we actually complete the activities of stage No. 1A2. It might be that when No. 1A2 is completed, an alternate other than No. 2A2 will be seen as the superior course to follow. In fact, this is the case shown in Figure 6. At stage No. 2, alternate No. 2A1 was determined to be superior to No. 2A2. The final revised sequence turned out to be B–1A2–2A1–3A1–R. The computer has made DP feasible; all forces affecting the plan can be processed, and the plan updated as events occur.

Who performs planning? The answer: every manager. Some do all or most of their own planning, others share the work, whereas others have specialists and subordinates perform the lion's share of the planning efforts. No single or simple arrangement applies equally to all enterprises, nor is any approach to planning consistently followed. The personal wishes of the management members, custom, and individual circumstances determine, for the most part, the practice, in any specific case. However, in general, managers at the top level devote their planning time to plans of relatively long duration (six months or more),

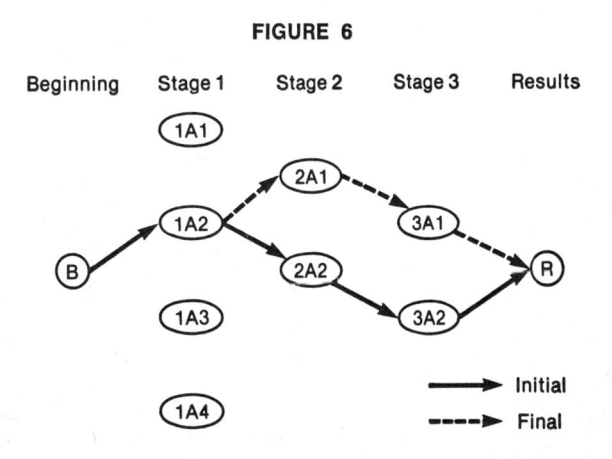

FIGURE 6

Beginning   Stage 1   Stage 2   Stage 3   Results

⟶ Initial
--→ Final

Answer frame 2¹⁰

1. True. Premises of the planner should be specifically stated so that the plan can be understood.
2. False. There are several ways of achieving every goal. Unless more than one way is identified, the planning is incomplete.
3. False. Identifying and understanding the problem is a *prerequisite* to formation of the plan.
4. True. Provisions for follow-up are essential in ensuring that satisfactory results are obtained.

Turn to Frame 3¹⁰, page 47, and continue.

Frame 3¹⁰ continued

whereas managers at the bottom levels concentrate on plans of relatively short duration (several hours to several months).

The trend is toward wider participation in planning. The typical manager today seeks facts, opinions, ideas, and reactions, in formulating plans. It is believed that, in this way, better plans are evolved, human relations are promoted, and endorsement and enthusiasm for the plan are won by those who are going to use it.

A common arrangement is to have a basic planning committee supplemented by project-planning teams. The committee consists of top management members whose duties include clarifying major goals and integrating basic recommendations, submitted primarily by the project teams. Each team consists of one member from the planning committee, plus managers who have charge of activities pertinent to the project team's work. Members of project teams represent diverse backgrounds and experiences. The responsibilities include gathering information, recommending courses of action, and studying basic questions, supplied by the planning committee. In addition, both committee and project team members encourage other management members, especially technicians and specialists, to participate in the planning.

More and more enterprises are setting up a department of planning. The duties of such a department vary widely. Some are limited to a specific type of planning, such as financial planning, whereas others develop long-range inclusive plans for the company. A planning department adds status to planning work, and it provides a center for motivating others to plan by offering suggestions, supplying information, and assisting in the formulation of practical plans.

Indicate whether each of the following statements is true or false by writing "T" or "F" in the space provided.

_____ 1. Dynamic programming consists of the prejudging of alternatives at each stage of a multistage planning project.

_____ 2. Managers at the top levels tend to devote their planning time to plans of relatively short duration, whereas managers at the bottom levels tend to concentrate on plans of relatively long duration.

_____ 3. When a planning committee and project-planning teams are used, managers who are not members of the committee or teams are encouraged to contribute to the planning process.

_____ 4. A department of planning is used only in financial planning.

Check your answers by turning to Answer Frame 3¹⁰, page 50.

Frame 4¹⁰

The performance of planning has certain characteristics worthy of note. They include:

1. The place to start planning. It is better to start planning with the major issues. This not only permits a broad structure, but also resolves important considerations essential for subsequent planning. Frequently, the planner finds it advantageous to work backwards from the objective, as in scheduling. This approach gives emphasis to the objectives. Some advocate the starting of planning at the top-organization level, whereas others suggest starting at the bottom level. Starting at the top gives needed direction and encouragement to all planning and is the preferred viewpoint. Starting at the bottom supplies plans quickly where they are frequently most needed and where the issues can be fully comprehended.

2. The influence of human element. The success or failure of any plan is directly related to the manner in which employees do their respective jobs. Strong belief in the plans and acceptance of responsibilities set forth are foremost in the effectiveness of most plans. Because of the human element involved, good plans can fail; likewise, mediocre plans can succeed.

3. The makeup of components. Plans contain two types of issues: (a) variable and (b) constant. The former regulate the number of alternatives derived from a plan and, normally, deserve the greatest amount of attention by the planner. Also, a plan contains (a) tangible factors and (b) intangible factors. The former are measurable and permit valid comparisons and summaries. In contrast, intangible factors are far less measurable, reflect chiefly the experience and judgment of the planner, and represent most of the risk of the plan.

4. The tentative process of planning. Most plans are evolved slowly. They start with initial concepts and data. These are refined, integrated, added to and subtracted from, and portions are changed completely, until the final plan is formulated. Planning is a trial-and-error, how-would-this-work type of activity. It is not solely a logical and rational activity.

Indicate whether each of the following statements is true or false by writing "T" or "F" in the space provided.

_____ 1. The main advantage of starting the planning process at the bottom of the organization is that it builds up direction and encouragement.

_____ 2. The success or failure of any plan is related not only to the technical quality of the plan, but also to the degree of commitment of the employees to the plan.

_____ 3. The formulation of a specific plan is likely to rely, to some degree, on the trial-and-error approach.

_____ 4. In reviewing a plan, the reviewer is more likely to question the planner's definition of the intangible factors than to question the planner's definition of the tangible factors.

Check your responses with those in Answer Frame 4¹⁰, page 50.

Answer frame 3¹⁰

1. False. Dynamic programming deals with the achievement of the best decision at each stage of a multistage planning process; prejudging of alternatives is eliminated.
2. False. Managers at the top levels tend to devote their planning time to plans of a relatively *long* duration, while managers at the bottom levels tend to concentrate on plans of a relatively *short* duration.
3. True. Members of a planning committee and project-planning teams encourage other managers, especially technicians and specialists, to participate in planning.
4. False. The duties of a department of planning vary widely. Some are limited to a specific type of planning, whereas others develop long-range inclusive plans for the company.

Now turn to Frame 4¹⁰, page 49.

Answer frame 4¹⁰

1. False. Starting planning at the top of the organization gives needed direction and encouragement to all planning and is the preferred viewpoint. Starting planning at the bottom supplies plans quickly where they are frequently needed and where the issues can be comprehended fully.
2. True. Because of the acceptance and support of employees, mediocre plans can succeed; likewise, lacking this acceptance and support, good plans can fail.
3. True. Planning is a trial-and-error, how-would-this-work activity. It is not solely a logical and rational activity.
4. True. Intangible factors are far less measurable than are tangible factors and they reflect chiefly the experience and judgment of the planner. These intangible factors represent most of the risk of the plan.

You have completed Chapter 10. You may want to work the examination, beginning on page 157, covering Chapters 1–10. Then go on to Chapter 11, page 51.

chapter 11

ORGANIZATION CONCEPTS

Frame 1[11]

Organizing is a basic activity of management. It is performed to assemble and arrange all required resources, including people, so that the required work can be accomplished successfully. Actually, people are foremost in importance and interest. By means of organizing, people are united in performing interrelated tasks. The goal of organizing is to assist people in working effectively together.

A manager must know what activities to manage, who helps and who is helped, the channels of communication, the clustering of work that is followed, the relationships among individual employees and among different work groups, and the general makeup of the work group. Answers to these questions are given by effective organizing. Further, the nonmanager needs to: (a) have an accurate and concise understanding of the job's requirements, (b) know the relationship of the job to other jobs, and (c) know his or her own relationship with the immediate manager and also with other nonmanagers in the work group. Again, organizing provides this information.

Organizing comes into being because the work to be done is too much for one person to handle. Hence, helpers are obtained, and the problem of gaining effective group action is created. Many minds, hands, and skills may be assembled, and these must be coordinated not only to accomplish the defined work, but also to provide work satisfaction to each member in keeping with respective wants, skill, and knowledge. In these efforts, the typical organizer strives to achieve a total effect greater than the sum of its individual parts. In other words, the manager strives for *synergism* —the simultaneous action of separate but related parts to produce a sum greater than that of its separate components.

Historically, organizing pervades all human activity, because of the individual's dependency on society and because of our desire to gain protection against antisocial forces that threaten us. Writings of ancient history are filled with references to organizing as it affected armies, government, and religious groups. This interest continues unbroken right down to the present.

Prominent throughout the centuries, and especially so at the present time, is the underlying and knotty question of the proper balance between organizing efficiency and individual freedom. Can a person possess freedom and still be a part of an efficient organization? Specifically, how is the proper balance to be achieved between freedom and organizing efficiency? For maximum benefits, how much guidance and restraint should be blended with individual initiative and freedom? These questions are difficult ones. A universal answer, applicable to all cases, is lacking. Every attempted answer must be heavily qualified.

Indicate whether each of the following statements is true or false by writing "T" or "F" in the space provided.

_____ 1. Organizing is necessitated by the fact that employees are basically lazy.

_____ 2. Organizing is based on the assumption that efficiency must be subservient to individual (employee) freedom.

_____ 3. Organizing is a function that was nonexistent prior to the Industrial Revolution.

_____ 4. The goal of organizing is to assist people in working together effectively.

Turn to Answer Frame 1[11], page 54, to check your answers.

Frame 2[11]

Long experience and interest in organizing have led to many different beliefs and theories of organizing. Among the most important are the following:

1. The neoclassical theory. This theory emphasizes the accomplishment of work. Maximum work achievement is sought through maintaining a logical and balanced arrangement of the necessary functions. Division of labor is followed, and jobs are defined. The approach, however, is not mechanistic.

The impact of human relations on the structure is recognized, and human behavior, both individual and group as well as formal and informal, has a role in the theory. In addition, environment and social values are woven into the overall pattern of interdependency of the various organization components, and the influence of these values on the organization is included.

2. The fusion theory. This theory points out that an individual uses an organization to achieve personal goals and, in turn, the organization uses the individual to further its goals. By a "personalizing process," the individual seeks freedom of decision and optimum performance, whereas the organization, by a "socializing process," requests completion of work assignments and gives rewards or penalties. These personalizing and socializing processes are fused by means of organizing, according to this theory.

3. The quantitative theory. Here measurable factors affecting organizing are related and processed, so as to derive the best organization in keeping with the restraints that are assumed to exist. Illustrative of measurable factors are the number of decisions made by each manager and the number of people reporting to a manager. In some instances, satisfactory mathematical models and formulas have been developed. The theory strives to increase organizing's preciseness and degree of rationale.

4. The systems theory. In this theory, organizing is viewed as a system of mutually dependent variables that include: (a) the individual, (b) the formal arrangement of functions, (c) the informal arrangement of functions, (d) the behavior patterns resulting from the reactions to the role requirements of the organization and the role perception by the individual, and (e) the physical environment in which the organization exists. These variables are held together by the system's imbalance or influence upon its components, assisted by communication and decision making. The theory considers all the factors, existing within the system, as a dynamic unity that reacts to and shapes its environment.

All these theories are meaningful and offer helpful knowledge about organizing. Some are further developed than are others, and some are more familiar and enjoy wider acceptance than do others. Which is superior depends on: (a) the user's knowledge and understanding of organizing, (b) the particular background or setting involved, and (c) the problem of organizing that is being confronted.

Change in an organization is a vital concept. This change can be classified as taking place either in: (*a*) structure, (*b*) motivation, or (*c*) technology. A change in any one of these affects either or both of the remaining two. For example, to inject greater motivation or to change it requires, from the organizing viewpoint, a change in either structure or technology, or in both. More discussion of organization change is presented in Chapter 16.

Indicate whether each of the following statements is true or false by writing "T" or "F" in the space provided.

_____ 1. The organizing function is very important in the fusion theory.
_____ 2. The neoclassical theory focuses on the accomplishment of work.
_____ 3. The qualitative theory strives to increase organizing's preciseness and degree of rationale.
_____ 4. All of the theories of organizing contain some insights that are helpful to a manager.

Compare your answers with those in Answer Frame 2[11], page 54.

Frame 3[11]

There are four *tangible components of organizing*, and they can be remembered by the word, WERE, standing for Work, Employees, Relationships, and Environment. Let us look at these four components more closely.

1. Work. The functions to be performed are derived from the stated objectives. These functions form the foundation for the organization. The functions are segregated into subfunctions and in turn to sub-subfunctions. This is done because: (*a*) work distribution among a group requires that the work be divided, and (*b*) work specialization necessitates small parcels of tasks. From these various functions, clusters of work activities are now formed on the basis of either similarity of work or efficiency; that is, if placed in certain clusters, they will be performed best. These clusters are termed "organization work units." Figure 7 shows the use of the tangible components in organizing.

2. Employees. Each person is assigned a specific portion of the total work. Preferably, the assignment should give full recognition to the employee's interest, behavior, experience, and skill. This recognition is vital in organizing. The assignment to an individual usually consists of a

FIGURE 7

The Tangible Components of Organizing Are Used to Create a Formal Organization Structure

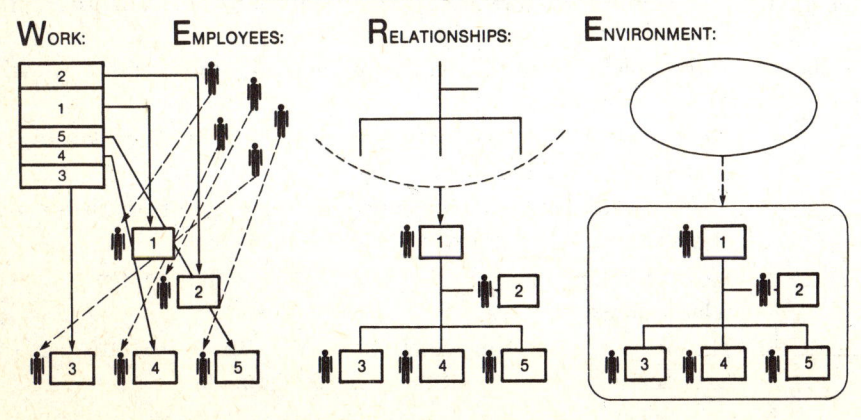

Answer frame 1[11]

1. False. Organizing comes into being because the work to be done is too much for one person to handle.
2. False. In organizing, it is realized that there must be some balance between the demand for efficiency and the right of individual freedom.
3. False. Historically, organizing pervades all human activity. Ancient history is filled with reference to organizing as it affected armies, governments, and religious groups. This interest continues unbroken right down to the present.
4. True. Organizing is a basic activity of management, and is performed to assemble and arrange all required resources, including people, so that the required work can be successfully accomplished. Foremost in importance and interest are people. By means of organizing, people are united in interrelated tasks.

Now go to Frame 2[11], page 52, and continue reading.

Answer frame 2[11]

1. True. According to the fusion theory, the personalizing and socializing processes are fused by means of organizing.
2. True. The accomplishment of work *is* emphasized by the neoclassical theory.
3. False. The *quantitative* theory strives to increase organizing's preciseness and degree of rationale.
4. True. All of the theories of organizing are meaningful and offer helpful knowledge about organizing.

Proceed to Frame 3[11], page 53.

Frame 3[11] continued

part of the work of an organization work unit or, in some cases, it includes all the work of that unit. Also, in certain instances, the work of several units is included. From this step results an "organization work-employee unit."

3. Relationships. These are of major concern in organizing. The relationship of an employee to the work, the interaction of one employee with another, and of work-employee unit to work-employee unit are crucial issues of organizing. The sought-for harmony and unity of effort are possible only if these relationships are adequate and correct. Most problems in organizing deal, in some measure, with relationship difficulties.

4. Environment. This last component of organizing includes the physical means and the general climate within which the employees are to perform the work. The location, machines, desks, paper forms, light, general morale, and attitudes are representative of the factors making up the environment. It has a significant effect on the results obtained from organizing.

Indicate whether each of the following statements is true or false by writing "T" or "F" in the space provided.

_____ 1. The tangible components of organizing are Work, Employees, Relationships and Environment.

_____ 2. The stated objectives of the enterprise are drawn from the definition of the work to be performed.

_____ 3. Most problems in organizing can be traced to problems regarding relationships.

_____ 4. The physical setting in which the work is to be performed must be considered in carrying out the organizing function.

Now check your answers in Answer Frame 3[11], page 56.

Frame 4[11]

Out of organizing emerges an *organization structure* that shows the flow of interactions within the organization—who decides what, who tells whom, who responds, and who performs what work. Things don't always happen, however, as indicated by the structure, not only because the structure may not be complete, but also primarily because we are dealing with human beings who have different interactions in keeping with their personalities. The interaction pattern is commonly set by the work and the employee assigned to it. In time, this interaction usually becomes quite stable. The employee adjusts to the work requirements and, in fact, resents any change in his habitual work pattern. A person may enjoy adequate satisfaction from work efforts. On the other hand, the employee initially may react extremely unfavorably to the work, and this gives rise to serious and immediate difficulties.

This brings up the subject of *behavior*, which is paramount in organizing. There are many types of behavior and most, if not all, of them exist in an organization. For simplicity, however, two types are considered here: (*a*) *formal*, and (*b*) *nonformal*. Formal behavior is prescribed by the formal organization structure and is the type we have been discussing. Nonformal behavior is not prescribed, but it exists within the formal organization structure.

Formal behavior results from using prescribed communication channels, standardized methods for performing tasks, work-oriented attitudes, clearly defined jobs, and stated lines of command among work-employee units. In some cases, desirable social conduct is spelled out, and employees are encouraged to conform to accepted norms of behavior, to develop a sense of duty, and to find self-enrichment in their work. Pay increases and promotions depend on such conformity.

Nonformal behavior is behavior neither prescribed nor included in the formal organization makeup. The fact that it is not a part of formal organization does not mean that it is undesirable. Much nonformal behavior is advantageous, contributing to efficiency and satisfying employees in its unique way. Nonformal behavior is psychologically and socially inspired and created. Cultural likes and dislikes, individual values, and socializing on the job are typical of factors leading to nonformal behavior. Such factors can be studied, and the resultant behavior analyzed in terms of *dysfunctions*, which are formal organization characteristics that cause or permit the nonformal behavior to exist.

Dysfunctions are many, but most common are those existing in structure, work process specifications, duties, responsibilities, and differentiation of decision-making responsibility among different employees. To illustrate: A formal work process specification may not apply to all the work that an employee performs, or it may conflict with instructions insisted on by a specialist who is not the immediate superior of the employee. In such cases, the employee draws heavily from his or her own scale of values, experience, dedication to work, and opinions expressed by work associates. The nonformal behavior is followed because formal behavior is not clearly defined or does not meet the situation with which the employee is faced.

Indicate whether each of the following statements is true or false by writing "T" or "F" in the space provided.

_____ 1. If actual interaction patterns differ from those depicted in the organization structure, the structure must be incomplete.

_____ 2. Nonformal behavior is behavior that is not prescribed by the formal organization; therefore, it is unacceptable behavior.

_____ 3. An employee resorts to nonformal behavior out of spite.

_____ 4. Dysfunctions permit the establishment of nonformal behavior.

Compare your answers with those in Answer Frame 4[11], page 56.

Answer frame 3[11]

1. True. The tangible components of organizing are Work, Employees, Relationship, and Environment.
2. False. Just the opposite is true. The work to be performed is derived from the stated objectives of the enterprise.
3. True. Most problems in organizing deal, in some measure, with relationship difficulties.
4. True. The last component of organizing, the environment, gives recognition to the physical setting in which the work is to be performed.

Continue by reading Frame 4[11], page 55.

Answer frame 4[11]

1. False. The actual interaction patterns typically differ from those depicted in the organization structure, because we are dealing with human beings who have different interactions in keeping with their personalities.
2. False. Many types of nonformal behavior are advantageous, contributing to efficiency and satisfying employees in a unique way.
3. False. An employee utilizes nonformal behavior because formal behavior is not clearly defined or does not meet the situation being faced.
4. True. Dysfunctions are characteristics of the formal organization that cause or permit nonformal behavior to exist.

Now go to Frame 5[11], below.

Frame 5[11]

An *organization chart* is drawn to help visualize the formal organization. Such a chart shows what activities are performed and by whom, the work groupings of activities, and their relationships. Chart lines, joining the organization work-employee units, indicate the formal flow of communication and decision making. The most popular arrangement places those having the greatest decision-making authorization at the top of the chart and those with the least at the bottom (see Figure 8).

Figure 8 also indicates areas where nonformal behavior exists. For example, the credit and collections manager marked with a "1," and one of the division sales managers, also marked with a "1," get together and discuss and make decisions regarding collections on the division manager's accounts. Likewise, the vice president of research marked with a "2," and one of the foremen in production, also marked with a "2," work together and jointly decide how to make certain pieces of equipment needed for research projects. In similar manner, those managers marked with the same number, such as 3, 4, 5, or 6, practice nonformal behavior.

Organization charts are helpful in: (a) identifying organization levels, such as top, intermediate, and bottom; (b) naming units of each level, such as division, department, and section; and (c) assigning titles.

Organization manuals are becoming more common. Various formats are used, but each supplies complete information on each major job and outlines its requirements, limitations, and relationships to other jobs in the enterprise.

The main advantages of organization charts and manuals lie in their preparation and maintenance. They force the person preparing them to think about organizing and to make difficult organization decisions. Further, they serve as good sources of information for: (a) training purposes, (b) settling disputes, and (c) referring to past organizational arrangements. On the other hand, they: (a) are difficult to keep up-to-

11 Organization concepts   57

FIGURE 8

An Organization Chart with Notations, Showing Existence of Nonformal Behavior
(i.e., "1" with "1", "2" with "2", "3" with "3", and so forth)

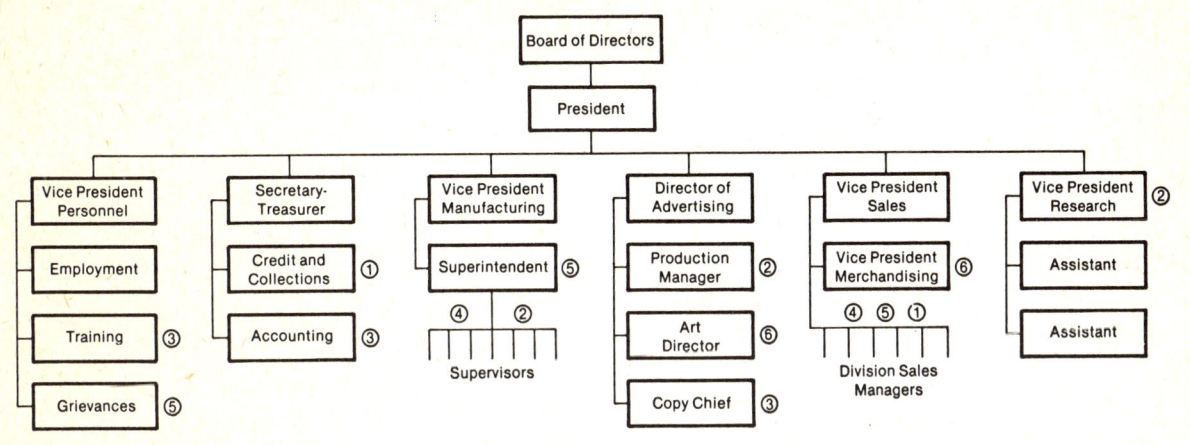

date, (b) might erroneously be viewed as the organization itself rather than a symbol of it, and (c) provide limited information—for example, only formal organization normally is included.

Indicate whether each of the following statements is true or false by writing "T" or "F" in the space provided.

_____ 1. An organization chart is an abstract of the formal organization of the enterprise.

_____ 2. All organization charts are set up in the same manner, with the higher levels of authority at the top of the chart and the lower levels of authority at the bottom.

_____ 3. The preparer of the organization charts and manuals receives the main benefits of those charts and manuals.

_____ 4. Organization manuals are similar to corporate charters, in that they are only compiled once.

Compare your answers with those given in Answer Frame 5[11], page 58.

Answer frame 5[11]

1. True. An organization chart *is* an abstract of the formal organization. It normally does not depict the nonformal organization.
2. False. Although the vertical arrangement for organization charts as illustrated in Figure 8 is the most popular, other types of organization charts are used.
3. True. Although organization charts and manuals are useful for training, settling disputes, and references to past organizational arrangements, the main advantages of the charts and manuals lie in their preparation and maintenance.
4. False. Organizational manuals must be kept up to date through periodic revision.

You have completed Chapter 11. Now begin Chapter 12, below.

chapter 12

ORGANIZATION: PERSONAL AND SOCIAL CONSIDERATIONS

Frame 1[12]

As a manager, the people with whom you work are very important. How people are organized is also very important. Whether goals are reached or not, whether team effort is present or not, and whether workers are satisfied or not, is, to a very great extent, influenced by the effectiveness of the organization devised and developed. In this chapter the discussion is directed toward satisfying, through organizing, the human and social needs of the managers and nonmanagers.

Satisfaction from working at a job is gained through: (*a*) off-the-job satisfactions, and (*b*) on-the-job satisfactions. The former are usually indirect and are made possible by such things as providing status or a sense of importance to an individual in the eyes of the community, giving favorable publicity to the person, contributing to and assisting in a wanted public endeavor, or building an employee's influence and ability to operate within an organization. In contrast, on-the-job satisfactions are attained directly from performing the work and are probably of greater importance to both the employee and the organization. They are reached only if organizing is done in such a manner as to produce such satisfactions, and if, at the same time, the organizing followed serves to further the goals of the enterprise.

Several ways in which these on-the-job satisfactions can be assisted by organizing are:

1. Scope of decision making. Freedom to

12 Organization: Personal and social considerations

decide issues pertaining to his or her work affords self-assertion, which is personally satisfying to most people. This freedom aids in fulfilling self-expression needs and permits people to gain the feeling that they are running their own job, preparing themselves for future growth, and enjoying the satisfaction of achievement.

2. Reciprocal relationships. For maximum satisfaction, the organizing should strive for reciprocal, not one-way, relationships. Employees enjoy a "give-and-take" discussion about issues affecting them as well as factors affecting their jobs.

3. Size of work-employee unit. The satisfaction of belonging, of personal achievement, and of doing something important are enhanced when the work group is kept within a reasonable size, say up to 15 persons. Beyond this number, the satisfying of personal needs of employees through organizing becomes more difficult. Likewise, having an employee work alone may create difficulties, in that the person is isolated and cannot interact with the co-workers.

4. Degree of work specialization. A too-specialized job can rob the employee of opportunity for growth, of seeing the relationship of the task to the overall work, and of achieving a sense of accomplishment.

5. Reporting to high-level executives. Most everyone likes to report to a person at the top level. This denotes status, adds to the reporter's prestige, and reflects the importance of the work being done. Organizing can provide this arrangement, when deemed desirable.

Indicate whether each of the following statements is true or false by writing "T" or "F" in the space provided.

_____ 1. An employee gains only on-the-job satisfactions from working at a job.

_____ 2. Management can assist the employee in achieving on-the-job satisfaction by properly organizing the work.

_____ 3. Most people try to avoid any decision-making responsibility.

_____ 4. Most people prefer to be assigned a job and then to be left alone to perform that job.

Turn to Answer Frame 1[12], page 60, to compare your answers.

Frame 2[12]

As pointed out in Chapter 3, culture can be thought of as a system of values and sanctions of society. Since organizing has a strong personnel makeup and is, in fact, people working together within a framework, there exists in every organization values and sanctions influencing the patterns of behavior that are associated with working and being a part of that organization. In other words, all organizations have cultures that are essential to the existence and operations of the organization.

In addition, behavior is greatly conditioned by custom and habit. Customs become established mainly through experience. Doing a certain task, in a particular manner and getting acceptable results tends to perpetuate that manner. The results are favorable, and we get to know the manner. That is, we develop a custom to follow for this task. Customs become established with use.

Significantly, this means that merely defining duties and methods as a part of organizing does not insure that they will become customary behavior. Actual repeated use is necessary. Further, if formal instructions are not insisted on by the management members, the nonmanager will develop a work pattern and, with usage, this pattern will become the customary and accepted manner of performing the work. For example, if a salesperson can adjust a price, without following instructions in the sales manual calling for consultation with the sales manager, the formal plan for price adjusting loses its significance.

Answer frame 1¹²

1. False. An employee gains both on-the-job satisfactions *and* off-the-job satisfactions from working at a job. Many of the latter are indirect and come about through the compensation received for the work.
2. True. The attainment of on-the-job satisfactions by employees can be assisted through management's proper performance of the organizing function.
3. False. Decision making regarding the work at hand affords self-assertion, which is personally satisfying to most people.
4. False. Most people prefer opportunities for interaction with other employees, their immediate supervisors, and high-level executives to being left alone or isolated.

Continue by turning to Frame 2¹², page 59.

Frame 2¹² continued

Formal duties and methods have full impact only when they become a part of custom, i.e., have repeated usage.

In addition, some jobs, as such, have widely accepted and expected *roles*. The general public has preconceived notions of how a person performing a particular job should behave. A research director is expected to behave in a certain way and a sales manager in a different way. The actions of holders of job titles are influenced by the roles associated with these titles. People strive to play their expected respective roles in order to attain acceptance and approval by other members of the organization.

Many believe that organization favorably enhances the behavior of an individual. The big person becomes bigger, the great one becomes greater, because in an organization one is placed in a situation that challenges and stimulates and is supplied mutual assistance, cooperation, and resources far beyond one's power to command alone.

When significant differences exist between the formal concept of a job and strong custom about it, what can the manager do to mediate the difference? Answer: The manager can: (*a*) get to know the custom better and develop ways of utilizing it in achieving objectives; (*b*) explain what modifications are needed, along with complete reasons for change; (*c*) relate how change to a formal concept will benefit both the job incumbent and the organization; (*d*) give examples and opportunities to show how the suggested new behavior is superior; and (*e*) offer rewards to the incumbent for adopting the proposed formal concept.

Indicate whether each of the following statements is true or false by writing "T" or "F" in the space provided.

_____ 1. *Culture* is a system of values and sanctions of a society or organization.

_____ 2. Behavior is influenced by culture, custom, and habit.

_____ 3. Customs are always detrimental to the organization.

_____ 4. A role associated with a specific job is always incompatible with the formal definition of that job.

Refer to Answer Frame 2¹², page 62, to compare your answers.

Frame 3¹²

An organization is a *social entity*, as well as an economic arrangement. It supplies a social stimulus that affects most people, that is to say, an organization is reciprocal, it affects the individual and, in turn, the individual affects the organization.

How does an organization affect a person's behavior? There are at least three different ways:

(1) through the individual's own behavior as a member of the organization; (2) by means of the individual's interpersonal relations with the group (formed by the organization); and (3) by the actions of the group of which the individual is a member.

The individual's own behavior can probably best be understood by keeping in mind four major considerations. They are:

1. *Recognize that each person is a separate entity.* Essentially each person is an individual: no person is exactly like any other person.
2. *Know a person's goals to better understand that person's behavior.* Different means are used by different people to achieve the same as well as different goals. These different means arise primarily because of individual differences in perception, personality, and mutual ability.
3. *A person's actions make sense to him or her and are entirely justifiable to that person.* The reason for this is that the action is usually consistent with the person's perceptions and beliefs of what sort of person they envision themselves to be.
4. *Frequent interrelations between two persons influence the behavior of each.* The degree of influence varies depending upon the particular situation and the interpretation given the words and actions between the people involved.

Groups formed by an organization influence the behavior of their members. The simple truth is that these groups are vital to the success of an organization. What employees do for each other and their commonness of purpose are fundamental in organization study. Within any group the interaction of one member with other group members is especially significant. To illustrate, a portion of one member's satisfactions comes from group responses, such as its approval and acceptance of his or her behavior. Whether the group approves or disapproves is highly significant. Further, the group typically supplies many beliefs and values to its individual members. In many cases, beliefs by an individual are based not on a member's personal knowledge about the subject, but on statements supplied by the group of which the person is, or wants to become, a member. Group influence is also important in winning acceptance to change. A person tends to dislike change that threatens to destroy either accustomed behavior patterns or established social relationships. However, when the change is initiated from within the group or is approved by the group, the individual member usually accepts the change with minimum resistance.

Indicate whether each of the following statements is true or false by writing "T" or "F" in the space provided.

_____ 1. Managers should regard their organizations as more than economic entities.

_____ 2. By definition, social groups within an organization corrode the formal structure of the organization.

_____ 3. The beliefs of an individual are often based on statements supplied by the group of which one is, or wants to become, a member.

_____ 4. The group may be used in gaining acceptance to change.

Now see Answer Frame 3[12], page 62.

Frame 4[12]

Group dynamics is the term commonly applied to the way in which interactions among a group's members produce acceptance or resistance to suggestions, improvements, or change. Useful guides from studies of group dynamics include: (a) all information affecting a group should be shared by the group's members; (b) the norms of the group are strong benchmarks—the group's

Answer frame 2¹²

1. True. *Culture* is a system of values and sanctions which can exist in a society or an organization.
2. True. All three of these influence behavior.
3. False. Specific customs may or may not be detrimental to the organization; they must be analyzed in relation to their compliance with the formal methods and goals of the organization.
4. False. A role associated with a given job may be in agreement with the formal definition of that job.

Now turn to Frame 3¹², page 60.

Answer frame 3¹²

1. True. Organizations are both social and economic entities, and both viewpoints must be considered by managers.
2. False. If properly recognized and utilized, social groups can be used to fortify and strengthen the formal structure of the organization. These groups are vital to the success of an organization.
3. True. In many cases, beliefs of an individual are based not on personal knowledge about the subject, but on statements supplied by the group of which he or she is, or wants to become, a member.
4. True. When a change is initiated from within a group or is approved by the group, the individual member usually accepts the change with minimum resistance.

Continue by turning to Frame 4¹², page 61.

Frame 4¹² continued

members are highly resistant to ideas and concepts that will make their behavior deviate from the group's norms; and (c) behavioral changes and reactions by certain members of a group can bring about strains among the remaining members of the group. Such strains can be lessened only by adjusting either the behavior and reactions of the total membership or by eliminating certain members from the group.

Almost all employees in industry are members of a group. Organization brings this about and it is not solely the result of economic considerations, but social preferences as well. As implied above, there is a strong feeling for a member to conform to the group, yet the total individual personality and behavior are not completely lost in group action. Attractions and rejections continually change among members of a work group. What prevails depends upon the particular issue and the then prevalent beliefs of the members.

How does a manager cope with a group? One key is to identify the real leader of the group and know the leader's beliefs and preferred means of operation. (The real leaders may be formally designated, as a crew boss, or informally as one chosen by the group.) Always remember the purposes of the organization and how the groups' efforts are directed toward achieving the basic goals of the total organization. Generally speaking, groups are open to conversation and suggestions. If one member will not listen, another might, and typically a person likes to be asked for an opinion or to give a description of the group's reaction to a given suggestion. It must be remembered that group feelings and emotions may run high. Determination can mount and in some cases lead to drastic action that the individuals making up the group would never have done acting as individuals.

The foregoing suggests that, in organizing, it is wise to identify the existing personnel and social forces and the roles they play. The organizer who recognizes these influences on organization and aggressively seeks to include contributions that they can make to the organizing effort, will more likely organize successfully.

Not to be confused with the effect of formal or informal behavior upon organization (see chapter 11) is *informal* behavior which results from members with common social interests banding together. Such groups are not prescribed by formal organizing. Members frequently see each other—riding home from work, meeting at the local P.T.A., or eating lunch together. They discover common interests and discuss ideas with each other. Informal groups arise naturally, whenever people work together.

It is in the nature of a person to like to be with others one knows and who, in turn, know her or him. Informal group members enjoy the sociability, having an audience to listen to them, a sense of belonging, and some protection from unreasonable demands from superiors. Common determinants of informal groups are: (*a*) identical interests, (*b*) common physical work location, and (*c*) same type of work performed. This last determinant, for example, supplies a mutuality among the members, in that they have common job satisfactions and problems. For survival, an informal group needs continuing relationships among its members. Characteristically, the group has a leader, communication within itself, and status values.

The behavior of an informal group, while tending to modify formal behavior, is in the nature of an adjunct—a sort of additional organization superimposed on the formal organization. Hence, it differs from the effect of dysfunctions which permits modification of behavior, but exists within the formal organization. Dysfunctions grow *out* of formal organizing. In contrast, the effect of informal groups on behavior is in *addition to* the formal organizing.

Nothing permanently destroys informal groups in an organization. They simply arise from organizing. The astute manager realizes this and tries to work with informal groups, releases accurate information, listens to the views of the group, and establishes interaction with its leader and members. The manager still manages, but seeks the opinions and reactions of the group members on matters that are of deep concern to them.

A *clique* is another type of informal group. Supporting a common "cause" and drawing its members from several widely spread and different departments identify the clique. The cause is usually something the enterprise should or should not do, such as promote a certain management member or hire certain people only. To obtain its aims, a clique follows various means, such as openly advocating its cause and obtaining appointments of its members to influential jobs. Its objective is good if it assists in achieving company goals; it is bad if it does not. If a clique exists, the manager should find out what it stands for. If good, members should be convinced that the aim can be achieved through regular channels; if bad, strong efforts should be directed toward eliminating the clique.

Indicate whether each of the following statements is true or false by writing "T" or "F" in the space provided.

_____ 1. The formation of a group is the result of the dissatisfaction of employees.
_____ 2. Individuals with similar characteristics or who are in similar circumstances are likely to form an informal group.
_____ 3. Because informal groups are not provided for by the formal organization, managers should try to discourage their formation.
_____ 4. A clique is an informal group whose goal may be the opposition of a goal of the company.

Refer to Answer Frame 4[12], page 64.

Answer frame 4[12]

1. False. Groups arise naturally whenever people work together. They also arise through organization.
2. True. Common determinants of informal groups are: (*a*) identical interests, (*b*) common physical work locations, and (*c*) same type of work performed.
3. False. The astute manager realizes that informal groups cannot be permanently discouraged or eliminated; and therefore, should accept and try to work with them.
4. True. A clique is an informal group formed for a common cause. This common cause may be in support of, or in opposition to, a goal of the company.

You have completed Chapter 12. Now proceed with Chapter 13 below.

chapter 13

DEPARTMENTATION

Frame 1[13]

In Chapter 11, we noted that work division leads to departmentation. Approaches to departmentation are termed: (*a*) *top-down*, (*b*) *bottom-up*, or (*c*) *work flow through*. The first one starts with the entirety of work at the top and works down; the second groups individual tasks into jobs, and then combines related jobs into work sections; and the third follows the work flow through the organization. In the work flow through approach, each necessary step in the work is assigned, and what each unit and person contributes is highlighted.

In almost every enterprise, there are three basic activities to be performed: *producing, selling, and financing*. They do not always have these identities, but they are present, because they are necessary for the enterprise to operate and survive. Numerous divisions and arrangements of these basic activities are possible. The specific way in which they are utilized depends mainly on the nature and amount of work, the people available for work, and the extent of specialization followed.

The major means of departmentation are:

1. Function. Common or homogeneous activities are placed in a common organizational unit. Functional departmentation is a normal way to departmentalize; it is readily understood and is used more often than any other means.

2. Operations and services. Operations are units in which work directly related to the product is performed. They may be allocated to different areas or physical facilities, and are frequently divided into major and auxiliary units. Services are units whose work facilitates, or assists indirectly, in the work of the operating units. This arrangement makes for better utilization of management members in that: (*a*) important duties are given priority, (*b*) available technical knowledge is utilized, and (*c*) adequate managerial attention is given to all necessary activities.

3. Product. A sensible degree of specialization is encouraged by departmentation according to product. Further, specialized knowledge, as it applies to a product and its requirements, can be more effectively utilized. Examples include separate departments for different types of merchandise in a department store and separate facilities for commercial loans and personal loans in a bank organization.

4. Territory. Departmentation by territory is popular in sales organizations. It enables the salesperson to reduce travel time and expense, and makes it possible to become better acquainted with local conditions. There is some duplication of functions, but sales personnel transfers are expedited and similar controls can be used for each of the territorially organized units.

5. Customer. Departmentation according to type of customer places emphasis on giving better service to customers as, for example, in the children's department in a clothing store. Generally speaking, departmentation by customer is most effective when the product is popular, widely used, and sold through many outlets.

6. Process. Departmentation by process stresses technical facilities, is logical, and commonly is employed at the operative levels. Three basic patterns exist:

a. Serial. The production moves through a single channel and progresses step by step to completion. Each step is performed by a different employee.

b. Parallel. Concurrent working calls for several work steps to be done by the same employee.

c. Unit assembly. Featured is simultaneous performance of work steps by different employees, without regard to the sequence of work flow.

7. Task team. A specific project or a block of work is assigned to a small group that operates as a unit which is self-contained and includes all the required skills for performing the work. The task team usually operates until the successful fulfillment of the project, after which it is disbanded with persons and facilities reassigned. The arrangement is contrary to the common approach of work division and of specialized and somewhat separated organization units. Organization by task team is sometimes termed *project* organization.

8. Matrix. One of the newer types, matrix departmentation, features dual supervision; for example, one on a technical basis (vertically on the organization chart) and one on a management basis (horizontally on the chart). Resembling a lattice-work pattern, this type departmentation gives flexibility, technical orientation, and a balanced format to the organization.

Indicate whether each of the following statements is true or false by writing "T" or "F" in the space provided.

_____ 1. The most widely used means of departmentation is by *function*.

_____ 2. Departmentation of the selling function is commonly by territory.

_____ 3. Departmentation by process is quite common in manufacturing organizations at the top levels of organization.

_____ 4. Departmentation by task teams requires each team to have the necessary technical ability to complete the assigned task.

_____ 5. Under matrix departmentation an employee would have two "bosses."

See Answer Frame 1[13], page 66, to check your answers.

Answer frame 1[13]

1. True. Functional departmentation is a normal way to departmentalize; it is readily understood and is used more than any other means.
2. True. Departmentation by territory is quite common in sales organizations.
3. False. Departmentation by process is employed by manufacturing organizations *at the operating levels of production.*
4. True. Departmentation by task teams assigns blocks of work to a team, whose members have all the required knowledge and skill to accomplish the work.
5. True. The employee would have one boss for technical matters and one for routine operating purposes.

Now proceed with Frame 2[13] below.

Frame 2[13]

The organizer is free to use any means of departmentation. Typically, several are used in the same organization. Commonly, "by function" is used for the top levels of organization and "by process" for the bottom levels. But it must be remembered that people are the important ingredient in organizing. We cannot successfully departmentalize solely on the basis of the work itself. What social values the people have must be taken into account. Likewise, their traditions, beliefs, and individual differences should be considered in selecting the form of departmentation.

During the past decade, the emphasis in organizing has been directed toward: (*a*) improving the efforts of the group as a unit, and (*b*) widening individual job requirements. With reference to the former, much work is accomplished by a group, and efforts to raise the group's productivity and increase the satisfactions of the group's membership are really worthwhile and are the concern of organizing. If we were to concentrate only on the individual efforts, we would be ignoring a most lucrative source for organization improvement, namely, the group's accomplishments. In addition, the greater knowledge and better understanding of personal and social implications of organizing point toward greater effort in achieving teamwork.

With reference to individual job requirements, ample research indicates that work specialization can be overextended to the point where the employee's interest in the work is dulled, sense of accomplishment is diminished, and fatigue comes on more quickly. These undesirable effects can be avoided by expanding the variety of work and eliminating the concentration on a single task. This is referred to as *job enlargement*. It should be noted that the managerial problem of coordinating the various jobs is lightened by job enlargement. Also, more self-contained operating units are obtained. Job enrichment is also motivational as pointed out in Chapter 17.

Indicate whether each of the following statements is true or false by writing "T" or "F" in the space provided.

    _____ 1. An organization must decide on one method of departmentation and exclude all other methods.

    _____ 2. In recent years, the main consideration in organizing has been the type of work to be performed.

    _____ 3. Research findings indicate that further work specialization is to be encouraged in all situations.

    _____ 4. Job enlargement eases the problem of coordination.

Compare your answers with those in Answer Frame 2[13], page 68.

Frame 3[13]

Actually, there is no predetermined pattern that a manager can follow in solving each organizing problem. The manager must decide what requirements are paramount and try to satisfy them. The objective is to seek the best composite —all important factors considered.

Factors to keep in mind are that effective departmentation:

1. Aids coordination. Assigning work to the unit that can best perform it simplifies coordination. Separate and dissimilar units that require close coordination may be placed advantageously in the same department. Further, where there is clearly a dominant objective related to several diverse units, it is usually effective to place these units under one segment of the organization structure.

2. Expedites control. It assists controlling to have a highly competent management member within each organizational unit. Hence, a unit may be so placed in the total organization in order to achieve this goal, even though it may seem an illogical location. Where the work of one unit is independently checked by another, it is clearly desirable to place the units in separate organization locations; for example, auditing and cash disbursing should be separated. Further, identical operating units can be set up, identical controls applied, and the results compared. Inefficiency is quickly spotted by comparison of achievements.

3. Provides the benefits of specialization. Concentration of effort helps a person to become expert in certain types of work, but as indicated above, the specialization should not be extended too far. Capitalizing on a person's specialty is good organizing, especially when a particular and scarce skill and knowledge are required.

4. Cuts cost. Costs must always be considered in determining the organization structure. The number of units utilized has a direct bearing on cost. Too frequently, new units are added and additional people hired without adequate study of costs. Such additions should not be made without some idea of the value of the contribution of the new unit compared to its added cost. Opportunities exist in organizing to reduce labor cost, by designating different grades of jobs paying different rates where the work has different skill requirements.

5. Places emphasis on human relations. To reiterate, we must not forget that organizing, to be effective, must take human relations into account. A strictly logical, materialistic approach that does not do so cannot be successful for any length of time. Allowances must be made for individual differences. Managers' ideas on how they want to organize, and how they want to run their units cannot be ignored. The real pay-off of organizing is in the results it brings, and these in turn depend more on how well people work together than on any other consideration.

Indicate whether each of the following statements is true or false by writing "T" or "F" in the space provided.

_____ 1. The proper organization structure can facilitate control and coordination of the enterprise.

_____ 2. The concept of job enlargement should be avoided, since it eliminates the benefits to be gained from specialization.

_____ 3. Costs are an important consideration in the structuring of an organization.

_____ 4. The most important consideration in structuring the organization is the structure's suitability to people.

Go to Answer Frame 3[13], page 68, to check your answers.

Answer frame 2[13]

1. False. An organization may adopt any means of departmentation. Typically, several are used in the same organization. For instance, "by function" may be used for the top levels of organization and "by process" for the bottom levels.
2. False. During the past decade the emphasis in organizing has been toward: (a) improving the efforts of the group as a unit, and (b) widening individual job requirements.
3. False. Ample research indicates that work specialization can be extended too far. In some situations, a movement toward job enlargement, rather than further specialization, can result in increased employee interest in the work, an increased sense of accomplishment, and a slower fatigue rate.
4. True. Coordinating the various jobs is lightened by job enlargement, and more self-contained operating units are obtained.

Continue by turning to Frame 3[13], page 67.

Answer frame 3[13]

1. True. Management functions are interrelated; coordination and control can be facilitated by the proper organization structure.
2. False. A balance must be reached between the benefits the individual receives from job enlargement and the benefits the organization can receive from specialization.
3. True. The costs incurred with a given organization structure are always a significant consideration.
4. True. The results of organizing depend more on how well people work together than on any other consideration.

Now continue with Frame 4[13] below.

Frame 4[13]

Committees can also be included in a discussion of departmentation. Common, yet controversial, they exist at every organization level and serve different purposes in various prescribed capacities. Some are permanent, with makeup, duties, meeting times, and membership carefully defined; others are temporary and informally assembled to talk about a particular problem. Committees are viewed by some managers as a very effective coordinating medium, whereas others consider committees a great source of frustration and an excellent way to waste time. For best results from use of a committee, observe these points:

1. Write down the purpose, scope, decision-making power (if any), and relationships with organization units for the committee.
2. Appoint an effective chairperson who prepares the agenda, supplies data to members prior to the meeting, and keeps the discussion focused on the subject at hand.
3. Select subject matter discreetly. Basic issues, evaluations, and review of past activities are well-handled by a committee.
4. Stress the prestige, publicity, and influence that being on a committee provide to the individual members.
5. Keep the membership within practical limits, usually three to seven members.
6. Arrange for adequate follow-up to the committee's work, and periodically review its contributions.

The *board of directors*, another organization group, is legally created and has these essential duties: (a) to exercise "an awareness of trust," i.e., to serve a position of trusteeship over the corporation's assets; (b) to question corporate officers, in order to justify their past or proposed actions; and (c) to deliberate and formulate decisions on major and basic issues of the corporation. The board is a group, it acts as a group, and renders decisions as a group.

Indicate whether each of the following statements is true or false by writing "T" or "F" in the space provided.

_____ 1. Committees are formed only at the top levels of the organization.
_____ 2. Not all committees are organized as permanent units of the organization's structure.
_____ 3. The board of directors is controlled by the officers of the company.
_____ 4. The board of directors has some decision-making duties.

Now check your answers with those in Answer Frame 4[13], page 70.

chapter 14

AUTHORITY

Frame 1[14]

To complete an organization, the work-employee units are joined together by means of authority that establishes relationships among the units. It is important to establish such relationships, because only when their relationships to one another are clearly understood, can units serve effectively as components of a whole organization. Authority is needed to direct each unit's actions toward total organization goals.

Authority can be thought of as *the power to exact action by others* or perhaps, more simply, *to make decisions and enforce them.* The compliance, however, need not be obtained by the use of coercion and force; it can be secured through persuasion and requests. These latter means are more in keeping with the modern tempo.

Some view authority as coming into being from ownership, legal decree, or status in the organization. That is, an owner of property has the privilege of deciding how the property is used. The owner can exercise this privilege, or can designate others to do it. The law gives authority to those charged with enforcing statutes. And, in some organizations, an officeholder, by status in the organization or by position, receives the authority required to perform the duties of that job.

In the opinion of others, authority comes to its holder through acceptance by subordinates of the manager's decision making and decision enforcement. In this view, a manager has no authority until it is conferred by the subordinates. This is the *subordinate-acceptance approach* to

Answer frame 4[13]

1. False. Committees exist at every level of the organization.
2. True. Some committees are permanent units, whereas others are temporary.
3. False. The officers of a company are responsible to the board of directors.
4. True. The board of directors has the responsibility for making decisions on major and basic issues of the corporation.

You have completed Chapter 13. Now continue by beginning Chapter 14, page 69.

Frame 1[14] continued

authority. It emphasizes: leadership; the importance of a manager winning support, not ordering it; and the recognition by the nonmanager that someone in the group must make decisions. In it, the manager's motivation derives from the opportunity to contribute to a group's efforts, to gain acceptance, and to receive awards.

Other forms of authority are recognized. *Authority of the situation* arises from an emergency or unusual event, and is voluntarily conferred upon the person assuming authority to meet the particular circumstances. It remains until the emergency terminates or the person regularly charged with authority takes over. *"Technical or computer authority"* is authority given to a person possessing and interpreting valuable information and knowledge. *"Accomplishment authority"* is that gained through past accomplishment, experience, and competency. The holder of such authority decides issues, and these decisions are followed by the group, primarily because it believes the manager knows what he or she is doing, commands respect, and can generate enthusiastic cooperation.

Indicate whether each of the following statements is true or false by writing "T" or "F" in the space provided.

_____ 1. The relationships among work-employee units can be established by means of authority.

_____ 2. The exercise of authority necessarily involves the use of coercion and force.

_____ 3. A manager's authority is always accepted by subordinates.

_____ 4. A new member of the organization is most likely to be accorded *accomplishment authority*.

See answers in Answer Frame 1[14], page 72.

Frame 2[14]

Before continuing with authority, let us note another important concept that is a twin of authority; that is, responsibility. This can be defined as follows: Responsibility *is the obligation of an individual to perform assigned activities to the best of his or her ability*. Effective management requires that, for every management member, *authority should be commensurate with responsibility*. Authority, without responsibility, lacks justification for existing; responsibility, without authority, has a hollow ring.

For formal organizing to exist, *authority must be delegated* or referred from one management member or organization work-employee unit to another in order to accomplish specific assignments. This gives the delegatee the power to decide issues affecting this assignment. However, the delegating manager does not permanently relinquish either authority or responsibility. What the manager does is grant the right for the delegatee to manage within the prescribed area, but the ultimate authority remains with the delegator or manager, who is the ultimate authority managing the activity and who has the ultimate responsibility.

Delegation of authority is vital in management, because it: (*a*) establishes the formal organization relationships among members of an enterprise; (*b*) gives managerial depth, i.e., a reserve of managers, able to carry on if the need arises; and (*c*) develops subordinates, by permitting them to make decisions and to apply their knowledge gained from training programs and meetings.

Delegation is not a natural tendency with most human beings. Some managers like to dominate; they have a deep desire to influence others, to be in on every decision, and to run the show. Often, a manager may erroneously feel that no one can do the work quite like he or she can and that, therefore, the manager must do it. Or, the manager wants to achieve an outstanding record and be remembered for super accomplishments. Such attitudes defeat effective delegation and stifle an organization.

Indicate whether each of the following statements is true or false by writing "T" or "F" in the space provided.

_____ 1. Authority and responsibility must be segregated from each other, or control breaks down.

_____ 2. A manager completely discharges his or her duty when delegating authority.

_____ 3. Delegation of authority cultivates new management talent.

_____ 4. Almost all managers are receptive to the idea of delegating their authority.

Check your answers by turning to Answer Frame 2[14], page 72.

Frame 3[14]

To combat tendencies to refuse to delegate authority, a manager must:

1. Recognize the need for delegation. A manager must have confidence that delegation of authority will be rewarding, will assist in building an effective group effort, will help multiply his or her efforts, will benefit subordinates, and will enable subordinates to contribute to their full measure.

2. Devise a means for knowing what is going on. Delegators want to be kept informed, simply in order to be knowledgeable of what is taking place and to be in a position to institute corrective steps, if required. To supply information, a built-in audit, prescribed written reports, or periodic conferences can be utilized.

3. Decide what type of decision making to delegate. A list can be prepared so that identification of those decisions to be delegated is predetermined. This ties in delegation with planning, and makes it a part of the managerial practice followed.

4. Select carefully the delegatee. The assignment should be measured to the person. The delegatee should be one whom you believe can succeed. Give opportunity to those persons not utilizing their full potential.

5. Help the delegatee. Assist, but do not tell the delegatee exactly what to decide and what to do. Typically, if the delegatee asks for help, give it; but to give the answers negates the benefits of delegation. Rather, the delegator remains available, gives encouragement, and asks pertinent questions designed to identify and explore possible solutions to the problem.

Span of authority, closely relates to the degree of delegation followed, *relates to the number of subordinates that report to a manager.* If the practice is to use a large number, i.e., a wide span of authority, the organization structure will tend to have relatively few organization levels. This is referred to as a *"flat organization structure."* In contrast, utilization of a short span makes for relatively many organization levels

Answer frame 1[14]

1. True. Work-employee units are joined together by the existence of authority that establishes relationships among the units.
2. False. The use of authority need not involve the use of coercion and force; it can involve merely the use of persuasion and requests.
3. False. The *subordinate-acceptance approach* holds that authority comes to its holder by the *acceptance* of subordinates; this acceptance may be withheld.
4. False. *Accomplishment authority* is only gained through accomplishment, experience, and competency. A new member of the organization could only be accorded this kind of authority if it were gained in some other organization and this fact was known by members of the present organization.

Continue by going to Frame 2[14], page 70.

Answer frame 2[14]

1. False. For every management member, authority should be commensurate with responsibility.
2. False. In delegating authority, a manager does not permanently relinquish either authority or responsibility.
3. True. Delegation of authority develops subordinates by permitting them to decide and apply their knowledge gained from training programs and meetings.
4. False. Delegation is not a natural tendency with many human beings.

Now go to Frame 3[14], page 71.

Frame 3[14] continued

and a *"steep organization structure."* How many persons should be subordinated to an executive varies, with consideration for: (*a*) the type of work, (*b*) the location in the organization structure, (*c*) the ability of the manager, and (*d*) the amount and type of communication required among the members. Generally speaking, spans of authority tend to be short at top organization levels, especially if the work has many nonrecurring problems or mainly requires mental effort, and these spans tend to be wide at lower organization levels if the operations are fairly well-defined and the decisions deal with repetitive situations.

Indicate whether each of the following statements is true or false by writing "T" or "F" in the space provided.

_____ 1. Delegation of authority benefits only the manager who delegates it.

_____ 2. A manager should delegate all authority and act only as a monitor or auditor over subordinates.

_____ 3. The *span of authority* is the number of superiors to whom a manager must report.

_____ 4. An organization structure can have both "flat" and "steep" characteristics.

Now go to Answer Frame 3[14], page 74.

Frame 4[14]

Centralized authority and decentralized authority are further important considerations of authority. The former means concentration of authority; the latter, dispersion of authority. They are related to the delegation of authority inasmuch as the real issue is how much authority

FIGURE 9A

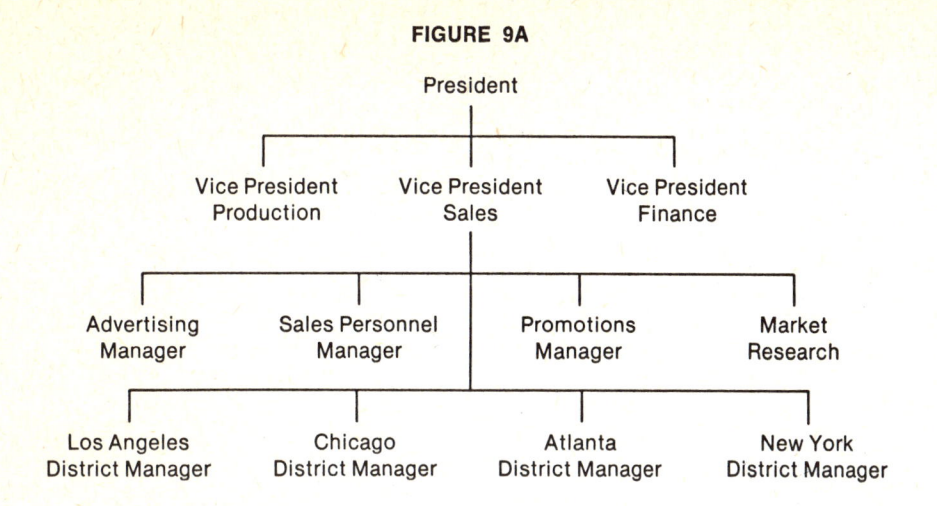

```
                        President
            ┌──────────────┼──────────────┐
      Vice President  Vice President  Vice President
        Production       Sales          Finance
        ┌───────────┬──────┴──────┬───────────┐
   Advertising  Sales Personnel  Promotions   Market
    Manager       Manager         Manager    Research
        ┌───────────┬─────────────┬───────────┐
   Los Angeles   Chicago        Atlanta     New York
   District      District       District    District
   Manager       Manager        Manager     Manager
```

is delegated to subordinates. Diagrams help to comprehend the meaning of centralization and decentralization. Figure 9A illustrates centralization, in that the decisions about advertising, sales personnel, promotion, and market research are concentrated, with the managers of the respective units reporting to the vice president of sales. Their decisions apply to the district managers in charge, respectively, of Los Angeles, Chicago, Atlanta, and New York. A decentralized arrangement is shown in Figure 9B. Each sales district now has its own sales personnel and promotion units. Managers, heading these units, decide issues in these activities for their respective sales district and report to their respective district managers. However, advertising and market research are still centralized.

Advocates of centralized authority cite its advantages as follows: (*a*) duplication of functions is avoided, (*b*) uniform policies and practices are promoted, (*c*) prestige and full utilization of managers are won, and (*d*) specialists' contributions are maximized, primarily because of the scope and volume of work processed. In contrast, advocates of decentralized authority are quick to relate its advantages as follows: (*a*) effective human relations are encouraged, (*b*) greater opportunity to develop and to manage are provided, (*c*) teamwork and self-sustaining organization segments are promoted, and (*d*) risks of losses of personnel and facilities are spread out.

It should be pointed out that there are *specific limits to authority*. For example, it is common to

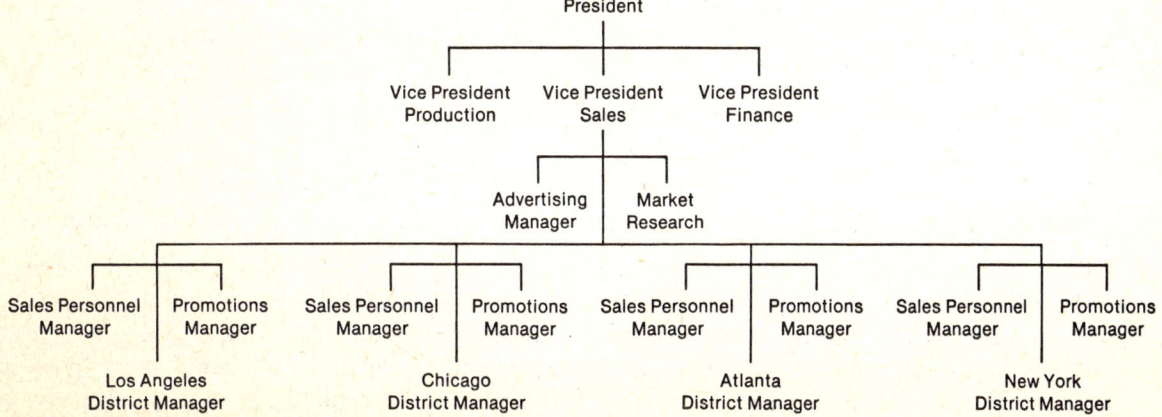

FIGURE 9B

```
                                President
                  ┌────────────────┼────────────────┐
            Vice President    Vice President    Vice President
              Production         Sales             Finance
                             ┌─────┴─────┐
                        Advertising    Market
                         Manager      Research
   ┌──────────┬──────────┬──────────┬──────────┬──────────┬──────────┬──────────┐
  Sales    Promotions  Sales    Promotions  Sales    Promotions  Sales    Promotions
Personnel   Manager  Personnel   Manager  Personnel   Manager  Personnel   Manager
 Manager             Manager             Manager             Manager
   Los Angeles          Chicago            Atlanta            New York
 District Manager   District Manager   District Manager   District Manager
```

Answer frame 3¹⁴

1. False. Delegation of authority benefits not only the manager but also the subordinates to whom the authority is delegated.
2. False. A manager should not delegate all authority. Those areas that warrant delegation should be determined.
3. False. The *span of authority,* or *span of control,* is the number of subordinates that report to a manager.
4. True. An organization can intermingle the "flat" and "steep" organization structure. A structure usually tends to be "steep" at top organization levels and "flat" at lower organization levels.

Now turn to Frame 4¹⁴, page 72, and continue.

Frame 4¹⁴ continued

find that several major management members must agree on a basic decision before it is implemented. What authority is used must be compatible with the major objectives and policies of the enterprise. Further, what is decided and enforced by a manager must be within the physical and mental capabilities of the recipient of his orders. These are constraints within which the manager exercises authority. In addition, what is ordered must be in keeping with the codes and social beliefs of the individual and the group. Collective bargaining, for example, places limitations on what the owners of property or those acting as their agents can do. To illustrate: It is a violation of current labor laws to interfere with the establishing or operating of a trade union, or to refuse to bargain collectively with employees.

Authority is also limited by the scope and type of decisions that the authority covers. These limitations are necessary to make the organization feasible and to achieve specific goals through group effort. Certain managers decide certain issues, other managers decide other issues. Some orderliness about decision-making power and enforcement is required because of: (a) the relative importance of the activities involved, (b) the nature of the activities, (c) the desired relationships among activities and employees performing them, and (d) the background and ability of the management members.

Indicate whether each of the following statements is true or false by writing "T" or "F" in the space provided.

_____ 1. Decentralized authority has been clearly proven superior to centralized authority.

_____ 2. Authority is only constrained by the rules of the organization.

_____ 3. A manager's authority should be limited by the goals that he or she is supposed to achieve.

_____ 4. Authority is usually assigned to management members rather than to management positions.

Turn to Answer Frame 4¹⁴, page 76.

Frame 5¹⁴

The common classification of authority, indicating its limitations, is: (a) line authority and (b) staff authority. The former is limited mainly by the position in the organization of the manager and unit—the latter by the type of decision-making authority. When a superior delegates to a subordinate, who in turn delegates authority to another subordinate, and so on, a line of authority from the top to the bottom of the organization structure is formed. It is from this source that the

FIGURE 10

Comparisons of Line and Staff Authority

Line Authority	Staff Authority
1. Pertains to superior-subordinate relationships.	1. Characteristically, is a manager-to-manager relationship.
2. Is directly related to objectives of enterprise.	2. Is indirectly related to objectives of enterprise.
3. Deals mainly with the exercise of authority *along* the channel of line authority.	3. Deals mainly with the exercise of authority *to a* channel of line authority.
4. Identifies units that initiate and carry through to conclusion the basic activities.	4. Includes all units that are not line.
5. Manager is a doer, or a putting-into-action type of manager.	5. Manager has a supporting role and aids the doer.
6. Designates a line manager.	6. Designates a staff manager.

term *line authority* is derived. Each manager with line authority is responsible for the work of his or her unit and its *direct contribution* to the objectives of the enterprise. In contrast, *staff authority* is in a supporting role, and contributes *indirectly* to the objectives of the enterprise.

To assist in clarifying the meaning of line authority and of staff authority, a comparison is shown in Figure 10.

To reiterate, the main concern in organizing is to get employees to work together effectively. Some managers decide certain activities, whereas other managers decide other activities. Yet all the decisions must be compatible, utilize the best abilities of each manager, and, to some degree and manner, assist in achieving the objectives. Who decides what and maintains the proper coordination among all the decisions gives rise to qualifying the authority used—specifically, to the utilization of line authority and staff authority. Genuine teamwork is desired. A mutual goal is known. Team members contribute what they can do best, so that the highest joint efforts can be applied.

Indicate whether each of the following statements is true or false by writing "T" or "F" in the space provided.

_____ 1. Staff authority is directly related to the objectives of the enterprise.
_____ 2. Staff authority is characterized by manager-to-manager relationships.
_____ 3. A staff manager is likely to render aid to the line manager.
_____ 4. In utilizing the line and staff classification of authority, the need for coordination is eliminated.

Check your answers with those in Answer Frame 5[14], on page 76.

Frame 6[14]

As complexities and advances in technologies have increased, various types of staff authority have emerged. Staff authority can be classified into six major types, as follows:

1. Advisory staff. A manager with this type of staff authority analyzes problems, gives suggestions and advice, and prepares reports to assist the line manager, who can accept, modify, or reject what is offered. However, it is best that the line manager be required to listen to or read proposals of the staff manager. Such a policy is known as *"compulsory staff advice."* In most cases, it is helpful for the advisory staff manager to talk over a proposed recommendation with the line managers who will be affected by it. Such action helps gain acceptance of the advice. Further, the advisory staff manager should prepare the recommendation in a *completed* form,

Answer frame 4[14]

1. False. There are advantages to be derived from centralized and also from decentralized authority.
2. False. Authority is also constrained by the codes and social beliefs of the individual and the group.
3. True. A manager's authority should be sufficient to permit the achievement of the assigned goal; it should not be without limit.
4. True. Authority is normally assigned to specific management members.

Go to Frame 5[14], page 74.

Answer frame 5[14]

1. False. *Line* authority *is directly* related to the objectives of the enterprise. *Staff* authority is *indirectly* related to the objectives of the enterprise.
2. True. Staff authority *is* characterized by manager-to-manager relationships, while line authority implies superior-subordinate relationships.
3. True. A staff manager has a supporting role and aids the line manager.
4. False. Line and staff decisions must be compatible; this means that coordination is essential.

Proceed with Frame 6[14] on page 75.

Frame 6[14] continued

so that the recipient need only approve or disapprove it. Management scholars call this staff submission of a complete recommendation the *"completed staff work doctrine."*

2. Service staff. This authority covers the manager of an organization unit having a service relationship to the line. An example is purchasing. This service work may be separated from the line activities. The authority is not advisory, but it is expected to be used by the line managers to achieve better purchasing. Hence, it limits the line authority and is of assistance to it. And, like much staff authority, it places emphasis on expertness and specialization.

3. Control staff. It is helpful to designate some managers as having control staff authority, meaning that they decide issues of a designated type and, in so doing, directly or indirectly exercise control over other managers, usually those with line authority in the organization. Control staff authority is directly exercised through serving as an agent for a line manager, or indirectly, by means of policy interpretation, reports, or compliance with established procedures. In these efforts, approval or disapproval of line actions is taken, and hence actual constraint of line authority is exercised. The manager with control staff authority does not simply advise; the manager controls.

4. Functional staff. In the interest of efficiency and convenience, certain line or staff authority over *specified activities* may be delegated to another manager who has either line or staff authority. Commonly, it is a portion of line authority delegated to a staff manager, and usually pertains to a particular activity only and for a specified period only. Thus, the authority is definitely limited; if this were not so, it would damage normal established authority and result in chaos within the organization. Most managers agree that functional authority is extremely helpful in certain situations, but, in general, it should be kept to a minimum.

5. Assistant-to. In most instances, the manager with assistant-to authority has functional staff authority and can be thought of as a line manager's special assistant, with a limited set of duties and no major supervisory responsibilities. He or she is not the "heir apparent" to the superior line manager; that is, the "assistant-to" is not identical with the assistant line manager. True, the assistant-to acts for the line manager, but this is not as the assistant in exercising line authority. It is as a helper in interpreting objectives, in formulating plans, processing routine papers and documents, and explaining technical material outside the experience of the superior. In the opinion of many, the title *assistant-to* is inadequate. *Executive assistant* or *staff assistant* would be a more accurate description.

6. General staff. This has been used successfully by the armed forces and, to a much lesser degree, by other governmental, business, and educational organizations. General staff authority provides a manager, line or staff, with a group to assist in exercising the managerial work. It is well to rotate general staff members to various levels and areas of the organization in order to foster better understanding for the problems of the managers of that organization. They need to be fully aware of the various situations that they must face as general staff members. Further, they should be made familiar with the results of their work, which recommendations or actions proved quite successful, and which did not.

Indicate whether each of the following statements is true or false by writing "T" or "F" in the space provided.

_____ 1. The *advisory staff* is encouraged to present its recommendations in partial form so that the line manager will be involved during the entire process.

_____ 2. The *control staff* exercises control over the line manager.

_____ 3. The assistant line manager is the individual exercising the *assistant-to* staff authority.

_____ 4. The *general staff* replaces a line or staff manager.

Go to Answer Frame 6[14], page 78.

Answer frame 6[14]

1. False. The *advisory staff* should prepare its recommendations in a *completed* form. Then the recipient need only approve or disapprove it. This is called the *"completed staff work doctrine."*
2. True. The *control staff's* approval or disapproval of line actions is adhered to and, hence, actual constraint of line authority is exercised.
3. False. The *assistant-to* is not identical with the assistant line manager.
4. False. The general staff *assists* a manager, line or staff, in exercising managerial work.

You have completed Chapter 14. Continue with Chapter 15.

chapter 15

STAFFING THE ORGANIZATION

Frame 1[15]

It is important in organizing to utilize the best departmentation and to provide the correct authority, but it is still more important to place the right people in the various managerial jobs. The quality of the managers usually makes the difference between success and failure of an organization. The accomplishments by an organization may be reasonably satisfactory even though there is room for improvement in the organization units utilized and the authority relationships present. However, if incapable managers are directing the organization, it is almost certain that the results will be poor. Therefore, it is of critical importance that this task be expertly performed.

These managerial position assignment efforts are referred to as *staffing* by some management scholars, who consider them a separate function of management. According to this viewpoint, *staffing is the recruiting, selecting, promoting, transferring, and retiring of management members.* This approach highlights the importance of keeping the managerial jobs filled with the right people.

In this discussion, staffing the organization is included under organizing. Justification for this viewpoint is (*a*) the total concept of organizing includes consideration for the people so organized, and (*b*) the acquiring and assigning of managerial personnel are done in reference to a specific organization with all its uniqueness, problems, and goals. Whether or not staffing is given separate managerial status is an academic decision. Certainly, the work of maintaining the personnel of an organization is vital and merits attention and study in management.

The responsibility for staffing an organization rests on every manager at every level. Usually, the personnel department provides at least technical help, in every case, and contributes in accordance with the desire and permissiveness of the manager who has assumed charge in a particular situation. In many cases, the personnel department confines its efforts to screening the applicants and selecting those considered promising; the manager does the selecting. This is justified on the basis that inasmuch as the manager is responsible for the work, he or she should have some say in the choice of subordinates. Policies to cover staffing efforts are essential, and their development is the duty of the top executive and immediate subordinates—the top-management team. With such policies established, putting them into effect can be the responsibility of either the top-management team, which is usually the case for high-level jobs, or any department head, commonly the personnel manager, for lower-level jobs.

Indicate whether each of the following statements is true or false by writing "T" or "F" in the space provided.

_____ 1. The goal of staffing is to place the right people in the right managerial jobs.

_____ 2. Staffing and directing do not refer to the same activity.

_____ 3. The personnel department is solely responsible for staffing the organization.

_____ 4. The personnel department often does not have the final say in hiring employees.

See Answer Frame 1[15], page 80.

Frame 2[15]

For practical purposes, *staffing an organization starts with the makeup of the jobs, expressed by job descriptions*. Following this, specifications are needed. Candidates, meeting these job-worker requirements, are then recruited, selected, and hired. The entire plan is shown in Figure 11. The discussion presented here follows this plan.

Beginning with the makeup of the job, the common job identification is widely used, but there is no universal agreement as to its specific content. For example, the positions of both the vice president of production and the director of data processing are referred to as managerial jobs, but the contents of each are far different. And the duties of the vice president of production, in one enterprise, may be quite different from those of the vice president of production in another organization. This demonstrates the need for *job descriptions* of managerial jobs. Such descriptions answer questions such as: (*a*) What is the manager on this job expected to do? (*b*) What is the job content? (*c*) What are the important relationships the occupant of this job must develop and maintain?

Answering these questions, i.e., spelling out precisely the job content and the relationships that successful occupancy of the job demands, results in a *job description*. It includes the duties, the activities to be performed, the responsibilities, the chief characteristics of the work, and the results expected. The job description, however, is not actually complete; it does not include *all* the duties and *all* the responsibilities entailed. To attempt to do so would make the writing cumbersome and impractical. Further, the job description is always subject to interpretation and, with time, the typical manager modifies her or his job content to some degree, a natural result of change both by the manager and the organization.

Answer frame 1[15]

1. True. It is important in organizing to place the right people in the various managerial jobs; this is the goal of staffing.
2. True. Some consider *staffing* a separate function of management, whereas in this discussion it is included under the organizing function.
3. False. The responsibility for staffing an organization rests on every manager at every level.
4. True. In many cases, the personnel office confines its efforts to screening the applicants; the manager responsible for that particular organizational level does the final selecting.

Now go to Frame 2[15], page 79.

Frame 2[15] continued

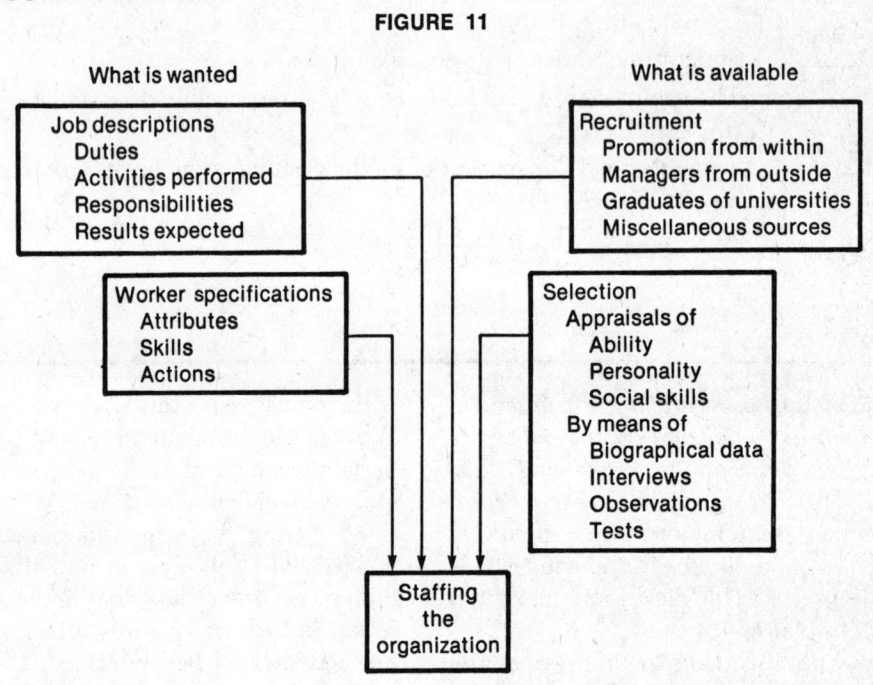

FIGURE 11

What is wanted

Job descriptions
   Duties
   Activities performed
   Responsibilities
   Results expected

Worker specifications
   Attributes
   Skills
   Actions

What is available

Recruitment
   Promotion from within
   Managers from outside
   Graduates of universities
   Miscellaneous sources

Selection
   Appraisals of
     Ability
     Personality
     Social skills
   By means of
     Biographical data
     Interviews
     Observations
     Tests

Staffing the organization

Indicate whether each of the following statements is true or false by writing "T" or "F" in the space provided.

_____ 1. The first step in staffing the organization is recruiting.
_____ 2. The job description specifies the skills needed to fill that job.
_____ 3. A job description does not describe all of the features of a specific job.
_____ 4. A manager's scope of activities is strictly limited over time by the initial job description.

Go to Answer Frame 2[15], page 82.

Frame 3[15]

Having a reasonable comprehension of the job specifications, the next step is to identify the *manager specifications*. This includes the attributes, skills, actions, and characteristics believed necessary to perform effectively the managerial work. At the outset, it must be pointed out that there is no general concurrence on what these factors are. No neat list of qualities exists that is applicable in all cases. Different mixes of attributes appear to produce successful managers. Nevertheless, it is helpful to discuss certain attributes that are commonly mentioned in studies pertaining to managerial qualification. They are as follows:

1. Desire to manage. This somewhat obvious characteristic appears significant in managerial success. A liking for managing, for making decisions, and for assuming responsibility are of great importance. These characteristics, plus a deep interest in management, its problems, its contributions, and its achievements, are closely related to successful performance of management. Attraction to management because of status or salary is insufficient. There should be a basic satisfaction derived from getting work accomplished by means of teamwork with associates.

2. Conceptual and analytical ability. The ability to visualize the enterprise as a whole, to recognize the interrelationships and relative values of a management problem, and to grasp the essence of ideas and to relate them to practical operations are basic qualities that most successful managers possess. In addition, a manager must be able to analyze a situation, to initiate a logical approach, to separate pertinent from unimportant issues, and to identify relationships of activities and their probable outcomes.

3. Ability to identify and concentrate on what is important. The managerial mind quickly identifies the vital issues, the main stems of a maze of intricate and complicated situations or challenges. Knowing what's important, managers concentrate on the crucial components and do not spread their efforts too thinly. Further, managers are objective and deal with things as they are, not as they feel they should be.

4. Ability to influence others. This includes winning cooperation from those in the work group, motivating others to want to achieve stated goals, developing an effective work team, and getting work accomplished through the efforts of others. Also included is the know-how to communicate ideas and beliefs to others and to understand the thoughts and attitudes others are trying to convey. Clarity of thought, good choice and easy flow of words, and ability to maintain interest while conveying information are basic to adequate communication. Managers with the ability to influence others recognize what views they bring to groups and when such views should be modified as a result of working with a group.

5. Ability to find and develop subordinates. This usually is considered essential for a manager to succeed. It requires much time and patience. Having for each job a competent assistant to take over in case of need demonstrates possession of this ability. On the other hand, a manager's practice of doing everything personally indicates failure to possess this characteristic. The person with true ability for management takes the best people available and develops them. The alibi, "I can't attain an effective unit, because I don't have the right kind of people" is never used.

6. Adaptability to many conditions. Many researchers in the field of executive selection rate highly the ability to adapt to situations at hand. The manager must, as a requirement of the job, remain flexible in thought and action. The need is to be able to meet the challenge of unexpected and nonrecurring events.

7. Technical knowledge and skill. The manager needs to have proficiency in, and understanding of, the specific subjects, techniques, and processes required to carry out a particular job. A manager also should possess any scientific or specialized background essential to the job.

Answer frame 2[15]

1. False. The first step in staffing is preparing job descriptions.
2. False. The job description describes the nature of the job, its duties, its activities, and its responsibilities.
3. True. The job description does not include *all* the duties and *all* the responsibilities entailed in a specific job. To do so would be impractical.
4. False. A job description is always subject to interpretation and, with time, the typical manager modifies the job content to some degree.

Turn to Frame 3[15], page 81.

Frame 3[15] continued

Indicate whether each of the following statements is true or false by writing "T" or "F" in the space provided.

_____ 1. One of the more obvious manager *specifications* is the *desire to manage*.

_____ 2. A manager's ability to influence others must be judged at two levels: the ability to influence individuals and the ability to influence groups.

_____ 3. To build an effective unit, the manager must recruit persons who already have highly developed managerial skills.

_____ 4. A manager must formulate ideas and actions at an early stage in her or his managerial career and stick by them.

Now see Answer Frame 3[15], page 84.

Frame 4[15]

With the job and manager specifications completed, the next step in staffing the organization is to *recruit and select candidates*. In the majority of cases, an almost constant lookout for potential candidates is suggested. This is necessary because of the intense competition for, and the importance of, acquiring competent managers. *Aggressive recruitment* is required if the firm is to find and attract the most likely candidates. No enterprise can afford to coast on its reputation and expect a sufficient number of qualified candidates to apply. Managerial material must be sought and, in this connection, the interests and wants of the enterprise should be publicized.

Legal constraints on employment. It is important to note that laws exist to assure equal job opportunities to equally well qualified candidates. The person doing the selecting must be fully informed regarding what legal provisions are applicable and further must understand how they are enforced. The Civil Rights Act of 1964 forbids discrimination in employment on account of sex, race, color, religion, or national origin. The act applies to selecting, hiring, upgrading, demoting, transferring, selection for training, and rates of pay. The Equal Employment Opportunity Commission (EEOC) receives and also initiates complaints alleging that a violation of Title VII of the Civil Rights Act has occurred. After investigation if the complaint is believed to be valid, the Commission tries to remedy the alleged unlawful practice by means of conference, persuasion, and conciliation. If no mutually acceptable agreement is reached by these means, the Commission may bring suit in an appropriate federal district court. In addition, the Employment Act of 1967 forbids discrimination due to age. Minimum hourly wages to be paid are stated in the Fair Labor Standards Act. This was initially passed in 1938 and has been subsequently updated and amended several times.

The sources for personnel are many; none should be ignored, although some will prove superior to others. In general, the following sources tend to be favored:

1. Promotion from within. Filling managerial jobs by advancement from the rank and file upward through the organization is common and popular. Such advancement usually is qualified by the statement, "when reasonable success in the new job appears likely." Such a qualification is intended to decrease the inherent difficulties in following a strict promotion-from-within policy. Using this source promotes morale and a positive attitude among employees. It also supplies potential managerial candidates, but overemphasizing it or using it exclusively can be dangerous.

The facts are that some employees are hired initially for their present jobs only; they are not hired for future managerial work; some lower-level managers are not interested in jobs with more authority and responsibility; and not all current middle managers qualify for top-management work. Employees may become upset and resentful when one, and only one, of their own number is to be promoted. Frequently, the feeling among the group becomes so intense that an easier way is followed—that of selecting an outsider.

2. Selection of managers from outside. When *new applications, fresh ideas,* and *improved vision* are believed necessary, but unavailable within the organization, experienced management members may be acquired from the outside. Many times this is the case when the enterprise enters a different and, to it, a new type of activity; or a stagnant position is reached and bringing in a manager from the outside to revive the enterprise is believed to be the best decision. Inbred thinking and acting are thus avoided.

On the other hand, morale problems can be created by selecting managers from the outside. Old-timers, not selected for a given promotion, can become uncooperative and frustrated. Also, outside superiority may be an illusion. It may not be true that a candidate from the outside is better qualified than anyone already with the enterprise. Standards for judging qualifications are required.

3. Hiring of graduates from colleges, universities, and special schools. By virtue of their special education, college graduates are believed to possess a background on which managerial skills can be built; i.e., they have managerial potential. The courses taken, proficiency attained in them, the quality of the university, and the requirements of the enterprise are but a few of the many factors that should be taken into account. Not all graduates, because of their graduation, are of management caliber. However, as a group, graduates have become an outstanding source of future managers.

4. Miscellaneous means. Advertisements and announcements reach many likely candidates, and are effective and widely used. Such sources are highly impersonal, and may attract some who are not qualified. Hence, the use of good selection devices is recommended. Employment agencies, both public and private, are favored by some enterprises. They perform creditable work, but may supply an inadequate number of qualified candidates.

Executive selection can follow many different patterns. Most include several *appraisals,* including those for: (*a*) *ability,* (*b*) *personality,* and (*c*) *social level,* by means of biographical data, interviews, observations, and tests. The appraisals do not always follow this order, but they are integrated into a composite of the candidate's qualifications. Biographical data, showing personal data, past places of employment, and past accomplishments, give information necessary for employment records but are generally believed to have limited selection value. Interviews, commonly several interviews by different interviewers for each candidate, can serve to provide insight into the manner of expression, aims, interests, and values of the candidate. Observations provide information on: (*a*) a candidate's reactions to situations, (*b*) ideas advanced, (*c*) mode of operation, and (*d*) general impression given to others. Tests measure a number of traits and are helpful, but not conclusive. The main limitation of tests is lack of agreement as to which traits are required for managerial competency. A battery of tests designed to measure many attributes is commonly relied upon to provide an insight into as many as possible of the candidate's attributes.

Answer frame 3[15]

1. True. The *desire to manage*, although a somewhat obvious characteristic, appears significant to managerial success.
2. True. A manager must be able to deal with individuals and with groups composed of many different types of individuals.
3. False. The person with true ability for management takes the best people available and develops them.
4. False. A manager should maintain flexibility, and must have the ability to adapt to unexpected and nonrecurring events.

Now turn to Frame 4[15], on page 82.

Frame 4[15] continued

Indicate whether each of the following statements is true or false by writing "T" or "F" in the space provided.

_____ 1. The Civil Rights Act of 1964 changed the rules of hiring.

_____ 2. Promotion from within is always the best method of obtaining new management members.

_____ 3. Selection of managers from the outside can cause conflict and dissatisfaction.

_____ 4. Graduates from universities and special schools usually are highly regarded for their managerial skills.

Refer to Answer Frame 4[15], page 86.

chapter 16

ORGANIZATION DYNAMICS

Frame 1[16]

Organizing is never finished. Viewing an organization as a network of decision-making communicating centers, from which effective group effort is to be obtained from the efforts of individuals, it can readily be seen that organizing is dynamic. Changes are certain to take place, because we are dealing with people, their relationships, and physical resources, none of which remain static. An organization must be adapted to the changing needs of those identities of which it is made up, as well as to its changing environment.

The four major reasons for organization dynamics are as follows:

1. The handiwork that organizing creates. In an organization, there are many mutually dependent variables, and each is affected by the collective effect that all the variables help to maintain. The structure is built on, and emphasizes, interdependence among its various units. And the exact operation of the unit is conditioned by the human element of those performing the work. Thus, the various ingredients that constitute an organization, and the purpose for which it is created and maintained, contribute to its dynamic characteristic. It is never static and should never be thought of as a static entity.

2. The inherent effects of personnel. Human beings change—their attitudes, capacities, and interests do not remain the same. Part of this is normal, and part is promoted and forced by development programs. Further, employees quit, are transferred, promoted, demoted, get married, grow old, retire, and die. Also, in some cases, the individual is moved up too fast due to an emergency, or too slowly because of few openings. And there are numerous examples where the arrival of a new top manager brings about reorganization of the unit and many changes in personnel.

3. Economic considerations, growth, and stresses. Without doubt, many organization changes are initiated for the purpose of bringing about improved organization effectiveness. Duplication of work, employees on jobs not requiring their special training and experience, and excessive cost are but a few of the common reasons for organization change. Furthermore, there are economic cycles, revealing fluctuation in demand for the products or services of most enterprises. Adjusting to these variations causes organization change; for example, during boom periods, the tendency is to add assistants, staff people, and special units, and these additions are often made without adequate planning. Likewise, when the boom subsides, the paring of the organization may be done in a quite unorthodox manner.

Addition of new products and new markets is a prime reason for change. This brings about new objectives that result in the obsolescence of certain existing functions. Mergers and acquisitions bring about the same effect. When there is a wide variety of products, the problem of coordinating and of decision making can become somewhat complex. New departmentation, additional people, and new authority may be added. In fact, growth of an enterprise is, of itself, a cause for organization change. Functions multiply, authority widens and increases, and rela-

Answer frame 4[15]

1. True. It forbids descrimination on account of sex, race, color, religion, or national origin.
2. False. *Promotion from within* can have shortcomings, such as the creation of hostility in those who were passed over.
3. True. Morale problems can be created by selecting managers from the outside; old-timers not selected can become uncooperative and frustrated.
4. False. Graduates from universities and special schools usually are highly regarded for their managerial *potential*.

You have completed Chapter 15. Now turn to Chapter 16, page 87.

Frame 1[16] continued

tionships become more complex. The initiation of manufacturing and sales operations in foreign countries creates new problems arising out of trade restrictions, the customs of the country, currency control, taxes, market characteristics, and so on. The structure of the organization must be altered to cope with these problems.

4. Technological changes. New developments in technology are an important contributor to organization dynamics. New materials and new processes call for new activities and organizational units. For example, automation may completely eliminate former functional manufacturing units and cause them to be replaced with new ones. Material handling may become highly important, production scheduling much less so. When a computer takes over paper work formerly done manually, the makeup and pattern of relationships of the organization must be altered, and different skills will be needed.

Indicate whether each of the following statements is true or false by writing "T" or "F" in the space provided.

_____ 1. Organizing is a static function; once completed, it can be put aside.

_____ 2. Changes in personnel can necessitate changes in the organization structure.

_____ 3. A change in the organization structure is a clear indication that the organization is regressing or losing ground.

_____ 4. Changes in technology affect the qualifications of employees, but not the organization structure.

Now refer to Answer Frame 1[16], page 88.

Frame 2[16]

What might be termed the normal growth pattern of organization consists of three steps, in the following sequence: (*a*) *vertical growth,* (*b*) *horizontal growth,* and (*c*) *functional to divisional departmentation.* When the work becomes too much for one person to handle, the usual decision is to get a helper who reports directly to the person being helped. Thus, an organization level is added, or *vertical growth* has been experienced. As the work expands further, more helpers are obtained, so that eventually departments are formed. Figure 12 clarifies this concept. Initially, the owner and president secured one helper each in production, sales, and finance. With time, each of these helpers secured helpers, and finally departments were formed, as for example, Production Departments No. 1, No. 2, and No. 3. The same development occurred in sales and in finance. The vertical growth is shown by solid lines.

FIGURE 12

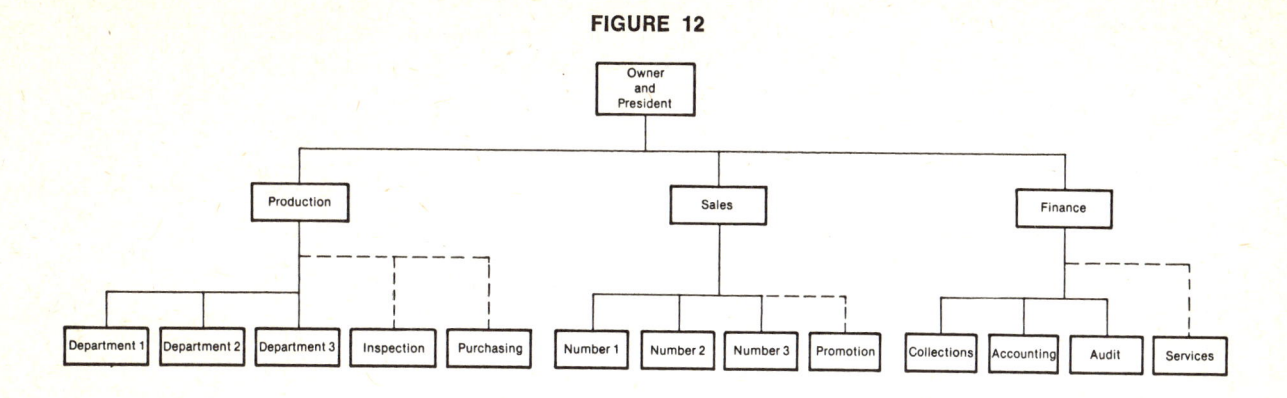

Complexities in performing the work tend to increase with growth in the amount of work. That is, Department No. 1, under production, will be required to maintain quality and to buy materials it needs. The same is true of Departments No. 2 and No. 3. Soon it will be reasoned that it would be beneficial to have a specialist in that particular work perform it for each department. Consequently, such units are added to the organization. These are indicated by dashed lines in Figure 12. Under production, a unit of inspection and one of purchasing are shown. They represent *horizontal growth* of an organization.

With still further work expansion, additional vertical and horizontal growth is experienced, until eventually the organization structure becomes cumbersome and fails to meet the needs of an enlarged, diversified company. Adjustment to the company's growth is now accomplished by going from *functional* to *divisional departmentation*. The many functional units are regrouped into several large, self-contained organization segments with a common or central group or staff to supply needed specialized assistance. In Figure 13, under production, this divisionalization is by product, with components No. 1, 2, and 3 served by the specialized units of cost, scheduling, and purchasing. Thus, an organization is formed that is flexible and practical, one that makes further growth possible, without distorting the basic structure.

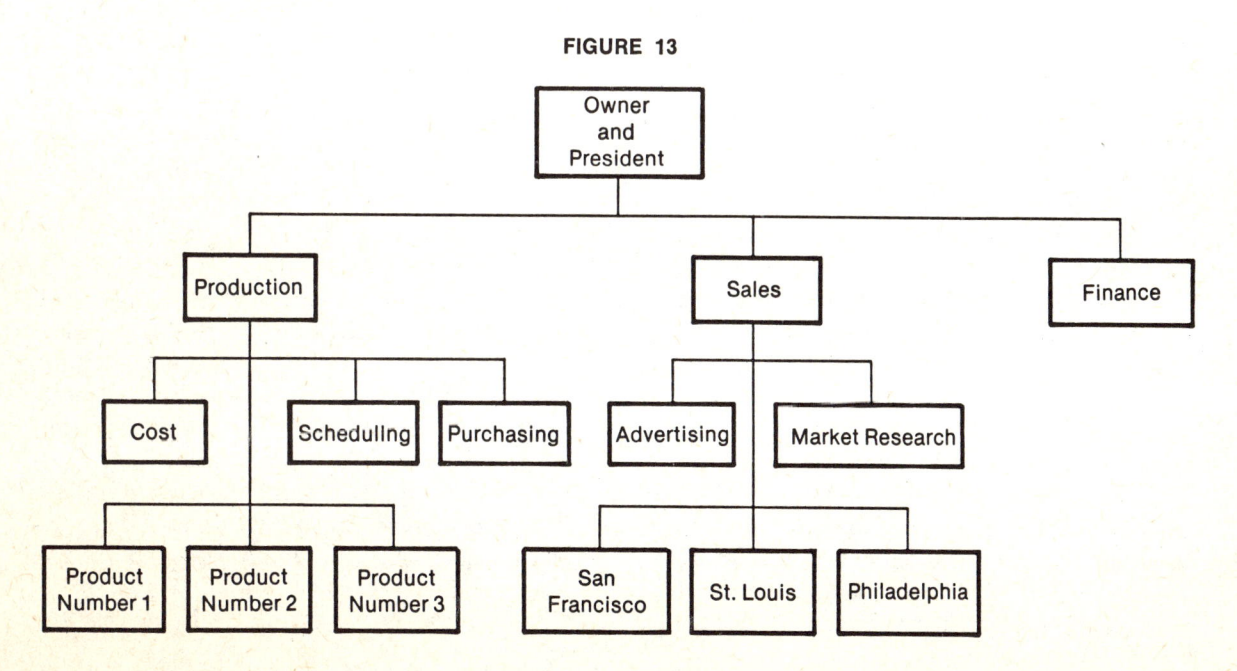

FIGURE 13

Answer frame 1[16]

1. False. Organizing is *dynamic,* since we are dealing with people, their relationships, and physical resources, none of which remain static.
2. True. Reorganization can be caused by changes in the employee mix.
3. False. The growth of an organization is of itself a cause for organization change.
4. False. Technological changes are important contributors to organization dynamics; for example, entire departments may be eliminated and replaced by others.

Continue by turning to Frame 2[16], page 86.

Frame 2[16] continued

Indicate whether each of the following statements is true or false by writing "T" or "F" in the space provided.

_____ 1. An organization usually witnesses vertical growth before horizontal growth.
_____ 2. *Horizontal growth* implies the addition of organizational levels.
_____ 3. The addition of specialists is an example of *horizontal growth.*
_____ 4. The large, diversified company is likely to utilize divisional departmentation.

Turn to Answer Frame 2[16], page 90.

Frame 3[16]

When to make an organization change is always significant. Frequently, it is a matter of the manager's judgment; although, in some instances, the economics of the situation or the critical need for a change may override all other considerations. There are two extremes that can be adopted. The extremes are to make changes: (a) *gradually over a fairly long period of time,* or (b) *quickly over a brief period.* The former, sometimes termed *the infiltration approach,* is conservative, stresses "let's-be-sure," and permits a high degree of employee consultation and consideration. The latter, or *earthquake approach,* features decisiveness, getting the change accomplished, and letting employees know immediately what the changes are. Frequently, a compromise course between the two extremes is followed.

Successful reorganization normally requires that the manager follow certain salient steps. First, *the manager must determine and review the objectives the new organization is set up to accomplish.* This forces a broad, overall viewpoint, so important in organizing. The intent is not to achieve just an improved organization but to achieve an improved organization to meet the specific requirements of the reorganizer.

Second, *the manager must try to develop the organization that will be most effective in achieving the stated objectives.* In doing so, some ideal concepts can be included—even that of aiming at the perfect organization, but the manager must take care to keep the plan for the proposed organization within reasonable and practical limits. This step brings into clear focus what the manager theoretically would like to have.

Third, *the manager must obtain complete facts about the present organization.* These facts will help determine where the organization now stands. The facts must be sought and accepted without bias. The available organization materials of the enterprise can be reviewed, interviews with key employees conducted, and questionnaires circulated. Especially valuable is the information gained about work performed, authority possessed, and duties assumed by the present staff.

Fourth, *the manager must decide on the*

phases required to go from the present to the proposed organization. People who can be made available for promotion through development; what changes of which activities will probably give better results, and when such changes should probably be made; and what the best way is to modify authority relationships existing must be identified. The timing of these changes, i.e., what phases will be used, and how long will each one be utilized before moving onto the next phase, is vital.

Fifth, *the manager must prepare for the reorganization and implement it.* Acceptance of the reorganization should be won by explanation, communication, and participation. To a degree, this was accomplished under the third step, but discussion about the specific reorganization plan is strongly recommended to take place during this fifth step. Generally, it is best neither to hurry this work nor to delay it unduly. The manager should pay special attention to those affected by the reorganization. At this stage, modifications, additions, and even rejections will occur. Implementation can follow verbal or written announcement by the top manager or the superior of the unit being changed. Exact information and all necessary details should follow in a written supplemental communication.

The organization audit—designed to check whether an organization encourages the attainment of goals, utilizes present employees to their fullest, and contributes to their growth—is similar to reorganization. As in reorganization, an early step in the audit is to collect and study organization material, such as job descriptions, performance appraisals, work actually done, and qualifications required. One important purpose of this step is to compare job requirements with individual qualifications for each management member. Requirements not adequately possessed by the manager are segregated from those not needed by the manager on the current job. Likewise, those requirements not adequately possessed are divided into those that can be achieved through development and those that probably cannot be developed within a reasonable period. From all this, various organization patterns and position breakdowns are evolved and evaluated, and note is taken of where existing personnel would be placed and what new personnel would have to be obtained.

Indicate whether each of the following statements is true or false by writing "T" or "F" in the space provided.

_____ 1. As the name implies, the *earthquake approach* to organization change is doomed to failure.

_____ 2. Reorganization should aim at achieving or aiding the achievement of the enterprise's objectives.

_____ 3. The last step in reorganization is to select the phases necessary to go from the present to the proposed organization.

_____ 4. An organization audit is an audit of the organization's financial records.

Now see Answer Frame 3[16], page 90.

Answer frame 2¹⁶

1. True. In the normal growth pattern, vertical expansion precedes horizontal expansion.
2. False. When an organizational level is added, *vertical growth* has been experienced. Horizontal growth involves the addition of more units *without* increasing the number of organizational levels.
3. True. The addition of specialists is an indication of *horizontal* growth. No new organizational levels are added.
4. True. The growth of an enlarged, diversified company is frequently accommodated by utilizing divisional departmentation.

Now go to Frame 3¹⁶, page 88.

Answer frame 3¹⁶

1. False. The earthquake approach is a legitimate and acceptable method of introducing change. It involves making changes quickly.
2. True. The first step in reorganization is to review all of the objectives that the new organization is to achieve or assist in accomplishing.
3. False. The last step in reorganization is to *prepare* for the reorganization and *implement* it.
4. False. An organization audit is a review of an organization, designed to check whether or not an organization encourages the attainment of goals, utilizes present employees to their fullest, and contributes to their growth.

You have completed Chapter 16. Now proceed with Chapter 17.

chapter 17

MOTIVATION AND MODERN MANAGERS

Frame 1[17]

Motivation deals with people's behavior, and it is a vital element in management. It can be defined as *getting a person to accomplish work enthusiastically because that person wants to do it.* The manager's task is to create work conditions that will help arouse and maintain this enthusiastic desire. To do this, knowledge of people and skill in dealing with their behavior are essential. Motivation differs among persons; it depends on many factors such as personality, ambition, education, and age.

A manager not motivated for progress and success will find it extremely difficult to motivate others. Self-motivation stems from an intense desire to achieve a certain goal, no matter what obstacle must be overcome. Positive thoughts and actions, along with persistence in adhering to a stated course of action, are also motivating factors.

The basic approaches to motivation differ among managers. The three approaches, selected for discussion here, are: (*a*) partnership, (*b*) productivity, and (*c*) wants-satisfaction. In the partnership approach, the assumption is that the typical employee dislikes work, but will perform well if there is the feeling by the employee that he or she is participating in the rewards of the enterprise. Hence, to motivate, friendliness and personal considerations are extended the employee, conflicts are avoided, comfortable conditions of work are provided, and, as the enterprise prospers, so does the employee. Such actions attract applicants, reduce labor turnover, and make for an agreeable work force; but it has not been proven that productivity per employee is thereby increased.

The *productivity approach* stresses rewards based on productivity. Work assignments are specific, and the wage or salary rates are explicitly stated. Firm policies are followed, job descriptions are well-defined, work performance is carefully measured, and special compensation is given for higher performance. A basic thought behind this approach is that a person who performs an activity and is rewarded tends to repeat that activity. On the other hand, if the person is punished as a result of actions, the tendency is not to repeat them. The productivity approach is used successfully, but it requires measured performance, the individual's control over performance, and a clear understanding of the basis for granting the rewards.

In the *wants-satisfaction approach,* an attempt is made to ascertain human wants and to satisfy them through the work situation. The concern here is not with the wants as such, but with the satisfactions a person will really strive for. People always have wants; as soon as one desire is satisfied, another appears in its place. As a result, people seek continuously to satisfy their needs. Under the wants-satisfaction approach, the manner and the climate under which the work is accomplished are established by skillfully arranging for interplay among the satisfactions and the wants, the relationships among the group's members, and the work to be done. The objective is to obtain a self-generated will-to-do, so that the work is accomplished in a manner that satisfies both the employees' wants and the enterprise's requirements.

All three approaches are used, but increasing emphasis is being given the wants-satisfaction approach. As we learn more and more about human behavior and witness the almost unbelievable results obtained from the wants-satisfaction approach, it becomes evident that this is the most effective approach.

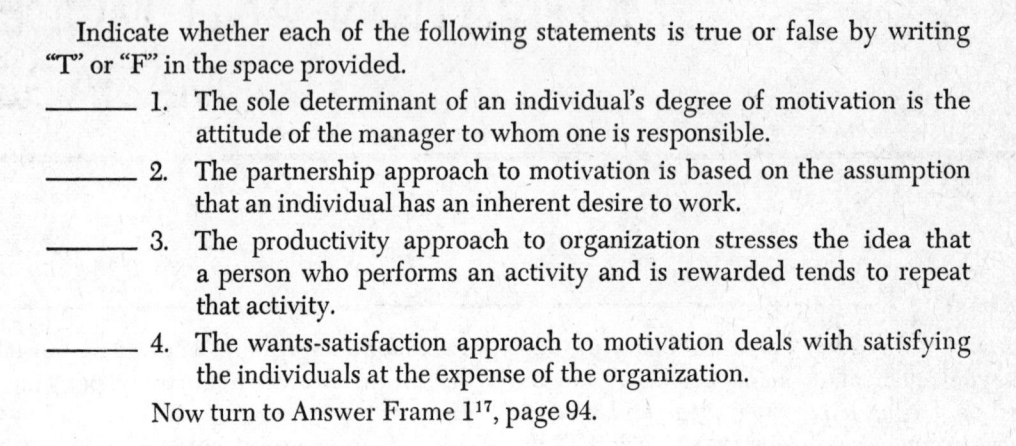

Indicate whether each of the following statements is true or false by writing "T" or "F" in the space provided.

_____ 1. The sole determinant of an individual's degree of motivation is the attitude of the manager to whom one is responsible.

_____ 2. The partnership approach to motivation is based on the assumption that an individual has an inherent desire to work.

_____ 3. The productivity approach to organization stresses the idea that a person who performs an activity and is rewarded tends to repeat that activity.

_____ 4. The wants-satisfaction approach to motivation deals with satisfying the individuals at the expense of the organization.

Now turn to Answer Frame 1[17], page 94.

Frame 2[17]

As implied in Chapter 12, individuals seek to satisfy at least a portion of their wants by working with others in a group. Each member contributes something, and depends on others to gain wants satisfaction. Frequently, in this process, the individual loses some individual personality and takes on a group complex, and personal wants become a part of the group's wants.

Group behavior must be recognized as an important concept in motivation. It is characterized by teamwork and by mutual dependence of its members on one another. To influence a group, the manager must treat it as a group, not as a mere collection of separate individuals. Group behavior asserts itself in many ways. For example, an individual affiliated with a group will not normally strive harder to satisfy personal wants in any way that brings conflict with the group's accepted norms of behavior. Therefore, when managers wish to bring about a change, the proper approach is to establish the need for the change with several group members and to let them win acceptance for the change from the group. Group members tend to listen to and to believe far more of what one of their members says than of what an outsider says.

Knowing what persons to put in a certain work group, shifting a misfit, and recognizing a bad group situation are basic in achieving motivation where groups are involved. Research confirms that wants satisfaction is maximized when the individuals are free to select their own work group. Likewise, under such conditions, each group member's job satisfactions increase, presumably because each individual is working with employees he or she likes, prefers to work with, and the behavior adjustment is relatively small.

Indicate whether each of the following statements is true or false by writing "T" or "F" in the space provided.

_____ 1. An individual receives some satisfaction from membership in groups.

_____ 2. The proper way to deal with a group appears to be to treat it as an entity and not as a collection of individuals.

_____ 3. Management must allow groups to initiate all changes.

_____ 4. Management should aid the establishment of cohesive, compatible work groups.

Now refer to Answer Frame 2[17], page 94.

Frame 3[17]

Wants to be satisfied differ among individuals because they place different values on various types of accomplishments. Perhaps the most common classifications of wants are: (*a*) *physiological wants*—for food, clothing, and shelter; (*b*) *safety wants*—for safety and for protection from possible harm; (*c*) *social wants*—for belonging and group relatedness; (*d*) *ego wants*—for self-esteem, and competence; and (*e*) *self-fulfillment wants*—for self-development and creativity. These types constitute a hierarchy of wants. The first group (physiological) is the first to be satisfied. After these are satisfied, the higher, or safety, wants are of chief importance, followed, in turn, by social wants, ego wants, and self-fulfillment wants. It is important to note that, *after a need is satisfied, it ceases to motivate until it is again felt.*

What can a manager do to create work situations in which these wants can be satisfied? One major action, of course, is to find out what the wants of each employee are. These change with time and conditions; but from observations of the employee, the work record, informal talks, performance ratings, and comments of others, the manager should be able to arrive at a reasonable evaluation. Knowing one's want or wants, it is possible to proceed with trying to satisfy them through a job-related activity. This necessitates proficiency in the art of management. The common approach is to provide several simultaneous opportunities, in the hope that one will cause the employee to respond favorably.

All these opportunities require the worker to make a contribution. The impact of an individual's efforts to contribute abundantly in work accomplishment, to offer suggestions, and to achieve good relationships with fellow employees, appears essential for genuine motivation.

A very important influence upon actuating is the viewpoint of the manager toward members of the work group. The two extremes of possible viewpoints are commonly expressed by the terminology of Professor McGregor as Theory X and Theory Y. The major characteristics of Theory X are that most employees: (1) work as little as possible and resist change; (2) must be persuaded, rewarded, punished, and controlled so that their behavior meets the needs of the organization; and (3) want direction and avoid job responsibilities. In contrast, Theory Y holds that most employees: (1) do not inherently dislike work; (2) have the capacity to assume work responsibility and have potential for development, but management by its actions must make them aware of these capacities; and (3) want to obtain social, esteem, and self-actualizing satisfactions from their work. A manager following Theory Y will realize by far the better results.

The behavior research scientist, Dr. Frederick Herzberg, states that achievement and job satisfaction lead to motivation, not the reverse. More specifically, this means that either the job content (the makeup of the work being performed) or the job context (environment under which the work is performed—supervision received, personal relations with peers, and technical aspects of the work) provide the means for motivation to originate. These two—job content and job context—are closely related, but job content is of relatively greater importance. Job content is intimate, always timely, and serves to support behavior as it takes place. Therefore, to motivate, be certain that the work itself challenges and stimulates the employee performing it. The work–employee relationship should provide opportunity for the employee to be creative in his own way.

Answer frame 1[17]

1. False. It is dependent on many factors besides the attitude of the individual's superior. Motivation differs among persons, and also depends on such factors as the individual's personality, ambition, education, and age.
2. False. The partnership approach to motivation is based on the assumption that the typical employees dislike work, but will perform well if they have a feeling of gratitude for the enterprise.
3. True. The productivity approach looks on reinforcement of an activity as the means of assuring that the activity will be repeated. Rewards are based on productivity.
4. False. The wants-satisfaction approach strives to have the work accomplished in a manner that satisfies *both* the employee's wants *and* the enterprise's requirements. It appears to be the most effective approach.

Go to Frame 2[17], page 92.

Answer frame 2[17]

1. True. An individual seeks to satisfy at least some wants by working with others as a group.
2. True. It seems to be more effective to treat a group as a single entity and not as a number of individuals who are banded together.
3. False. Management should initiate change, but group acceptance should be sought to implement that change.
4. True. Groups that are internally compatible are more easily delt with by management than groups wrought with dissension.

Turn to Frame 3[17], page 93.

Frame 3[17] continued

Indicate whether each of the following statements is true or false by writing "T" or "F" in the space provided.

_____ 1. Individuals strive to satisfy their highest level of wants and to sacrifice the satisfaction of the lower levels.

_____ 2. Managers should not allow employees to satisfy their needs because, once satisfied, the need ceases to be a motivating factor.

_____ 3. Time and conditions change, and so do an employee's wants. Managers must be aware of this, so that the means for satisfying these wants can be changed.

_____ 4. An employee should be offered several opportunities or means of satisfying a particular want.

_____ 5. Theory X and Theory Y are groups of assumptions that a manager can make concerning attitudes of workers.

Refer to Answer Frame 3[17], page 96.

Frame 4[17]

Selected attributes that facilitate motivation include:

1. Job enrichment. It follows from what has just been stated about the importance of job content that deliberately enriching the job to include greater responsibility, scope of tasks, and challenge in keeping with the personal needs of the employee on that job will have motivational effect.

2. Job rotation. This method of motivation

is gaining in popularity. Having an employee rotate periodically from one job assignment to another aids in minimizing boredom and disinterest. A composite of jobs should be included so that employee development and satisfaction of the person's needs are possible and encouraged.

3. Management by objectives. The practice of having the employee participate not only in determining personal objectives, but also in determining how they will be accomplished, all with final approval by the superior, has enormous motivational qualities. By such an approach the employee stresses results not activities, strengths not weaknesses, management not nonmanagement.

4. Participation. The best way for an individual to contribute is to participate. For the person to know that his or her ideas help shape the decision reached and to realize that self help is effective are highly motivating. With participation present, the individual's *desire to feel important and to contribute to progress* is recognized and favorably utilized. Best results are experienced when the individual: (*a*) is keyed in with the objectives sought, (*b*) has adequate knowledge to deal with the problem at hand, and (*c*) is given ample time to think about the issue—its constraints and important ramifications.

5. Multiplier manager. To each member of the work group, the multiplier manager asks, "How good have I made you look?" Helping members do a better job and fully developing their respective talents are key guides in the multiplier manager mode of managing and these efforts promote motivation. Also, being a multiplier manager assists in attaining a close relationship between skills of the employee and the requirements of the enterprise.

6. Achievement. The manager should make certain that the goal is challenging, yet attainable to the individual. The work must be meaningful and valuable in the eyes of the performer who should be given an immediate evaluation on completion of the work. Emphasis upon achievement will be effective in satisfying such wants as the desire for *interesting work to do* and the *accomplishment of useful work.*

7. Growth. The desire to develop and to advance exists in all employees in varying degrees. These wants are reflected in the need to realize *one's potentialities* and the desire for *promotion.* The progressive manager seeks to satisfy these wants by creating and maintaining a working environment in which the individual's drive and capacity for growth thrive.

8. Recognition. People generally want *acceptance as a member of a group* and *status.* Status is associated with recognition. People like acknowledgment of their presence, their accomplishments, and their contributions. The motivation is greatest when this acknowledgment comes from those within the same or closely related work group. Also, the person receiving recognition must know why she or he is getting it and must feel that it is deserved.

9. Responsibility. When responsibility is not specifically known, many individuals will take the attitude that others will see a job through, that it is not up to them to do so. Every employee needs to be aware of personal responsibilities. This helps the person perform the work that must be done. The employee's inherent desire to be assigned definite tasks and to be judged by accomplishment of them is illustrative of the motivation gained by effective use of responsibility.

The formal motivator of a work group is its supervisor. In general, tight supervision features getting out a specified volume of work and giving little freedom to the members. Under these conditions, the group does what is expected of it, but no more. But its members often have much mental satisfaction because the output expected of them is attained. In contrast, loose supervision gives members much freedom to utilize their ideas about the work, and the productivity is usually relatively higher. However, the members may not have as much mental satisfaction as under tight supervision. They find their hopes and imagination sparked, but unsatisfied, because they can do little about the nature of the work. The conclusion: For reasonably high production and employee satisfaction, a compromise between tight and loose supervision seems desirable; how tight or loose the supervision should be is conditioned by the makeup of the employees and the type of work.

Answer frame 3[17]

1. False. Individuals seek to satisfy higher level wants only when the lower level wants have been satisfied.
2. False. An individual who has satisfied one need proceeds to seek satisfaction of another and, therefore, a new motivating factor emerges. Individuals are never lacking for needs waiting to be satisfied.
3. True. A manager must be aware of the wants of each employee and changes in these wants, so that the proper opportunities for satisfaction can be offered to the employee.
4. True. After wants have been identified, the employee should be offered several job-related avenues to satisfy these wants, in the hope that at least one will motivate the employee to respond favorably.
5. True. Each might be valid in different circumstances. A manager of a work gang made up of prisoners from the state prison should probably assume Theory X. A manager of a group of research scientists should probably assume Theory Y. If either assumed the opposite theory, managing those respective employees could have disastrous results.

Now continue with Frame 4[17], on page 94.

Frame 4[17] continued

Indicate whether each of the following statements is true or false by writing "T" or "F" in the space provided.

_____ 1. Job enrichment is best described by stating that it involves having the employee participate in setting personal objectives and how they will be accomplished (with final approval by a superior).

_____ 2. For a goal to be a motivator, it must be set so high as to be practically unattainable.

_____ 3. Responsibility tends to contribute to motivation.

_____ 4. A major source of satisfaction for employees under tight supervision is in work accomplishment.

_____ 5. Loose supervision has been proven to be superior to strict supervision.

Now refer to Answer Frame 4[17], page 98.

chapter 18

DIRECTING

Frame 1[18]

Directing is the activity of integrating the efforts of members of a group, so that by accomplishing their assigned tasks they will meet individual and group objectives. All group effort requires direction if it is to be successful in attaining group ends. Each member of the group must have the information required to execute an assigned task. To this end, appropriate plans are made known to all members, in the form of instructions and orders that are recognized as official.

Good direction is not dictatorship. An employee expects to be given the information needed regarding quantity, quality, and time-use limits of the work. It is expected that this information is definite and complete, yet concise, that the job requirements are within one's skills and abilities, and that the best facilities available within the enterprise are provided.

Custom and habit influence all directing. As the manner of performing work breaks down into a series of routine situations, customary ways of cooperating and accomplishing the work become established. The directing may consist of a single routine, repetitive order such as: "Prepare 10 units of FM-99 for immediate shipment to Dallas." In contrast, if the directing initiates a new action, the manager must direct more fully. Participation by the employee, adequate communication, and strong leadership are essential to success in directing.

A manager is a part of the work group, yet it is convenient to consider the manager as apart from subordinates. The manager is the one to whom resources are made available. He is the one who must select and integrate them for the work at hand. Usually this is relatively uncomplicated for buildings, machines, and capital; but for people, direction is required, and this is a more complex matter. The manager is in a position to greatly influence the behavior of the group members. The character, trustworthiness, and attitude of the manager toward the group members will be judged by the subordinates and will influence the manager's effectiveness in directing them. The manager must gain the respect of both peers and subordinates. The role expected of the manager is different from that expected of the group members. The manager knows more about company policies; has foreknowledge of expected changes; and possesses, or at least should possess, greater experience. Also, managers stand apart from the group because they decide, at least to some extent, who gets what work, who is promoted, who is fired, and who receives a pay raise.

Answer frame 4[17]

1. False. The description given is that of *management by objectives.* Job enrichment involves giving the employee greater responsibility, scope of tasks, and challenge in keeping with the personal needs of the employee.
2. False. A goal should be challenging yet attainable. A goal that is viewed by the employees as being unattainable leads to frustration.
3. True. Responsibility helps an employee identify with the job and therefore contributes to motivation.
4. True. Under tight supervision, employees achieve much mental satisfaction from attaining the output expected of them.
5. False. For reasonably high production and employee satisfaction, a compromise between tight and loose supervision seems desirable.

You have completed Chapter 17. Now begin Chapter 18, page 97.

Frame 1[18] continued

Indicate whether each of the following statements is true or false by writing "T" or "F" in the space provided.

_____ 1. Directing is a management function that is general in nature, *i.e.*, it is only incidentally concerned with the accomplishment of a specific task.

_____ 2. The type and degree of the directing effort depends on the specific activity at hand.

_____ 3. A manager is a unique member of the work group.

_____ 4. The degree of influence a manager exerts over a group is determined solely by one's technical competence.

Refer to Answer Frame 1[18], page 100.

Frame 2[18]

Effective directing can best be carried out by one person for one group. Usually, this is the manager, because that person: (*a*) knows the subordinates, (*b*) is familiar with their skills and abilities, (*c*) understands their capacities and interests, (*d*) knows what they can produce, and (*e*) has observed their behavior. With all this as a background, the manager is well qualified to select the directing technique to best further the aims sought.

Providing information necessary for taking effective action is a cardinal contribution of directing. This is readily seen in the case of the new employee, but it applies equally in the case of the employee of long tenure. The new employee is assisted by briefings about the physical and human environment of the workplace. What information is needed for good performance and how it is to be transmitted are decisions made by the manager. Usually included are: (*a*) location of pertinent equipment within the office or factory, (*b*) identification of major departments, (*c*) a job description, (*d*) the relationship of a given job to other jobs within the organization unit or, in some cases, within the enterprise, (*e*) suggestions on how to fill out required reports, and (*f*) information on how a person's performance will be evaluated. If there is to be considerable contact with any other employees, the relationships are explained, and personal introductions among the parties are made. Further, if support services are required, the new employee needs to know what these services are and how to go about making use of them.

Orientation is also required for employees who have been with the enterprise for some time.

New assignments and changes in products, methods, and organization, make continuing orientation necessary. But this is not easy. The superior may neglect continuing orientation because other activities seem more important or the superior is busy or fears that poor responses and results will follow. And employees tend to grow indifferent toward suggestions and checkups repeated indefinitely.

It is paramount that subordinates keep their superiors informed; otherwise, the superiors are handicapped in their directing efforts. Reports and meetings commonly used for this purpose are frequently inadequate. The big question in the mind of the subordinate is: What should I report? Should all actions be reported and the risk taken of unduly burdening the superior? If any information is omitted, what parts should it be—that which adversely affects the reporter? The answer is: The subordinate should convey only such information as is pertinent and essential for accomplishment of the task. To carry out this mandate requires discernment and courage.

Indicate whether each of the following statements is true or false by writing "T" or "F" in the space provided.

_____ 1. A manager is not usually assigned the duty of directing the work group; this function is usually handled by specialists from outside the group.

_____ 2. One of the cardinal contributions of directing is obtaining information from employees.

_____ 3. Orientation is a form of directing used only in the case of new employees.

_____ 4. Just as the directing function contributes information to employees, employees must contribute information to the manager to aid in directing efforts.

Now turn to Answer Frame 2[18], page 100.

Frame 3[18]

An important tool of directing is *the order*. This can start, stop, or modify an activity. It is used by all managers. As a directional tool, an order is in the nature of a command, requiring a subordinate to act in a certain manner in a given circumstance. The common practice, however, is to express the order informally in nonauthoritarian language, as in "Let's go ahead with the revised design right away." Normally, a personal relationship between the order giver and receiver exists, and the sequence is always from superior to subordinate. To be complete, an order tells *what* is to be done; *who* is to do it; and *when, where, how,* and *why*. Preferably, it should have such clarity that it can be interpreted only as intended.

Orders are either: (*a*) *oral*, or (*b*) *written*, depending mainly on: (*a*) the degree of trust existing between the giver and the receiver, (*b*) the permanency of their relationship within the organization, and (*c*) the need for a record for future reference. In some companies, verbal orders, dealing with important subjects, are repeated by the receiver to insure completeness and accuracy. Also, verbal orders can be confirmed in writing if issuance must be verified and a record maintained.

Once an order is issued, the giver should see that it is carried out or is rescinded. Such a practice contributes toward good management. It is foolhardy to permit wide variations in the care and completeness with which orders are observed. For any subject area of an operation, it is best that the receiver be given orders from one source only. Orders should only be used when needed. An excess of orders causes confusion and waste. The necessity of the orders should be evident, and belief in their meaning

Answer frame 1[18]

1. False. The goal of directing is to insure the efficient accomplishment of a specific task.
2. True. Directing of routine activities is more a matter of following what has been done in the past, whereas a new activity necessitates the use of a more intensive and innovative directing effort.
3. True. Although a manager can be considered a member of the work group, the manager's authority and responsibility set him or her apart from the other group members.
4. False. A manager's influence on the behavior of the group is not only a function of technical competence, but also is determined by character, trustworthiness, attitude, and the respect of both peers and subordinates.

Turn to Frame 2[18], page 98.

Answer frame 2[18]

1. False. Effective directing can best be carried out by one person for one group; usually this person is the manager of that group.
2. False. One of the cardinal contributions of directing is *providing* information to employees, so they may take effective action.
3. False. Orientation is also required for employees who have been with the enterprise for some time; such things as new assignments and changes in products and methods are typical reasons for such orientation.
4. True. It is paramount that every subordinate keep the superior informed; otherwise, the superior is handicapped in the directing effort.

Now go to Frame 3[18], page 99.

Frame 3[18] continued

and intent is highly desirable. To gain belief in an order, a careful explanation of the "reason why" may be included.

Also used in directing are *instructions that serve to supply the how-to-do-it aspect for performing a particular task*. Typically, a variety of situations is covered, detailed data are given, and a sequence of steps to follow is featured.

Instructions are difficult to write, and they take considerable time. However, their use is increasing, primarily because: (*a*) they enable the recipient to go ahead with work in an approved manner, (*b*) the best how-to-do-it information is determined and standardized, (*c*) product uniformity is secured, and (*d*) indoctrination and development of personnel are promoted.

Indicate whether each of the following statements is true or false by writing "T" or "F" in the space provided.

_____ 1. An order is expressed as a formal command requiring a specific action on the part of a subordinate.

_____ 2. Written orders have more force and authority than do oral orders.

_____ 3. A manager should always translate ideas into orders when dealing with a subordinate.

_____ 4. Instructions explain the manner in which a particular task is to be performed.

See Answer Frame 3[18], page 102.

Frame 4[18]

Important to the method and approaches that a manager decides to use in his or her directing efforts is *the effect on the group*. As indicated in Chapter 12, interactions among the group's members result in acceptance or rejection of managerial suggestions or of changes affecting the members. These reactions should be taken into account in managerial directing efforts. Studies in this area supply helpful guidelines and now will be enumerated. First, the manager who wishes to use the group as an instrument of change in group attitudes, values, or behavior must keep in mind that: (*a*) those being changed and those exerting influence for change should have a feeling of belonging to the same group, and (*b*) a group highly attractive to its members exerts great influence on them. Studies of actual factory situations reveal that, where below-standard nonmanagers were given the opportunity to enumerate their gripes about factors affecting their production (materials, machines, and working environment), were promised correction of these ills, and were asked to estimate what they could produce under the improved conditions, *they set* goals 25–40 percent above what they had been attaining. In most cases, they achieved them. In contrast, where the group members were told what to produce by nonmembers, there was no increase.

Evidence such as this shows that the reaction and the behavior of the group must be taken into account in the work of directing. *Social pressure* exists within any group. It influences the individual's decisions and tends to breed conformity or common consent among the meubers. Social requirements apparently require consensus.

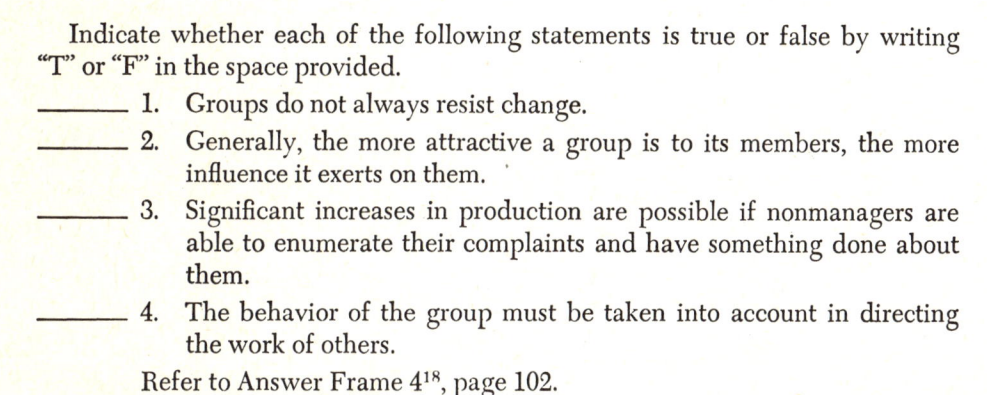

Indicate whether each of the following statements is true or false by writing "T" or "F" in the space provided.

_____ 1. Groups do not always resist change.

_____ 2. Generally, the more attractive a group is to its members, the more influence it exerts on them.

_____ 3. Significant increases in production are possible if nonmanagers are able to enumerate their complaints and have something done about them.

_____ 4. The behavior of the group must be taken into account in directing the work of others.

Refer to Answer Frame 4[18], page 102.

Answer frame 3[18]

1. False. Orders are commonly expressed in an informal manner, such as "Let's go ahead with the alternative plan as soon as possible."
2. False. Both oral and written orders carry the same degree of force and authority; the choice of one type over the other depends on such things as the relationship between the parties and the need for future reference.
3. False. Orders should be used only when needed; **an** excess of orders can cause confusion and waste.
4. True. Instructions supply the how-to-do-it aspects for performing a particular task.

Go to Frame 4[18], page 101.

Answer frame 4[18]

1. True. Groups can either resist or accept change. A prime determinant is the manner in which the change is introduced.
2. True. One does not wish to risk expulsion from a group to which one is highly attracted.
3. True. Increases in production of 25–40 percent were achieved in many cases.
4. True. Social pressure influences the individual's devisions and behavior.

You have completed Chapter 18. Continue by beginning Chapter 19, page 103.

chapter 19

COMMUNICATING

Frame 1[19]

A major skill required of a manager is the ability to communicate effectively. Gaining acceptance of policies, seeing that instructions are clearly understood, and bringing about improvements in performance depend on effectively communicating. The manager who is unable to communicate to associates what work is required will not succeed in getting the associates to accomplish it. In turn, if the associates are unable to communicate freely with the manager, information needed to manage successfully will be missing.

Communication is a means by which management is facilitated; it is not an independent activity but an essential adjunct to almost everything a manager does. Some estimates state that two thirds of a manager's time is spent in communicating. Keeping associates fully informed and gaining mutual understanding are so important, that some reach the erroneous conclusion that management is primarily communicating. But communicating is only a part of management.

Communicating is more than telling or writing. It also includes *understanding*. There is no communication if you are not understood and this lack of understanding poses the biggest difficulty encountered in communication. The *illusion of communication* is believing that mutual understanding has taken place because one person has spoken to another or because what has been written by one has been read by the other. Remember what is expressed is not always what is understood. From the management point of view, some of the reasons for failure of communication are: (a) the communication contains indirections—it does not reveal and stay with the real problem, (b) the receiver interprets communication in light of personal background and experience, and (c) the receiver has a disposition to read into the communication what one anticipates or expects. In other words, communication is conditioned by the receiver's interpretation of the message and the prevailing attitudes of the communicator and the receiver not only toward each other, but also toward the subject at hand.

These difficulties of communication may result in what is commonly termed *the communication gap*. To minimize this gap, the manager should strive for a climate of confidence in which communication can take place. To prejudge that which will be said or written weakens the communication. Communications should be specific and simple. A good rule to follow is "one message, one subject." Timing is also vital. Communication is especially dynamic, and saying the right thing at the right time has paramount value. It is advantageous for the recipient to take time to reflect on the answer, not to give forth with the first reaction that comes to mind. With reflection, the receiver will comprehend better what is really being communicated, and hence, is likely to give better answers.

It is helpful to keep in mind that communication is performed basically to influence behavior. Messages are generated from the outside, but meanings come from within. Messages are transmitted, meanings are not.

The perceptions of the receiver, not the intentions of the sender, govern what is understood. A person's self-perceptions, his or her perceptions of others, and how others perceive that person influence the interpretation of a message and what behavior is taken. Two conditions are important. First is how one perceives things and how they really are. Second is how one perceives things and how others perceive the same things. There may be in each human being a well-organized package of perceptions which are entirely acceptable to their possessor, but which may make no sense at all to others. In turn, this may give rise to "defensiveness" or a self-concept preservation by the possessor for her or his perceptions against those held by others. Defensiveness hinders effective communication and determines how supportive or defensive the communication environment is.

All communication is two-way. When one speaks, another listens. When one writes, another reads. The speaking and the listening, or the writing and the reading, must take place for communication to exist. More significant, however, is that, as stated above, the speaker or writer be sensitive to the listener's or reader's response. If not, the speaking or writing can lead to misunderstanding and antagonism. Free movement in both directions, statement and response, and the exchange of ideas open the way for effectively transmitting information and gaining understanding. For it is only in this free exchange, this give-and-take, that we find out how others react to the message communicated and what ideas they have to contribute.

Observe that listening and reading are essential parts of communication; they are the great media of learning, directing, and motivating. Unfortunately, people retain only a small amount of what they hear and read, and that not for very long. Listening and reading take energy; they are work. They should not be considered something to do when you have nothing else to do. To improve, the manager should listen and read with a purpose in mind, try to remove attributes and beliefs that interfere with effective listening and reading, and recognize the deep importance of these activities in managerial work.

Observe that communication involves not only factual but also emotional considerations. It involves the whole personality. When communication takes place a response is stimulated in addition to information being transmitted. In addition, a relationship is set up by the messages sent and the responses received. Therefore, it can be stated that communication is a major means for improving human relations.

Indicate whether each of the following statements is true or false by writing "T" or "F" in the space provided.

_____ 1. A manager's role in communicating consists in getting others to do what the manager wants them to do.

_____ 2. The *illusion of communication* arises because of the assumption that the meaning of what has been transmitted is common to the sender and the recipient.

_____ 3. One cause of the *communication gap* is that most communications are not specific and simple.

_____ 4. Not allowing the recipient of a communication to respond can lead to misunderstanding and antagonism.

See Answer Frame 1[19], page 106.

Frame 2[19]

Good communicating motivates. It encourages a feeling of participation; it excites greater interest in the work. Sharing information of mutual interest and benefit gives vital support to an employee's sense of belonging. Many advocate daily contacts between managers and nonmanagers. Explaining plans and policies, telling of changes to take place in the future, encouraging suggestions, and asking opinions are but a few of the many ways in which motivation can be enhanced.

For academic purposes, communication has

been classified into various types, as, for example: (*a*) *downward and upward communication*, (*b*) *formal and nonformal communication*, and (*c*) *oral and written communication*. In the first type, communication flows from the top to the bottom managerial levels of an enterprise and from the lower to the higher managerial levels. Downward communication may consist, for example, of orders, instructions, and memos; upward communication may be through reports, suggestions, and grievances.

Formal communication is that using established organization channels and standard media, such as departmental meetings, telephone calls, company magazines, posters, and direct-mail letters. Nonformal communication is that which exists because of personal and group interests of people. Commonly dubbed the *grapevine*, it is direct, fast, and flexible; yet it does not have access to official information sources. The believability of the grapevine is high, but sometimes it carries rumor or distorted information. Therein lies its danger.

The terms *oral communication* and *written communication* are self-explanatory. The ability to speak effectively is a requisite for most managers. Many find it helpful to jot down the major points to be included, so that the overall oral presentation can be well organized. Some repetition for emphasis is normal. Oral communication permits a face-to-face exchange, fosters a friendly spirit, and encourages questions and answers.

Formal meetings, within an enterprise, have become commonplace. This is in keeping with the high value currently placed on group decision making, encouraging group participation, and keeping employees informed. To be of greatest value, a meeting should be: (*a*) *planned*, with each member given the purpose, program, and time; (*b*) *specific*, with presentation and discussion kept directly applicable to the particular issue at hand; (*c*) *illustrated visually*, especially if complicated concepts are involved or statistics are used; and (*d*) *written up*, to supply a record of what was covered and decided and what responsibility for what participant was established.

Written reports exemplify written communication. By having them in written form, they become available for future reference, and details, if warranted, can be included. The keys to effective written communication are the familiar four C's—completeness, clarity, conciseness, and correctness. Common words, simple sentence structure, a writing style that flows naturally, and a presentation of material that is easy to follow should be used.

Indicate whether each of the following statements is true or false by writing "T" or "F" in the space provided.

_____ 1. Communication between organization levels generally can be made more highly motivating if it is a daily occurrence.

_____ 2. Nonformal communications arise when formal communications break down.

_____ 3. Formal meetings generally are most beneficial when any discussion is conducted in an "open-ended" manner.

_____ 4. The intended audience must be considered in evaluating the effectiveness of a written communication.

See Answer Frame 2[19], page 106.

Frame 3[19]

The following suggestions are helpful in attaining effective communication:

1. Know fully what you are trying to communicate. Clearly visualize what information you want the recipient to have or what issues you want to resolve. This implies that the communicator must have a greater fund of information than is actually used for the communica-

Answer frame 1[19]

1. False. A manager's role in communicating consists of getting others to *understand* what is wanted of them.
2. True. The *illusion of communication* is believing mutual understanding has taken place because a person has spoken to another or because what has been written by one has been read by the other.
3. True. One way to reduce the *communication gap* is to keep messages specific and simple.
4. True. If the recipient of a communication is not allowed to respond, the communication *can* lead to misunderstanding and antagonism.

Now go to Frame 2[19], page 104.

Answer frame 2[19]

1. True. Communication should not be treated as a reward. Many writers advocate daily contact between manager and subordinates.
2. False. Nonformal communications generally arise because of personal and group interests of people.
3. False. Formal meetings generally are most beneficial when discussion is limited to that which is applicable to the particular issue at hand.
4. True. A written communication should be tailored to the audience for whom it is intended.

Now go to Frame 3[19], page 105.

Frame 3[19] continued

tion. A person needs a reserve to answer unexpected questions and to expand on any relevant topic.

2. Communicate adequately—no more, no less. A constant challenge in communicating is to avoid talking or writing too much or too little. Excess is all too common. Overcommunication may result from too great an eagerness to utilize fully available communication channels and media. Some management members are literally buried under communication. They can't digest all of it and much is not essential to their work. Likewise, inadequate communication is undesirable. Failure to give enough information to perform the work or to develop on the jobs can be devastating. Both extremes must be avoided. Whether communication is adequate can be determined by being alert to the receiver's reactions and using past communication experience as a guide.

3. Realize that communication may be altered in its distribution. Change in a communication is likely to take place as it is interpreted by each in a line of receivers. The change may be either favorable or unfavorable, depending on the recipient's influence. Usually, people dislike passing on facts about unfavorable results, so the communication is sweetened. This happens more frequently in upward than in downward communication. The manager should be aware of this possible change, and practice the necessary control to minimize it.

4. Use proper symbols and visuals. All communication employs symbols to represent persons or things that can be distinguished. Symbols include signs, words, colors, and characters. They were developed to meet the needs of transmitting information; they stand for something meaningful. For example, the algebraic sign = stands for equals. Words are meaningful, but some words are far more definite or exact in meaning than are others. The word *iron* conveys a fairly precise meaning, whereas the word *excellent* is subject to different meanings by different persons and by the same person at different times. To the extent that symbols used in communication do not have universal meanings, we have communication difficulty. Visuals help the human mind to comprehend information. A simple chart or diagram often conveys the message better than many words.

5. Carefully select information communicated. Ideally, the information communicated consists of what the receiver wants to know and what the giver believes the receiver should know. Employees like to be informed about working conditions, promotion possibilities, company policies, work methods, employee benefits, and the general welfare of the enterprise. However, because employees want to be informed, doesn't mean that every last bit of information must be communicated. The company, too, has rights and interests that sometimes must be protected.

Indicate whether each of the following statements is true or false by writing "T" or "F" in the space provided.

_____ 1. An individual sending a communication typically has more information available than one wishes to pass on to the recipient.

_____ 2. A communication which passes from one individual to another is subject to distortion by each individual who receives it and passes it on.

_____ 3. A verbal explanation is usually superior to a simple chart or diagram.

_____ 4. The individual sending the communication should limit the degree of detail of the message.

Refer to Answer Frame 3[19], page 108.

Answer frame 3[19]

1. True. An individual rarely communicates all the information available regarding the topic of the communication.
2. True. Change in a communication takes place as it is interpreted by each recipient in a line of receivers.
3. False. A simple chart or diagram commonly conveys a message better than many words.
4. True. Too much detail tends to overwhelm the receiver and makes that person lose sight of the main issue.

You have completed Chapter 19. You may want to work the examination on page 161 which covers Chapters 11–19. Then proceed to Chapter 20, below.

chapter 20

LEADERSHIP IN MANAGEMENT

Frame 1[20]

Every individual has some influence on others; with practice, this influence grows. Some individuals are more influential than others, and some conditions are more conducive to influencing than others. By developing this ability to influence, it is possible to acquire leadership. We can view leadership as *the ability of a person or leader to show the way and to induce followers to work together with confidence and zeal on tasks that the leader sets.*

Leadership is a natural outgrowth of people being associated for some purpose in a group. A few in the group will lead, the majority will follow. Actually, most people want somebody to determine what should be done and how to do it; and to be motivated and assisted in actions they realize should be done, but that they will not do unless they have a leader. The leader accepts the responsibility and is eager to implement solutions to problems. The leader identifies and understands the wants of the nonleaders. Frequently, this is the result of developing an environment of mutual understanding, evolved from many sessions of participation and consultation.

A leader puts plans into action and contributes toward making a plan a reality. The leader communicates the plan to associates, explains the purpose of the action, tells what each member is to do, attempts to generate enthusiasm, and tries to resolve any friction among the members. In essence, the leader motivates and guides the behavior of the nonleaders to fulfill the plan and to accomplish the required work.

Leaders also perform another very important function. They seek to understand the problems that the followers are facing and also their feelings toward these problems, their work, their associates, and their work environment. This activity is often overlooked in discussions on leadership. Familiarity with the problems and feelings of associates enables leaders to obtain information and responses that can be used to modify their behavior in order to improve the quality of their leadership. For example, knowing how associates feel about a certain issue assists the leader in decision making, and operational facts derived directly from those performing the work are essential in appraising the work efforts being made. Further, a favorable motivating effect on the group is present when the leader evinces interest in what the members are doing and in what they think about the work they are doing.

Actually, there are mutual interactions between the leader and the nonleaders. It is not uncommon for the nonleaders to sway the leader. Their response to the leader's requests tends to significantly influence the leader's own behavior. Also, many leaders closely observe the behavior initiated by the nonleaders. Such observations give the leader clues about the group and suggest possible modifications in the leader's own behavior for more harmonious relationships.

Indicate whether each of the following statements is true or false by writing "T" or "F" in the space provided.

_____ 1. A distinguishing characteristic of a leader is that the person is a member of a group who has some influence over others.

_____ 2. Most people do not want to be leaders.

_____ 3. A leader should be interested in, and actively investigate, the problems that the followers face.

_____ 4. It is characteristic that a leader not be influenced by interactions with nonleaders.

Refer to Answer Frame 1[20], page 110.

Frame 2[20]

The leader needs to gain satisfactions in accomplishing specific work and in meeting the wants of the group. The degree of confidence the group has in the leader, as well as the willingness of the group to do what the leader tells them, are fundamental for proper leadership to exist. Followers must believe in their leaders. It is imperative that the leader be aware of the role expected. What is the leader supposed to decide? Does one have the authority to grant wage increases and to fire and hire? What objectives does the leader seek? Answers to such questions are given by the role the leader assumes and the actions taken.

It is equally important that the leader possess the ability to determine what actions will best help accomplish the group's goals. This requires an understanding of how one's actions as a leader affect the members of the group, as well as the work itself. But this ability involves more than making decisions; it also requires that the manager be able to utilize unique situational and interactional factors, so that the best ways to solve problems and accomplish one group's ends are followed and unfavorable responses are eliminated insofar as possible.

Leading is a continuous activity. Obstacles, toward achievement of the intended goals, appear that suggest modifications in the leadership. The feelings of the group members change, as do also their abilities and attitudes. Leadership is dynamic, and to be effective it must be constantly updated.

The type of leadership employed varies with the particular work situation; that is, the same leadership behavior is not equally effective in all situations. Because the typical leader becomes involved in different situations, it follows that, over a period, a leader must have some flexibility in her or his leading, something that many lead-

Answer frame 1[20]

1. False. Every individual has some influence on others. A leader has developed and augmented this influence.
2. True. Most people are satisfied to be followers and look to others for leadership.
3. True. A familiarity with the problems of followers aids the leader in making appropriate decisions. In addition, it has a motivating effect, because it indicates that the leader is interested in them.
4. False. It is not uncommon for nonleaders to sway the leader through their mutual interactions.

Now turn to Frame 2[20], page 109.

Frame 2[20] continued

ers find extremely difficult. This suggests tailoring the manager's job to a leadership style instead of trying to adapt the leader's style to the job requirements. If this is done, any of the following can be practiced: (a) alter the group's membership to improve the leader's relationship to it, (b) change the leader's formal authority, or (c) modify the task structures—detail some, define others in broad outlines, and leave still others to the initiative and preference of the leader.

Indicate whether each of the following statements is true or false by writing "T" or "F" in the space provided.

_____ 1. The leader must have the confidence and support of the group for proper leadership to exist.

_____ 2. In making a decision, the leader is only concerned with the effect of the decision on the members of the group.

_____ 3. An individual's method of leadership should remain consistent and unchanging.

_____ 4. When a manager's style of leading ceases to be effective in a particular work situation, that leader should always be removed.

See Answer Frame 2[20], page 112.

Frame 3[20]

Inasmuch as reference has been made to the type of leadership, let us enumerate the different main types:

1. Situational leadership. In this type of leadership the situation is believed to be the most important factor in determining leadership style. Both the leader and the follower adjust to the situation. There is also some adjustment by the followers to the leader, and vice versa. Dr. Frederick E. Fiedler's leadership research studies have contributed much to this viewpoint of leadership. According to Fiedler, three dimensions are helpful in measuring leadership effectiveness including (1) the leader-led relationship or the amount of confidence the followers have in their leader, (2) the degree to which the followers' jobs are task structured or routine, and (3) the extent to which power is inherent in the leadership position. The interaction of these three dimensions suggests what mix is probably most effective for a given situation. Fiedler found that the dimensions of leadership consisting of high confidence in the leader, nonstructured tasks, and much power by the leader were most effective. In contrast, for situations of intermediate or moderate favorability, leadership characterized by average confidence in the leader, moderately structured tasks, and moderate power by the leader, were desirable.

2. Personal-behavior leadership. As implied by the name, the *behavior* of the leader is emphasized in this type of leadership. The personal-behavior leader is flexible, using in each situation the action believed appropriate—keeping in mind the capabilities, amount of control desired, and whether the leader wishes to decide the issue. The personal-behavior leader can, for example, be highly authoritarian and even autocratic in one situation, and in another seemingly similar situation permit the subordinate to function with much freedom. Likewise, the leader may represent a combination of behaviors which commonly are believed to be incompatible, such as being benevolent yet autocratic in behavior.

3. Work-centered or worker-centered leadership. Different people in different situations respond differently to different kinds of leadership. While leadership emerges from many forces acting and interacting simultaneously, emphasis can be directed to either the (1) work that is being done, or (2) the person doing the work. This gives rise to work-centered or worker-centered leadership. The work-centered style focuses on task performance and accomplishment. In contrast, the worker-centered style is sensitive to people and human relations. The former commonly involves work of a routine nature, the leader announces the decisions, and rules are carefully followed. The latter, or worker-centered, style usually offers a minimum of procedures and edicts to follow, participation in decision making is encouraged and the leader is viewed as a coordinator and thought stimulator. Which type to use depends upon the individual circumstances and what you are trying to achieve. Some feel that the worker-centered leadership is always better, but research studies do not confirm this. In many cases the work-centered approach gives excellent results. Characteristics of the group's membership including its expectancies, status, experience, ambitions, and behavior, appear vital in deciding which style to select.

4. Personal leadership. Motivations and directives are given person-to-person contact. A close relationship exists between the leader and each nonleader. Personalities and an informal atmosphere characterize the situation when personal leadership is followed.

5. Democratic leadership. Stresses participation and utilization of ideas by the group members, who consequently should be well informed about the subjects discussed. Possible actions are presented to the group before implementing them. The group's interest and initiative are emphasized.

6. Authoritarian leadership. The basic belief here is that leadership is possessed by the leader to the extent that he or she has authority. It holds that because of the position held, the leader knows best and should decide what should be done. This type of leadership is characterized by stern, factual leaders and carefully defined controls.

7. Paternalistic leadership. A fatherly influence exists between the leader and the group. The intention is to protect and to care for the followers' comfort and welfare. Paternalism is well suited for certain situations, but it can prevent development of the self-reliance of the group members.

8. Indigenous leadership. Infinite in variety and form, this type of leadership originates from informal organization groups (see Chapter 12). Different indigenous leaders can exist for different purposes within the same group. The success of many actions are conditioned by indigenous leaders, even though the group is led by formally recognized leaders.

From all these different types of leadership, we can deduce that leadership is a multidimensional, complex relationship. It involves a leader, followers, and the situations created by the tasks of the organization, social values, economic conditions, technological facilities, and political considerations.

A leader must have followers, and regardless of how one became a leader, one must be able to retain followers. How does a person do this? *First, a leader represents a worthy cause.* Awareness of this is made clear to others. Followers believe in the cause and want to take part in its attainment. *Second, the leader's personality attracts,* and followers see in the leader the personification of good attributes they would like to have, or recognize in the leader those attri-

Answer frame 2[20]

1. True. The degree of confidence the group has in the leader, as well as the willingness of the group to do what the leader tells it, are fundamental for proper leadership to exist.
2. False. A leader must consider the effects of a decision on the group members and on the work itself.
3. False. Leadership is dynamic and must be constantly updated.
4. False. Sometimes the work situation can be tailored to the leader's style or one can change one's style of leadership.

Now go to Frame 3[20], page 110.

Frame 3[20] continued

butes required to get the job done. Third, *ability to inspire* convinces others that one knows what to do, has the ability to give courage and confidence to the followers, and convinces followers that the leader understands them and will help them.

Indicate whether each of the following statements is true or false by writing "T" or "F" in the space provided.

_____ 1. *Personal leadership* is more likely to be present in small groups than in large groups.

_____ 2. *Paternalistic leadership* does not contribute to the independence of individual members.

_____ 3. *Authoritarian leadership* is based on the belief that authority is necessary to exercise leadership.

_____ 4. Personal-behavior leadership and situational leadership are identical.

_____ 5. The common way a leader retains followers is to impress them with the leader's superiority.

Compare your answers with those in Answer Frame 3[20], page 114.

Frame 4[20]

To qualify for leadership necessitates possession of certain mental and philosophical concepts. Above all, a leader needs a basic philosophy of life and of work that will provide a framework for leadership. One should believe deeply in the possibility of advancement and progress; should be convinced that the goals can be achieved and should have the capacity to achieve them. Further, the leader must also be willing to pay the price that leadership demands. Sacrifices must be made, frustrations must be met, and imponderables have to be dealt with. All these exact tribute in time, effort, and money. Further, the leader should be willing to operate in the light of publicity. Some will praise one's efforts, others will be envious and loudly voice criticism. Last, the leader accepts the fact that what is accomplished depends in part on the era in which one lives. Emergencies may spawn opportunities for the leader; changing social and economic conditions may frustrate a leader's best efforts.

Current research reveals that successful leadership requires a high degree of perception about people involved in certain situations. Development of the following skills is paramount:

1. Objectivity toward human relations and behavior. The leader must be able to view people and their behavior in an unbiased, unemotional manner. The leader should not have a habit of prejudging. For each major action, one must be able to identify the influences and the responses elicited. The leader should have the ability to decide what caused the responses to take place and be able to verify conclusions.

2. Communicative and social proficiency. The leader should be able to talk and write forcefully and to accurately summarize the statements of others. In addition, the leader should be approachable, know the groups and their informal leaders, let goals be known, and strive to cooperate with associates.

3. Empathy. The ability to project oneself mentally and emotionally into the position of a follower helps a leader to comprehend the employee's views, beliefs, and actions. Empathy gives respect for the other person's point of view, even though one may disagree with that person's values and beliefs.

4. Self-awareness. The leader needs to know the impression he or she makes on others. Efforts should be made to fill successfully the leadership role expected by the followers.

5. Teaching. One of the best ways to lead, develop, and inspire people is by teaching. The leader must be able to use teaching skills advantageously through inspiring, demonstrating, correcting, and showing by example.

Indicate whether each of the following statements is true or false by writing "T" or "F" in the space provided.

_____ 1. All an individual needs to qualify for a leadership position is the willingness to accept responsibility.

_____ 2. A leader must be capable of meeting crises and not wavering in the face of adversity.

_____ 3. A leader should have the ability to analyze problems in an objective manner.

_____ 4. Empathy is the ability to understand the feelings and situations of others.

Now see Answer Frame 4[20], page 114.

114 Programmed learning aid for principles of management

Answer frame 3[20]

1. True. *Personal leadership* requires person-to-person contact and, therefore, is most likely to be present in small groups.
2. True. *Paternalistic leadership* is well suited for certain situations, but the self-reliance of the group members is not enhanced.
3. True. The basic belief of *authoritarian leadership* is that leadership is possessed by the leader to the extent that that person has authority.
4. False. While they may seem to be quite similar, personal-behavior leadership emphasizes the *behavior* of the leader regardless of the situation, while situational leadership emphasizes the *situation* in determining leadership behavior.
5. False. A leader retains followers by impressing them that the cause is worthy, his or her personality attributes are authoritative and that they feel inspired to follow.

Now continue by turning to Frame 4[20], page 112.

Answer frame 4[20]

1. False. To qualify for leadership necessitates possession of the ability to lead in addition to the willingness to lead.
2. True. Emergencies spawn opportunities for the leader and reduce the necessity to create challenging situations.
3. True. A manager should have the ability to view people and their behavior in an unbiased manner.
4. True. Empathy is the ability to project yourself mentally into the position of another.

You have completed Chapter 20. Now proceed to Chapter 21, page 115.

chapter 21

APPRAISING AND DEVELOPING MANAGERS

Frame 1[21]

Typically, a member of management wants to know where one's work is outstanding and where it can be improved. Also, the manager is likely to appreciate anything that is done to further one's development in management proficiency.

Appraisal, in itself, has a motivating quality. When managers evaluate the performance and the potential of subordinates, these managers become better aware of what subordinates are doing, what subordinates are not but should be doing, and how best they, themselves, might improve their own managerial skills and ability.

Appraising consists of two steps: (a) evaluating the incumbent on a number of selected factors, and (b) interviewing the incumbent to discuss the evaluation. There are differences of opinion regarding the basis on which the factors should be. Some advocate the *basis of accomplishment,* and select such factors as the amount of cost reduction achieved, savings from improved inventory control, and the increase in sales per salesperson. On the other hand, many believe that *behavior is the proper basis,* and that factors revealing behavior should be chosen. These would include such factors as judgment, initiative, self-expression, and drive. The assumption is that a manager with such-and-such behavior will attain a certain level of management proficiency.

The second step of appraising is interviewing to establish an evaluation dialogue with the incumbent. The interview is an ideal means to let the manager know how he or she is doing and to point out areas for improvements. It should be planned. Simply sharing the evaluation with the manager is effective. Recommended action includes: (a) concentrating on the manager's strengths, (b) asking where the manager believes she or he can improve, (c) giving specific examples and reasons for improvement, and (d) encouraging the manager to express his feelings and beliefs.

Interviews can also be used to obtain additional specific information. Such information can be appended to the appraisal data as well as to any pertinent records of achievements and operations that may be maintained. Various printed forms are available to assist in securing data helpful for appraisal purposes.

Developing managers is basic; it is a fundamental pillar of good management. Planned efforts for development are needed, because current demands for proficient managers exceed the supply. And, dependence on development by informal association with other managers is slow and frequently ineffective. *Capable managers are an enterprise's greatest asset.* Efforts to improve this asset are actually an investment. From the viewpoint of possible growth and return, it is often the best investment that can possibly be made within any enterprise.

Indicate whether each of the following statements is true or false by writing "T" or "F" in the space provided.

_____ 1. Appraisal of management performance benefits only the manager being appraised.

_____ 2. There is common agreement that accomplishment is the only reasonable basis for appraising a manager's performance.

_____ 3. A manager should be advised of the appraisal through an interview in which the manager is encouraged to participate actively.

_____ 4. The most efficient method of acquiring management talent is to recruit established managers.

Refer to Answer Frame 1[21], page 118.

Frame 2[21]

Certain characteristics of management development efforts merit discussion. They include:

1. Top-management support. This must be strongly evidenced by supplying vigorous leadership, providing required resources and facilities, and setting realistic goals.

2. Trainee self-development. Planned efforts for development should include making it possible for the trainee to follow self-development. To succeed, the urge to acquire managerial skill must be strong within the trainee.

3. Use of an organization chart, manual, and job and worker descriptions. These media supply basic and detailed background information against which the developing requirements can be ascertained. Through their use, the existent relationships, makeup of jobs, and what is believed necessary for satisfactory performance can be assembled in a usable form. In most cases, the job and worker descriptions may be satisfactorily written by the present manager for managerial jobs immediately under his or her direction.

4. Establishing the need for managers. The approximate number, location within the enterprise, and time for manager placements and replacements should be determined. These are estimates that establish the overall goals of the development efforts.

5. Pervasive and continuous efforts for development. No one individual, or one department, is completely responsible for management development. The entire management team, in the ultimate, shares this responsibility. In addition, the developing efforts should have continuity. The successful programs include assignments for each meeting, or all the meetings, held within a certain period. Also, application of knowledge acquired is mandatory.

6. Placement of trainees. All promises of promotion or transfer should be withheld until the opening is definite and the trainee has successfully completed the development requirements. Development efforts should not be viewed as hurdles for the trainee to surmount, but rather, participation in them should be looked upon as an opportunity and a privilege.

Management development programs have changed considerably since about 1970. The current objective is to develop *learning* managers, not *learned* managers. In today's dynamic management, the manager is becoming more of a finder of answers than a giver of answers. The manager finds out, with the group, what decision should be made, learning from the job and from associates. But one brings to one's work managerial thinking and skill in the application of techniques.

Another trend is emphasis on an organized approach, but with less use of formal programs. The developing efforts are more informal, and are conducted more by operating managers and less by personnel specialists. Potentially capable persons are placed in demanding assignments and given the opportunity to show what they can do. Literature on technical advances, business environment, and social responsibility have become more readily available.

More and more of the formal management-developing work is being conducted during time granted from the trainees' work period. A specific period is allocated, during which it becomes the main effort, not an adjunct to regular duties. Some predict that a leave of absence with pay for developing and updating of management members will become an accepted custom.

Indicate whether each of the following statements is true or false by writing "T" or "F" in the space provided.

_____ 1. The personnel department has all of the responsibility for management development.

_____ 2. A trainee's attitude has more effect on acquiring management skills than does the quality of the development program.

_____ 3. The current trend in management development programs is to improve the manager's ability to learn.

_____ 4. Another current trend in management development programs is the use of operating managers to conduct *formal* training programs.

Check your answers with those in Answer Frame 2[21], page 118.

Frame 3[21]

The media used for management development work are numerous—the list grows daily. For convenience, we have classified the major methods into two groups, including those stressing: (*a*) acquisition of management knowledge and techniques, and (*b*) participation in actual management situations. In the following sections, these types are identified and briefly discussed.

Acquisition of management knowledge and techniques

1. Lectures, programmed instruction, study courses, and readings. A personal and concise presentation of knowledge, by a recognized expert and qualified speaker, is offered through lectures. Programmed instruction focuses the trainee's attention on major points, as the person responds to questions asked in a prescribed sequence. Teaching machines may be utilized with this technique. Study courses, supplemented with readings, make specialized knowledge available to participants.

2. University courses, conferences, and seminars. These popular media feature the exchange of ideas, practice in analyzing situations, and formulation of recommendations for coping with managerial problems.

3. Business games, role playing, and in-basket exercises. By use of business games, the players gain practice in decision making, experience in competition, and practice in dealing with quantitative data and results. Role playing simulates face-to-face conflict situations confronting a manager, and necessitates deciding upon and applying courses of action to resolve the conflict. A packet of background information and written communication, placed in the "in-basket," can be used to develop the trainee's managerial action on the issues raised.

Participation in actual management situations

1. Job rotation, special assignments, and strategic jobs. As stated in Chapter 17, job rotation involves occupying successive jobs throughout the enterprise. It supplies a broadening experience, increased acquaintance with other personnel, and an opportunity to ascertain the jobs preferred by the trainee. On special assignments, complete freedom to handle the problems and to observe results of management efforts is offered. Strategic jobs are those holding extraordinary opportunities for self-development, such as making far-reaching decisions and solving especially tough problems.

2. Committees, junior boards, and team task

Answer frame 1[21]

1. False. Appraisal of management performance benefits not only the manager being appraised but also the individual doing the appraising.
2. False. Many feel that behavior, rather than accomplishment, is the proper basis for appraising a manager's performance.
3. True. It is generally ineffective for the superior to merely share the evaluation with a manager; the manager being evaluated should be encouraged to express one's feelings and beliefs about the quality of one's performance.
4. False. Developing managers from within the company is generally more efficient because it is even more frustrating, difficult, and costly to find and hire competent managers from outside the company.

Now turn to Frame 2[21], page 116.

Answer frame 2[21]

1. False. No one individual or department is completely responsible for management development. The entire management team shares this responsibility.
2. True. Attitude is more important. The development program makes it possible for the trainee to develop; without a proper attitude the program cannot be effective.
3. True. The current objective of management development programs *is* to develop *learning* managers not learned managers.
4. False. The current trend in management development programs is the use of operating managers to conduct *informal* training programs.

Continue by turning to Frame 3[21], page 117.

Frame 3[21] continued

forces. Experience and practice in exchanging ideas, in adjusting to others' viewpoints, and in getting specific work accomplished by means of the efforts by others are provided by these media.

3. *Coaching and counseling*. Coaching consists of telling and showing subordinate management members the best methods to follow for their work and familiarizing them with the policies involved. To counsel means to skillfully talk with another person and, by means of questioning, listening, and observing, to be able to suggest what change in the counselee's behavior is advisable or what course the person should pursue in resolving a problem. The counselor's role is to help the counselee gain a better understanding of oneself.

There is considerable interest in trying to *measure the productivity of management development efforts*. Are the expenditures in time and dollars justified? We want to think so because we are convinced that management development must be undertaken. *Tangible gains*, such as the decrease in production cost and time and greater return on investment, reflect, in part, improved management; but whether these are directly related to management development has not been proved. If we turn to *intangible gains*—greater enthusiasm, better teamwork, improved decisions—the general feeling is that management development helps, but it probably is not the sole contributor.

Indicate whether each of the following statements is true or false by writing "T" or "F" in the space provided.

    _____ 1. Programs designed to help the trainee acquire management knowledge and techniques are most likely to be carried on in a formal manner.

____ 2. Business games rather than role playing are more likely to involve decisions regarding the internal environment of the enterprise.

____ 3. Job rotation is used to give the trainee varied job experience within a limited time.

____ 4. It is difficult to relate the benefits of management development programs directly to the programs.

Compare your answers with those in Answer Frame 3[21], page 120.

chapter 22

CONTROLLING

Frame 1[22]

A manager manages in order to achieve *desired or planned results*. The success or failure represented by these results is judged in the light of the goals set. This implies *controlling; that is, evaluating performance and, if necessary, correcting what is being done to assure attainment of results according to plan*. Controlling is in the nature of a checkup to make sure that what is done is what is intended. It must be objective oriented. A means to an end, it is designed to get people to do what must be done to accomplish goals.

Controlling is a basic process, identical wherever found and whatever controlled. The well-known temperature-regulating device for the home is a good example of the controlling process. This device includes a thermostat, a thermometer, and a heating and cooling unit (see Figure 14). Suppose the thermostat is set at 70°, with the expectation that this temperature will be maintained. We can mark this *step No. 1, Expectancy*. Next, the thermometer registers 60°, the temperature actually being received. We can mark this *step No. 2, Performance*. Next, comparing expectancy to performance, or 70° to 60°,

FIGURE 14

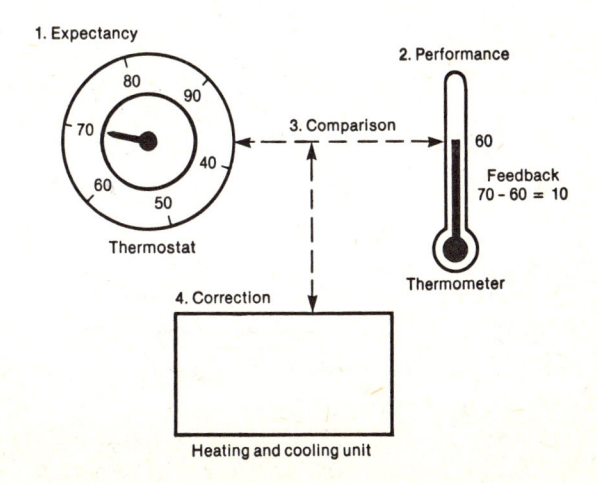

1. Expectancy — Thermostat
2. Performance — Thermometer
3. Comparison
4. Correction — Heating and cooling unit

Feedback 70 − 60 = 10

Answer frame 3[21]

1. True. Programs designed to help the trainee acquire management knowledge, and techniques are more likely to be conducted on a formal basis than on an informal basis.
2. False. Business games typically involve decisions pertaining to the external economic environment, whereas role playing concentrates on the alleviation of internal conflict.
3. True. Job rotation is used to give the trainee a broader knowledge of the firm's activities and personnel, and to give the trainee the opportunity to investigate those areas of interest to the trainee.
4. True. No direct cause and effect relationship has been identified between management development programs and benefits to the firm.

You have completed Chapter 21. Now proceed to Chapter 22, page 119.

Frame 1[22] continued

we note a difference between what is expected and what is being received. This is *step No. 3, Comparison.* This reveals a quantity known as *Feedback,* which in the illustration is 10° (70° minus 60°). Last, based on the results of the comparison, *step No. 4, Correction,* is taken. In the illustration, the heating and cooling unit goes into action and raises the temperature from 60° to 70°, which is the temperature desired.

Expectancy is commonly expressed by a standard that, as pointed out in Chapter 9, supplies a basis for reckoning. It entails answering questions such as: How many units should a machine operator complete in one hour? How many calls should a salesperson make each day? What should be the ratio of dividends paid to earnings? Such questions require quantitative answers, and this implies that the expectancy is measurable. This is true for some types of activities, especially those of the intermediate and lower managerial levels. But, in other cases, measurement of expectancy poses extreme difficulty, for the kind of measuring unit that the measurement requires does not exist. In such cases, somewhat rough measuring units are employed. An example is when the expectancy is the improvement of attitude. When the expectancy is extensive, as when an entire program or total accomplishment is involved, the measurement standard commonly consists of objectives, stated in general terms.

Indicate whether each of the following statements is true or false by writing "T" or "F" in the space provided.

_____ 1. Controlling is the process of evaluating goals and objectives.
_____ 2. The control function is a corrective device which is used only when the system needs adjustment.
_____ 3. The measurement of expectancy can be in either quantitative or qualitative terms.
_____ 4. *Feedback* is another term for controlling.

Refer to Answer Frame 1[22], page 122.

Frame 2[22]

Performance should be expressed in the same terms as expectancy, so that the subsequent comparison, or step No. 3, will be valid. *Several means are available for the determination of performance: observations, reports, and statistical data.* Direct observation provides an intimate picture of the performance. The quantity and quality of work, methods followed, and general work environment lend themselves to such observation, and it is an excellent means for checking and reporting intangibles such as observing the morale of a working group and watching developing managerial efforts being applied to trainees. On the other hand, observations are time-consuming, the observer's purpose may be misunderstood, and the data acquired tend to be general rather than precise.

Reports take the form of either: (*a*) *oral,* such as interviews and group discussions, or (*b*) *written,* which may be purely descriptive or may contain statistical data. The oral report is satisfactory for situations having very wide coverage or where opportunity for questions is needed, to clear up any misunderstanding or to secure additional information. Written reports are best when comprehensive, detailed information must be conveyed. They supply a permanent record and facilitate compilation of trend analyses. Written reports should be reviewed periodically as to the continued need for them. The format should be so designed that it permits easy reading and expedites the controlling for which the report is used.

Statistical data effectively express certain types of performance. Most common are those dealing with time, work, space, capital, debt, and profit. Statistical measurements, ratios, and key figures are frequently featured.

The third step of the universal control process—comparison—in effect evaluates the performance. Where a difference is found between expectancy and performance, judgment is required to assess the significance of the differential. In some cases, a slight deviation may be serious; in others, it is not. In the interest of good management, the comparison should be made as near to the time of performance as possible. Of greatest importance in the comparison step are *the exceptional cases—the comparisons showing deviations much greater than what can be considered normal.* A manager concentrates controlling efforts on these cases. Normally, the exceptional cases are in the minority, thus simplifying the controlling. In addition, *controlling by using key points only* is widely practiced. Usually, there are certain critical or key activities that appear to regulate or to strongly influence a totality of related activities. The key points will vary with the type of enterprise. So-called bottleneck operations, customer orders received, inventories, and shipments are a few of them. By carefully controlling the key areas, satisfactory and economical controlling can be gained.

The last step, correction, consists of seeing to it that operations are adjusted to obtain results compatible with expectancy. Modifications in any one, or all, of the managerial activities may be required; but, commonly, a method must be changed, an authority entanglement straightened out, or better motivation achieved. The corrective action should be taken by the person having authority over the work. Within each department or division, it is advisable to hold one management member responsible for implementing the required corrective work in that unit. This tends to personalize the controlling, and assures that a person known to all has the obligation to see that required corrective action is taken.

Indicate whether each of the following statements is true or false by writing "T" or "F" in the space provided.

  _____ 1. Personal observation is a good method to use in monitoring certain activities.

  _____ 2. There should be a continual effort to increase the number of written reports prepared.

  _____ 3. A manager should thoroughly investigate all deviations brought to light by the comparison of the performance to the expectancy.

  _____ 4. It is advisable to decentralize, within an operating unit or division, the responsibility for correcting deviations.

See Answer Frame 2[22], page 122.

Answer frame 1[22]

1. False. Controlling is the process of evaluating *performance* by comparing the actual performance to what was expected (goals or objectives).
2. False. The control function is the means of determining whether or not any adjustments are necessary, and, therefore, it should be an integral part of the management system.
3. True. In many cases, the measurement of expectancy has no satisfactory quantitative characteristics associated with it. In such cases, intangible, qualitative characteristics are used.
4. False. *Feedback* results from the comparison of the actual performance to the expected performance. It is only one component of the controlling process.

Now turn to Frame 2[22], page 120.

Answer frame 2[22]

1. True. Personal observation is excellent for checking and reporting intangibles such as observing the morale of work groups and the development of new management members.
2. False. In fact, periodic review should be made of the continued need for existing written reports. There is a tendency to continue these reports even after the need for them ceases to exist.
3. False. A manager should concentrate controlling efforts on those deviations which are considered exceptional or critical.
4. False. It is advisable to hold one management member within the work group responsible for implementing the required corrective action within that unit or division. This centralizes and personalizes the responsibility for the controlling activity.

Now turn to Frame 3[22], below.

Frame 3[22]

Proper controlling assists good human relations. The human response to controlling is a key consideration. Controlling can and should be used to promote favorable relationships among all employees. Controlling should be a positive, helpful activity. The effective manager in charge uses controlling to share information, to praise the high performer, and to spot those needing help and determine what kind of help they need. On the other hand, managers not in charge and nonmanagers want to contribute good performances; they want to know and to meet the requirements of their jobs, and they want recognition when they meet these requirements. In all these efforts, controlling can be of genuine assistance and, hence, can contribute to good human relations.

Controlling is commonly applied to many different types of activities. In one approach, the type of controlling is identified by *familiar functions* so that we have controls such as: production control, sales control, and purchasing control. Another, and perhaps more significant, approach is controlling by the following four factors; (*a*) *quantity*, (*b*) *quality*, (*c*) *time-use*, and (*d*) *cost*. The meaning of each of these is self-explanatory. They result in quantity control, quality control, time-use control (i.e., schedules and due dates), and cost control (i.e., expenditures, usually in dollars). The two approaches are interrelated; for example, production control usually emphasizes quantity and time-use controls.

Certain desirable characteristics of controlling should be mentioned. First, the type of control should be in keeping with the individual requirements of the activity. The size of the operation and its location in the organization are usually most important. Second, deviations requiring correction should be identified promptly, even before they occur, as is possible in some types of control—for example, statistical quality control. Also, controls should be worth their cost. Benefits from controlling are relative and depend on the importance of the activity, the contribution made, and the size of the enterprise. Further, controls should tie in with the organization pattern, thus making it easier to assign responsibility for control to persons in charge of the respective activities, and to provide usable control data to the management member concerned. Finally, the control should show the way to corrective action, including finding out where the action needs to be taken, who is to be responsible for taking action, and what the action should be.

Controlling assists in identifying managerial problems. Inasmuch as problem identification is a constant challenge to managers, this contribution of controlling is highly relevant. A manager becomes aware of a problem when deviation from a goal is noted. Often, more than one deviation is related to the problem, and the manager's task is to isolate these deviations and to determine the relevancy of each one.

Indicate whether each of the following statements is true or false by writing "T" or "F" in the space provided.

_____ 1. Controlling should be used as a corrective device for interior performance and as a means of reinforcing acceptable performance.

_____ 2. Control by function is more widely used than control by factor.

_____ 3. A system of control is not effective if it only indicates an area of below-par performance.

_____ 4. Whenever a deviation is indicated by controlling, it should be treated as a distinct problem area.

Check your answers with those provided in Answer Frame 3^{22}, page 124.

Answer frame 3²²

1. True. The effective manager uses controlling not only to aid those needing help, but also to praise and reward those whose performance is acceptable or exceptional.
2. False. Control by function and control by factor are interrelated and are used in conjunction with each other.
3. True. The system of control should show not only where there is trouble, but also where action needs to be taken, who is to be responsible for taking action, and what corrective action should be taken.
4. False. It is the manager's job to review all deviations and to attempt to identify any overriding problem that may account for many of these deviations.

You have completed Chapter 22. Now proceed to Chapter 23, below.

chapter 23

KEY CONTROLS OF MANAGEMENT

Frame 1²³

We noted in the previous chapter that controlling is commonly applied to the major functions of an enterprise—production, sales, finance, and personnel—and also to the major factors—quantity, quality, time-use, and cost. Further, we saw that these are interrelated. Several selected types of controlling are discussed in this chapter, and these may be considered key controls of management.

First is *quantity controlling*, which is intended to bring about an orderly and desired flow of products and/or services. Apply quantity controlling to operations of various scopes, depending on the individual situations, follows the basic control process, and it is familiar to many. To illustrate: In quantity controlling of products for sale, the purpose is to have sufficient quantities of each item, at satisfactory cost, and available where they are in demand. Stated negatively, we are trying to avoid: (*a*) unbalanced sales—selling only those products easiest to sell; (*b*) sales from each territory that are less than its tailor-made potential or sales quota; and (*c*) inadequacy in sales facilitation of each area, including sales personnel, number of retail outlets, advertising, and sales promotion efforts.

In the case of quantity controlling of sales, one of the difficulties is to define a unit to which the control process steps of expectancy wanted and performance achieved can be applied. Normally, a geographical area is employed as the base, so that we determine the amount of sales expected from this defined area. Sometimes, this base area is a city or county; but, more frequently, it is *a marketing or buyer trading area;* that is, a region surrounding a geographical center from which buyers normally make their expenditures. For each marketing area, considerable data are collected, processed, and reviewed to establish a *sales potential;* that is, *a goal for sales for a definite period.* What data are considered depends on the nature of the products being sold. Often used are (*a*) sales for previous years, (*b*) number gainfully employed, (*c*) general industrial activity, and (*d*) the consumer buying index. In addition, certain modifications may be made to reflect the estimated effect of such things as the method of purchasing, the caliber of salespeople, and the superior features of the product.

Dollar sales are generally the medium used in measuring and comparing sales; but number of sales, calls made, prospects interviewed, or miles traveled may also prove satisfactory. Daily and weekly summary reports are prepared by the field representatives, who mail them to the sales office, where they are used for analysis and for writing of composite statements essential for carrying out effective controlling. When required, the corrective action taken is usually in the form of a price adjustment, changes in sales presentation, motivation through sales contests, more thorough sales training, and/or revamping the product or its container.

Indicate whether each of the following statements is true or false by writing "T" or "F" in the space provided.

_____ 1. Quantity control is oriented toward controlling the output of the enterprise.

_____ 2. A geographical area is the typical frame of reference for quantity control.

_____ 3. The data used in quantity control are standardized in all firms.

_____ 4. A corrective action dealing with quantity control would more likely be initiated by sales office personnel than by an individual salesperson.

See Answer Frame 1[23], page 126.

Frame 2[23]

The second key control of management is *quality control.* With the increasing emphasis on high-precision products, high-speed production, and trouble-free products, quality control has become a foremost consideration. To dispel a common erroneous notion, it is well to state that, in quality control, the goal is maintenance of a *satisfactory quality for the intended purpose,* not the highest quality possible. Specifically, the goal sought is that which is the best in terms of: (*a*) consistency with the price being charged for the product, and (*b*) satisfactory and dependable results being provided.

Either *inspection control* or *statistical quality control* can be employed. In inspection control, identification of those parts or products that are acceptable is made by inspection. Normally, an inspection standard, in the form of a quality specification, represents the expectancy. What is being produced is compared to the inspection standard by means of a visual or a testing examination, resulting in distinguishing acceptable from nonacceptable products. When every part or product is inspected, we have *100 percent inspection;* when less than the entire lot is inspected, we have what is called *sample inspection.* Probability studies and experience help to determine the degree of sample inspection followed. Because inspection requires expenditures of time and money, the lowest percentage of sample inspection which will give satisfactory results should be followed. The inspection work itself can be performed: (*a*) manually, by either a trained inspector or the worker making the

Answer frame 1[23]

1. True. Quantity control is intended to bring about an orderly and desired flow of products and/or services.
2. True. Normally, a geographical area is employed as the base in quantity control.
3. False. The type of data considered in quantity control depends on the nature of the products being sold.
4. True. Most corrective actions in the area of quality control are so important as to be out of the control of individual salespeople.

Now go to Frame 2[23], page 125.

Frame 2[23] continued

unit, or (b) automatically, by ingenious devices and machines.

Statistical quality control, based on statistical theories and probability applied to sample testing, *is preventive as well as remedial.* This means that statistical quality control helps prevent defects from occurring. While the process is in operation, measurements are taken of the finished product and compared to predetermined standards. With these data and the quality control chart, the decision is reached as to whether the operation should continue or should be held up for correction.

Figure 15 shows a normal, or bell-shaped, curve and a statistical quality control chart. The normal curve shows the frequency or variation of a phenomenon from its middle or average value. That is, in measuring the length of a large number of "identical parts" supposedly two inches long, it will be found that there is some variation from the two-inch dimension. A large portion will measure exactly two inches, but some parts will be slightly overlength, some slightly under; a few will be quite a bit overlength, and a few quite a bit under. With size plotted on a horizontal scale and count or occurrence on the vertical scale, a bell-shaped curve is obtained. How much these over- and undersized parts are dispersed from the normal or average size is revealed by a statistical measurement called the *standard deviation.* Within three standard deviations to the left of normal and three standard deviations to the right are included 99.73 percent of the total number of parts. This means that, within plus or minus three standard deviations, practically all the parts are included, and their length measurements will fluctuate as a normal behavior between the length dimension on the

FIGURE 15

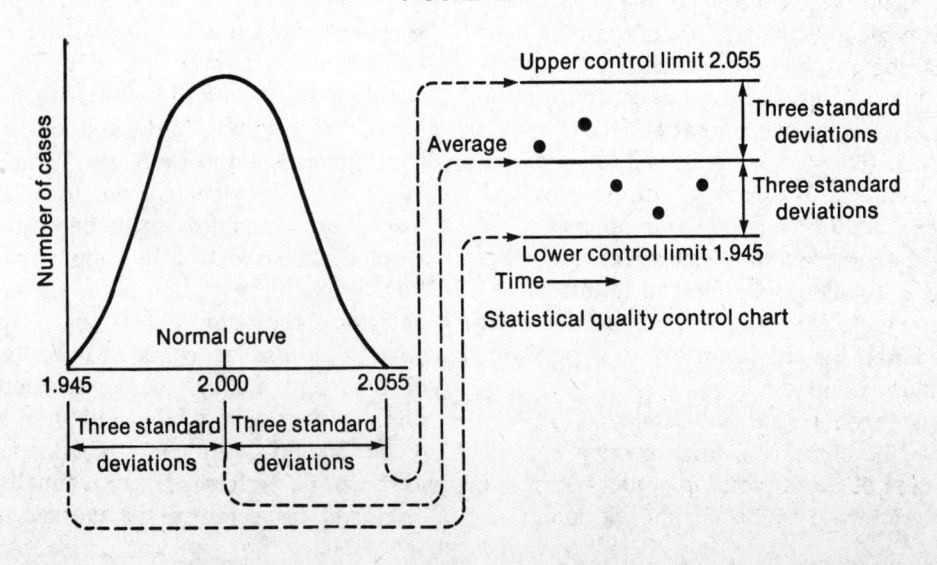

left (1.945) and on the right (2.055), as indicated in Figure 12.

More important, these variations between 1.945 and 2.055 can be considered due to chance. They result from the nature of the process followed. However, when from this same process a length is obtained outside these limits, say 2.060, it is not due to chance or expected variation but to an assignable cause. If this happens, we know something has gone wrong in the process, such as slippage of the cutting fastener, dulling of a tool, or movement of the setting of the cutting machine. The machine can then be stopped, and the assignable cause located and corrected, after which the work can be resumed.

Referring again to Figure 15, by swinging the bell-shaped curve 90°, and eliminating the extremes of the curve, the statistical quality control chart shown on the right of the figure is obtained. In this type of chart, variations from normal are shown on the vertical scale, and time is plotted horizontally. Samples from production are inspected periodically, and the results are plotted on the chart. If they are within the upper and lower control limits shown on the chart, the products are satisfactory in terms of quality. If they are outside the control limits, corrective action needs to be taken.

To construct the statistical quality control chart for a given case, the following steps must be taken: (a) collect data on the operation; (b) calculate the average and the standard deviation from these data; (c) compare the values to those of the quality specified; (d) if within specification limits, use data for statistical quality control chart; and (e) if outside specification limits, improve the process or loosen the specifications and draw a chart from these revised data.

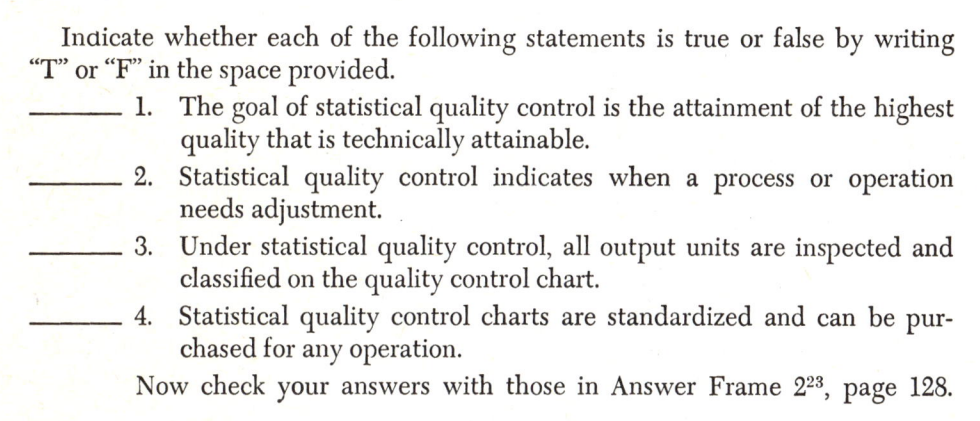

Indicate whether each of the following statements is true or false by writing "T" or "F" in the space provided.

_____ 1. The goal of statistical quality control is the attainment of the highest quality that is technically attainable.

_____ 2. Statistical quality control indicates when a process or operation needs adjustment.

_____ 3. Under statistical quality control, all output units are inspected and classified on the quality control chart.

_____ 4. Statistical quality control charts are standardized and can be purchased for any operation.

Now check your answers with those in Answer Frame 2[23], page 128.

Frame 3[23]

Time-use is the third key control of management. Using time effectively is a challenge to every manager. The manager is under pressure to reduce the time spent on reading material, attending meetings, and reaching decisions. Time is a limited resource. A manager often complains that time wasted on telephone calls and meetings could be avoided if some reliable way of appraising them in advance were available. Some management members are hard pressed to explain how they spend their days, other than in frittering away time on trivial details.

Three approaches to improved time-use control by the manager are discussed, including: (a) use of an assistant or a secretary to protect the manager against time wasters; (b) adoption of a return-on-manager-time criterion for decision-making efforts; and (c) collection of time data on current activities, evaluation, and improvement of methods of time utilization.

A good assistant or secretary can help the manager save time. Such help can take care of the endless paper work, assist in avoiding unwanted visitors, and screen telephone calls.

The concept of using a return-on-manager-time criterion places top priority on having a manager available to manage and to make necessary decisions. In essence, it emphasizes that, in

Answer frame 2²³

1. False. The aim of all quality control is the maintenance of a level of quality that is *satisfactory* for the intended purpose.
2. True. Statistical quality control indicates when output of a process or operation is in violation of quality limits, so that adjustments may be made.
3. False. Under statistical quality control, *samples* of output are inspected periodically and plotted on the quality control chart.
4. False. Statistical quality control charts must be constructed for each process and operation to be monitored.

Now turn to Frame 3²³, page 127.

Frame 3²³ continued

many decision-making situations, the alternative that will require the least managerial time in its implementation might well be the best selection. Advocates of the return-on-manager-time criterion point out that when problems arise, the manager's time is vital. This is the manager's stock in trade, and the value of one's time stresses the need for time-use controlling. In addition, it is logical to assume that the manager can better forecast the effect of alternatives in decision making when there is only the effect of time-use to evaluate than when there are more than this one consideration, such as profits of the enterprise and social implications of his decision.

Surprisingly few managers are aware of how they spend their time. It is essential for managers to recognize time-use controls in their work, and the first step might well be to get the facts concerning present time utilization. Having each manager keep a daily log by 15-minute intervals, showing what activity is performed and whether or not it is basically managerial, is recommended for this purpose. Recording such information for a period of several months provides a reasonable sample. Study of such data reveals what the time robbers are, the trivia, and nonessentials that should be eliminated, and what improvements can be made.

Other situations, where time-use considerations are essential, include production control and new-product development. Determining and coordinating the time values, to allow for performing each segment of work, are fundamental in production control. Material must be available at the time it is needed, and the same is true for machines and tools. The whole important area of scheduling is actually the placing of time values on a sequence of activities. In controlling time use in new-product development, ample time must be allotted for product inception, packaging, test marketing, and product production. Too little time given to test marketing, for example, may prove disastrous.

Indicate whether each of the following statements is true or false by writing "T" or "F" in the space provided.

_____ 1. A manager's time is one area of time-use that defies control.

_____ 2. Under the return-on-manager-time criterion, specific decisions are settled in favor of the alternative requiring the least amount of the manager's time.

_____ 3. It is practical and useful to have managers account for their time.

_____ 4. The only important time-use consideration for a new product is the production time.

Now refer to Answer Frame 3²³, page 130.

Frame 4[23]

Cost control, the fourth key control of management, is one of the most common. Cost is a consideration in almost every activity. There are many types of cost, and, before discussing their control, we should consider what these various types of cost are. A helpful classification is: (*a*) *direct labor cost*, (*b*) *direct material cost*, (*c*) *factory overhead cost*, (*d*) *selling cost*, and (*e*) *administrative cost*. The name of each of these is self-explanatory, with the possible exception of factory overhead cost, which includes expenditures for all manufacturing activities that cannot be classified as direct labor or direct material. A direct cost is an expenditure that is incurred in working directly on the product; an indirect cost is one that is not. Direct labor cost is illustrated by the wage paid a machine operator, indirect labor cost by the wage paid a cost clerk. All indirect manufacturing costs are included in factory overhead.

All these various types of cost are interrelated (see Figure 16). Along the bottom of this figure is total cost, which is made up of general administrative (or administrative overhead) expense and total selling and manufacturing cost.

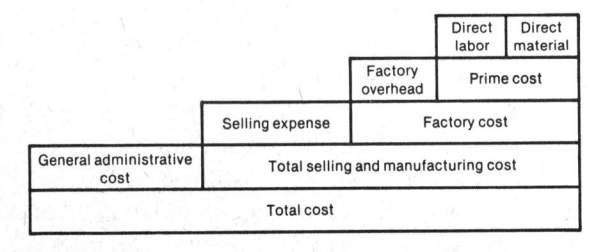

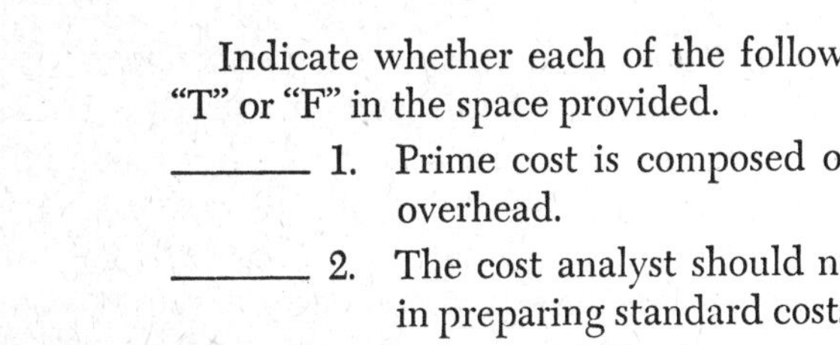

This latter amount is broken down into selling expense and factory cost; and factory cost is broken down into factory overhead and prime cost; prime cost, in turn, is make up of direct labor and direct material costs.

Cost control follows the universal control process. Hence, our first concern is for *cost expectancy*, which is determined by a cost analyst who employs: (*a*) scientifically determined standards, (*b*) past performance, and/or (*c*) judgment. Expectancy is sometimes expressed as *standard cost,* and represents *the normal amount of expenditures, including direct labor, direct material, and factory overhead, for accomplishment of specific work*. It is the cost realized when prescribed labor, materials, and methods are employed. There is, however, a tendency for cost expectancy to be reduced, i.e., to expect to reduce costs. This is a constant challenge to a manager.

Performance, evidenced by expenditures, is obtained from pertinent accounting records; for example, information on direct labor cost, direct material cost, and factory overhead are obtained from accounting data. For maximum usefulness, these cost data are expressed in *cost per unit*. This is quite simple in the case of direct labor or direct material; but for factory overhead cost, the allocation per unit poses some difficulty. Initially, factory overhead is expressed as a lump sum. It is usually allocated to units of production on the basis of direct labor hours or direct labor cost. For instance, the basis of application may be to allocate two dollars of overhead for each dollar of direct labor expended on a product.

FIGURE 16

		Direct labor	Direct material
	Factory overhead	Prime cost	
	Selling expense	Factory cost	
General administrative cost	Total selling and manufacturing cost		
Total cost			

Indicate whether each of the following statements is true or false by writing "T" or "F" in the space provided.

_____ 1. Prime cost is composed of direct material, direct labor, and direct overhead.

_____ 2. The cost analyst should not necessarily suppress personal judgment in preparing standard costs.

_____ 3. The most difficult cost to express on a per-unit basis is direct labor.

_____ 4. The *total* amount of overhead cost is the same under each of the methods of allocation.

Check your responses with those in Answer Frame 4[23], page 130.

Answer frame 3[23]

1. False. Although it may appear difficult for an individual manager to control time-use, efficient time apportionment should be attempted.
2. True. The return-on-manager-time criterion holds that the alternative that will require the least time of the manager in its implementation might well be the best selection.
3. True. By requiring managers to account for their time, it is hoped that they will learn to streamline their future time utilization.
4. False. New products require proper allotments of time for development and test marketing as well as for production.

Turn to Frame 4[23], page 129.

Answer frame 4[23]

1. False. Prime cost is composed of direct material and direct labor. Overhead is composed of indirect manufacturing costs, and is not a prime cost.
2. True. A cost analyst should exercise judgment in the setting of standard costs.
3. False. The most difficult cost to express on a per-unit basis is overhead. It must be assigned to units on an arbitrary basis, such as direct labor hours or direct labor cost.
4. True. The total amount of the overhead cost depends on cost incurrence, and not on cost allocation. The *per-unit* overhead cost of a product will vary, depending on the method of allocation selected.

Proceed to Frame 5[23], below.

Frame 5[23]

Comparison between cost expectancy and cost performance is self-explanatory. The next control step, correction, if any, may take many different forms. If the cost of direct materials is too high, the correction might consist of setting new standards or securing new sources of supply. A number of effective approaches can be followed. The following are of special interest:

1. Zero defect program. Emphasis is directed to the importance of the human element and the self-will of personnel to give high-quality performance. Actually, a zero defect program can be viewed as a technique for quality control, but it is included here because the elimination of mistakes is very important in keeping costs in line. Zero defect programs try to develop employees' cost consciousness and to get them to want to achieve high standards of work excellence.

2. Value analysis. The effort here is to improve the relationship of product worth to product cost. Value is interpreted as either: (*a*) *use* value, or (*b*) *esteem* value. From this value approach, what are believed to be unnecessary costs are identified. Then, substitute materials and methods are suggested for these excess cost areas. It boils down to substituting lower-cost labor or material, wherever possible, yet retaining satisfactory service of the given product or service.

3. Planning, programming, budgeting system (PPBS) and zero-base budgeting (ZBB). Useful in streamlining and rationalizing spending, PPBS is used primarily by government and large private enterprises. Its aim is to obtain the greatest cost effectiveness or to acquire the most benefit from what is expended. Information concerning both expenditures and benefits is quantified. For example, the government expresses expenditures in dollars and compares this to a dollar estimate of the benefits to be gained by society or by citizens as a result of these expenditures. Although not always easy to apply, PPBS is viewed by many managers as a significant approach to cost controlling.

Another technique, *zero-base budgeting* is coming into increased usage in both government and industry. Basically, it requires that each dollar included in the budget must be justified even if a similar amount appeared in the previous year's budget. It is designed to eliminate or curtail expenditures on low-priority programs.

Indicate whether each of the following statements is true or false by writing "T" or "F" in the space provided.

_____ 1. When cost expectancy exceeds cost performance there is a need for tighter cost control.

_____ 2. A zero defect program aims at cutting the cost of spoilage and waste.

_____ 3. Value analysis pinpoints and eliminates the less profitable products.

_____ 4. The most difficult part of implementing a PPBS program is identifying and quantifying the benefits.

Now refer to Answer Frame 5[23], page 132, to check your responses.

chapter 24

OVERALL CONTROLS

Frame 1[24]

Overall controls apply to the entire enterprise, or a large portion of it, taken as a base unit. The controlling is not confined to a particular activity or single function. Overall controls assist in keeping the viewpoint of management broad and in fostering a desired balance among various, but interrelated, efforts. These controls provide a better means for: (*a*) measuring the total effort of top managers, rather than a part of it; (*b*) keeping the controlling adapted to overall planning; and (*c*) controlling of semi-autonomous units resulting from a highly decentralized enterprise.

Most overall controls are financial. This is to be expected, because finance is the common denominator or language of each activity and is the binding force among activities. Also, financial controls help the manager keep expenditures properly related to goals.

In most cases, for overall controls to be satisfactory, inclusive plans and policies must exist. It is advisable to carefully monitor every area in which money or material is handled. Not only do overall controls pinpoint areas where deviation may occur, but they also tend to promote a favorable attitude toward controlling among em-

Answer frame 5[23]

1. False. When cost expectancy exceeds cost performance, there have been cost savings, and controls would appear adequate.
2. True. The elimination of mistakes is very important in keeping costs in line.
3. False. Value analysis aims at replacing a more expensive input factor with a less expensive one without changing the service value of the product.
4. True. The most difficult part of implementing a PPBS system *is* identifying and quantifying the benefits. The expenditures are much easier to quantify.

You have now completed Chapter 23. Turn to Chapter 24, page 131.

Frame 1[24] continued

ployees who normally realize that control of money and material is essential. In addition, exceptions to overall controls should be kept to a minimum; and enforcement of them must be certain, which means that proper directives and personnel must be provided. Trying to exercise controls without adequate means to do so can lead to chaos.

Various tools or media for overall controlling are available. Most of these stress comparison of performance to expectancy. Expectancy is commonly expressed by past performance, so that actually a trend is disclosed. The corrective action is seldom included in the system of overall control. To supply a comprehension of their nature and diversity, the following tools or media are discussed: (*a*) *income statements*, (*b*) *control reports*, (*c*) *budget summaries*, (*d*) *ratios*, (*e*) *return on investment*, (*f*) *break-even analysis*, (*g*) *audits*, and (*h*) *key areas*.

Indicate whether each of the following statements is true or false by writing "T" or "F" in the space provided.

_____ 1. Most overall controls are financial controls.
_____ 2. Overall controls generally are applied on an individual basis to the various functional areas or subdivisions of an enterprise.
_____ 3. The establishment of overall controls implies the existence of the will and resources to enforce these controls.
_____ 4. The last step in overall control is the implementation of corrective action.

Check your answers with those in Answer Frame 1[24], page 134.

Frame 2[24]

Earning or income statements show the components of net earnings or net loss for a given period. They are useful for identifying the revenue and expense factors that have accounted for success or failure. Frequently, the data for consecutive years are included, thus increasing the usefulness of the statements by revealing significant trends. An income statement can be forecast for a forthcoming period and can be used as a goal toward which to strive. The more complete the organization unit to which it applies, the more accurate the income statement. Usually, it is applied to an entire enterprise; but it is also satisfactory for a product or territory division where production and sales are under one jurisdiction. It has been successfully applied to departments, but quite often this requires arbitrary allocations of expense.

Control reports consist of special arrangements of data to expedite controlling. They may pertain to any one, several, or all of the departments of an enterprise, and show information on any of several activities. On items warranting further investigation, other written reports, giving more detailed data, generally are consulted. Some managers find the balance sheet an effective control report for overall controlling. This is especially true when comparative data for successive periods are provided. Figure 17 illustrates a simple control report. Selected data, expressed as percentages of sales, are indicated for two periods. By comparing data, one can see that the profit margin looks bad, yet sales have increased slightly. The culprits are production costs, up 5.2 points, of which labor costs are up 1.3 points. Further investigation of these costs should be considered.

Budget summaries are widely used in overall controlling. As summaries of the individual budgets of an enterprise, they reflect the expectancies and performances of selected items and reveal the degree of success in obtaining objectives. Through budget summaries, responsibility for performance is readily ascertainable. Deviations can be quickly spotted, and explanations for significant differences can be requested. Budget summaries should be evaluated by one familiar with the operations. Budgeting is fully discussed in Chapter 25.

Ratios involve the comparing of selected financial values in evaluating the overall perfor-

FIGURE 17

	Last Period	This Period
Profit margin	7.9	3.6
Administrative overhead	18.2	17.8
Sales	102.2	103.8
Personnel	35.5	35.6
Advertising	3.7	3.5
Production	24.0	29.2
Labor	9.8	11.1
Raw materials	3.1	3.0
Equipment	—	—

mance of an enterprise. The values usually are taken from the income statement and the balance sheet. Ratios sometimes used are: (*a*) *current assets to current liabilities,* (*b*) *net sales to working capital,* (*c*) *net sales to inventory,* (*d*) *administrative expenses to sales,* and (*e*) *long-term debt to total capital.* Careful interpretation of the significance of each ratio to the company's overall operations is mandatory. Normally, more than one ratio is used to gain comprehension of the entirety. With experience, satisfactory ranges, for each ratio used, are developed. For example, a manager may employ the value range of 6.50 to 7.00 for the net sales to working capital ratio in order to ensure the availability of funds to finance the current volume of sales activity.

Indicate whether each of the following statements is true or false by writing "T" or "F" in the space provided.

_____ 1. Income statements are most accurate when they cover only segments or divisions of an entire enterprise.

_____ 2. The balance sheet has been shown to be an effective control report for specific divisions of an enterprise.

_____ 3. A budget summary contains data that express only expectancies about items of future operations.

_____ 4. In utilizing ratios, a manager must be careful not to place too much weight on any one ratio.

Refer to Answer Frame 2[24], page 134.

Frame 3[24]

Return on investment is also a ratio, but it has become so popular that it merits separate discussion. This ratio is the rate of return a company or a division realizes from the capital allotted to it. The reference unit should be, at least, a large segment of an organization, because for this ratio the accuracy of data available for any smaller unit is open to question. Return

Answer frame 1[24]

1. True. Most overall controls are financial controls.
2. False. Overall controls are applied to the entire enterprise taken as a whole, or to a large portion of it.
3. True. Trying to exercise overall controls without adequate means to do so can lead to chaos.
4. False. Corrective action is seldom included in the system of overall control.

Continue your reading by turning to Frame 2[24], page 132.

Answer frame 2[24]

1. False. The smaller the segments being reported on, the more necessary it is to make arbitrary allocations. Thus, the more complete the organization unit to which it applies, the more accurate the income statement.
2. False. The balance sheet has been found to be an effective control report for *overall* controlling.
3. False. Budget summaries reflect expectancies *and* performances for selected items.
4. True. Normally, more than one ratio is used to gain comprehension of the entirety.

Now continue by going to Frame 3[24], page 133.

Frame 3[24] continued

on investment reveals areas where capital is being effectively employed, and this information is helpful in obtaining a desired balance in the use of facilities. The direct calculation of dividing net earnings by investment, or E/I, may be made. But a more common approach is to multiply the quantity of sales divided by total investments (which is referred to as turnover) by the net earnings divided by sales (which is referred to as margin), or S/I multiplied by E/S. This gives the same end results as the direct calculation, and allows the analyst to contrast ratios of turnover and of margin. Figure 18 shows the relationships of the factors in this calculation.

FIGURE 18

Calculations for Return on Investment

$$\frac{\text{Sales}}{\text{Total Investment}^*} = \frac{S}{I} = \text{Turnover}$$

$$\frac{\text{Net Earnings}}{\text{Sales}} = \frac{E}{S} = \text{Margin}$$

Multiplied—Return on Investment

*The alternative figures used for total investment are: total assets available, total assets employed, stockholders' equity plus long-term debt, and stockholders' equity. The most commonly used is total assets available.

Break-even analysis is used to determine the pattern of fixed and variable costs most desirable to maximize profits in keeping with sales expectancy. When fixed costs are increased, that is, when additional machines and facilities are acquired, the enterprise is committed to a larger sales volume in order to break even. The cost of utilizing the increased facilities will be the same, regardless of sales volume. In contrast, variable costs fluctuate directly with sales volume. The break-even point is the sales volume at which zero income is realized. To maximize profits, the company should try to maximize sales and reduce costs. Figure 19 shows a break-even chart. At sales of 4,000 units or $400,000, profits are $50,000, fixed costs are $150,000, and variable costs are $200,000. The break-even point is 3,000 units or $300,000 of sales. If future sales can only be stimulated to a level of about $250,000, the company should first try to adjust its fixed and variable costs downward. If this effort fails, the company should consider going out of business, for in the long run all costs must be covered.

FIGURE 19
Break-even Chart

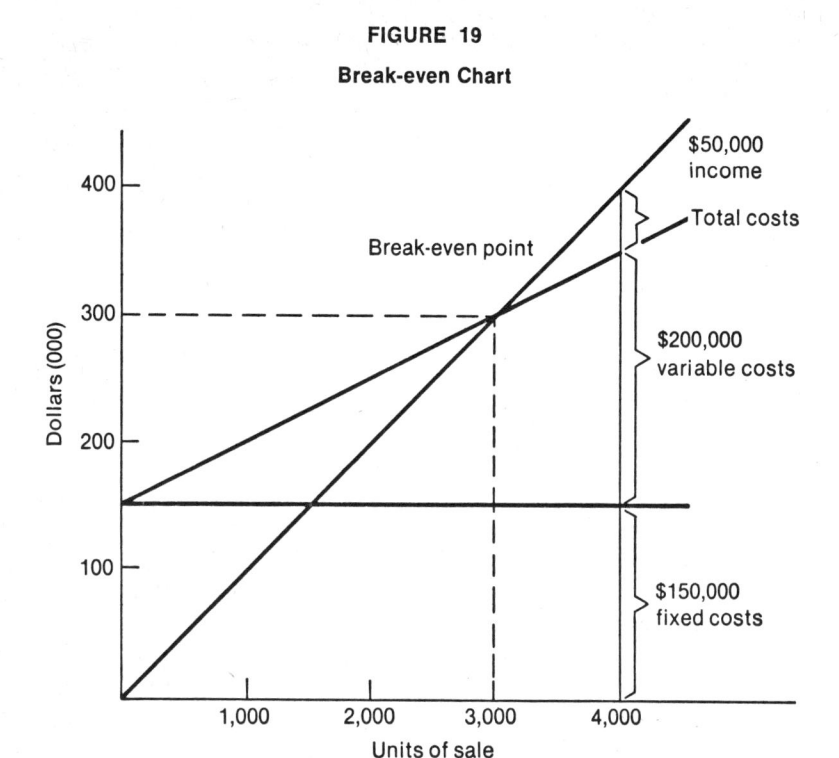

[Break-even chart showing Dollars (000) on y-axis from 0 to 400, and Units of sale on x-axis from 0 to 4,000. Break-even point at approximately 3,000 units and $300,000. At 4,000 units: $50,000 income, $200,000 variable costs, $150,000 fixed costs, with total costs line shown.]

Indicate whether each of the following statements is true or false by writing "T" or "F" in the space provided.

_____ 1. The concept of return on investment is best applied to smaller segments of an organization.

_____ 2. Of the two methods of calculating the return on investment, the direct method is more accurate.

_____ 3. As the level of fixed costs increases, the break-even point increases.

_____ 4. If an enterprise's sales are expected to fluctuate widely from year to year, it is likely to decide on incurring less fixed costs than it would if its sales were stable.

Now compare your answers with those in Answer Frame 3[24], page 136.

Frame 4[24]

Audits are employed to verify financial statements, to appraise the accounting and financial operations, and to evaluate the general management practices and results. *External auditing* is essentially a verification of the financial statements. Performed by members of an outside firm, external auditing indirectly influences overall controlling, since it is concerned with judging the accuracy and correct portrayal of financial information. The mere routine of external auditing tends to exercise a quasi-control or influence on the company's personnel.

Internal auditing is performed by accountants in the employ of the company. In addition to checking the accuracy of the data and verifying that acceptable accounting practices are being

Answer frame 3[24]

1. False. The reference unit for the return on investment computation should be at least a large segment of the organization.
2. False. Both methods of calculating the return on investment yield the same numerical answer.
3. True. The break-even point does increase as the level of fixed costs increases.
4. True. A company with unstable sales is likely to settle for a lower break-even point than it would if its sales were stable. In this way, it can avoid losses in years when sales are relatively low.

Turn to Frame 4[24], page 135, and continue.

Frame 4[24] continued

followed, internal auditing is used to check compliance with plans, policies, and procedures. It is in this latter area that its real contribution is made. Procedures seem to have a way of being ignored and misunderstood and of becoming outdated and obsolete. Internal auditors disclose areas needing controlling and help management avoid serious breakdowns. However, internal audits have their disadvantages; for example: (a) they can be expensive; (b) by themselves, they are ineffective—they simply detect trouble if it exists; and (c) they too often fail to completely persuade the responsible line manager to institute the needed corrective action, due mainly to poor communication between manager and auditor, or the manager's inability to comprehend the detailed data.

Another type of audit is the *management audit*. Basically, this is a periodic assessment of managerial efforts and results. The past, present, and future are taken into account. The aim is to determine if maximum results are being obtained from the managerial efforts being made.

Usually, only the broad concepts are included, with emphasis given to: (a) the interrelatedness of activities and their contribution toward achieving the goals, and (b) the inadequacy or absence of necessary efforts. The management audit is impersonal and is confined to auditing; it does not implement recommendations—this is the duty of the manager having the authority over the activity under question.

To conduct a management audit, a list of qualifications or attributes is formulated, and each is weighted according to a scale of values. Much judgment is required in developing such a list. Among questions that must be answered are: What values are really important? What significance should be given to new product development? Of what value are customers' opinions? Among the general attributes, the following are frequently emphasized: (a) financial stability, (b) sales trends, (c) employee relations, (d) vendor relations, (e) production efficiency, and (f) profit trends.

Indicate whether each of the following statements is true or false by writing "T" or "F" in the space provided.

_____ 1. External auditing is concerned with preparing the financial statements.

_____ 2. Internal auditing is primarily concerned with the verification of financial statements.

_____ 3. A management audit is an audit of management's accomplishments and efforts.

_____ 4. In conducting a management audit, many qualitative factors must be evaluated.

Go to Answer Frame 4[24], page 138, to check your answers.

Frame 5[24]

Key areas provide still another medium of overall controlling. Measurement of results, in areas compared to established goals or standards sought, provides helpful data in evaluating an enterprise's management or in comparing the management of one subsidiary to that of others within the parent enterprise. The following key areas show the types of entities used:

1. Share of market. Represented by the ratio of company sales to total sales in the industry, the important observation here is the trend, not the actual percentage. We are particularly interested in knowing whether the company is gaining, or at least holding its own, in its market. If a company is engaged in many different industries, examination of the share for each of its product divisions is made.

2. Product leadership. This gives recognition to a company's ability to meet the needs of buyers at attractive prices. It reveals success in utilizing new technical and scientific knowledge and in competing aggressively.

3. Productivity. Measurement of the ability to employ all its basic resources to maximum advantage and to maintain adequate coordination among them provides an excellent indication of overall management performance. This key area is not confined to labor productivity, but in cases where labor is the predominant controlling element, labor productivity can be used.

4. Input-to-output ratio. This ratio reveals the degree of effectiveness in utilization of the company's personnel and physical facilities. Input is reflected by labor-hours worked, payroll dollars, and initial cost of plant and equipment; output, in terms of units produced, units sold, and dollars billed. To illustrate: An increase in units produced, without a corresponding increase in labor-hours worked, shows better utilization of facilities and improved performance.

5. Personnel development. Attention here is focused on performance of employees in keeping with their respective capacities and on the degree of success in developing a supply of promotable personnel. The question asked is: Are qualified people available when needed?

6. Public responsibility. In this area, the aim is to measure the conduct of the enterprise in assuming its social responsibility and in being a good industrial citizen. For this purpose, a single index is developed from a variety of measurements, including: the employees' family security, the attitude of vendors toward the company, participation of employees in public organizations, comparison with community wage rates, and the number of job applications received by the company.

Indicate whether each of the following statements is true or false by writing "T" or "F" in the space provided.

_____ 1. In analyzing a company's share of the market, the most important consideration is its current position.

_____ 2. Labor productivity is a legitimate measure of overall productivity.

_____ 3. In using input-to-output analysis, a change in either input or output can only be analyzed by referring to the effect or change in the other element.

_____ 4. A company with a low evaluation in the area of public responsibility is undoubtedly an unprofitable enterprise.

Refer to Answer Frame 5[24], page 138.

Answer frame 4[24]

1. False. External auditing is concerned with *verifying* financial statements. Management is responsible for preparing the statements.
2. False. Internal auditing checks the accuracy of internal data, verifies that acceptable accounting procedures are being followed, and checks compliance with plans, policies, and procedures.
3. True. A management audit is an assessment of management's results and endeavors; the past, present, and future are considered.
4. True. Many areas covered in a management audit cannot be quantified and expressed in absolute values; therefore, qualitative measures must be used.

Now turn to Frame 5[24], page 137.

Answer frame 5[24]

1. False. The most important factor in considering a company's share of the market is the *trend*, and not the current percentage.
2. True. Where labor is the predominant resource, labor productivity is an acceptable measure of overall productivity.
3. True. A change in either an input or output factor cannot be evaluated without referring to the other factor.
4. False. A company's degree of public responsibility is no indicator of its profitability, but rather an indication of its public image.

Begin Frame 6[24], below.

Frame 6[24]

It is the work of *the controller* to develop many of the data, reports, and statements mentioned in this chapter. The controller requires great ability to envision the enterprise in its totality, as well as in its components, and to secure, formulate, and prepare information that makes possible effective control. Fundamentally, the controller provides the line managers with information needed to keep operations in balance. For example, production is kept in line with the progress of sales, and the selling expenses are not permitted to increase to the point where they no longer can be recovered and are economically unjustified. To be sure, all management members are concerned with the financial aspects of their work, and exercise judgment about it, which is as it should be. The controller supplements the manager's effort and represents the cost viewpoint of the company as a whole.

An organization control unit, to centralize information required for the controlling, is winning favor. The manager of the control unit has advisory staff authority, and usually reports to the president or a member of top management. The purpose of the control unit is the collecting and developing of control data. By having an organization unit for this purpose, substantial economies in controlling efforts are gained. Eliminated are overemphasis of one activity to the detriment of another, duplication of control effort, and erroneous interpretations of various controls. Further, the directing of control information from source to area of application can follow uniform practices, gain acceptance, and engender enthusiasm for controlling.

Computers have made feasible new types of overall controlling, because it is now possible to process huge quantities of data and to efficiently determine the dynamic relationships among many factors or forces. The effect of one activity, such as manufacturing output, results in changes in many related activities, including inventory levels, shipping, selling, credit extending, billing, and collecting. By measuring the change in one and relating it to each of the others, it is possible to identify the interrelationships and to exercise controls on the key activities bringing about the major changes and, consequently, to develop more stability, or controlled change, in the direction of existing goals. Extending the scope of the investigation leads to a better insight into cyclical business behavior under conditions of change than we have ever before been privileged to know. A considerable amount of research work is being done in the application of the computer to overall controlling.

Another interesting development is that of *distribution logistics,* sometimes termed *physical distribution management* or *rhochrematics.* It is concerned with the flow of materials from sales forecast through inventory, procurement, manufacturing lead time, manufacturing, transporting, and storing. These are viewed as a single system that correlates the various separate activities with reference to a stated goal. These activities can be thought of as the input; they are processed or implemented, so that materials procurement, warehousing, and shipping schedules are created, representing the output of the system. Hence, overall control of the materials flow is obtained. That this work can be exceedingly complex can be appreciated if, for example, there are some 10,000 raw material parts, three plants, 25 warehouses, and 100 sales outlets. Such a mass of interrelated information could only be economically manipulated by a computer.

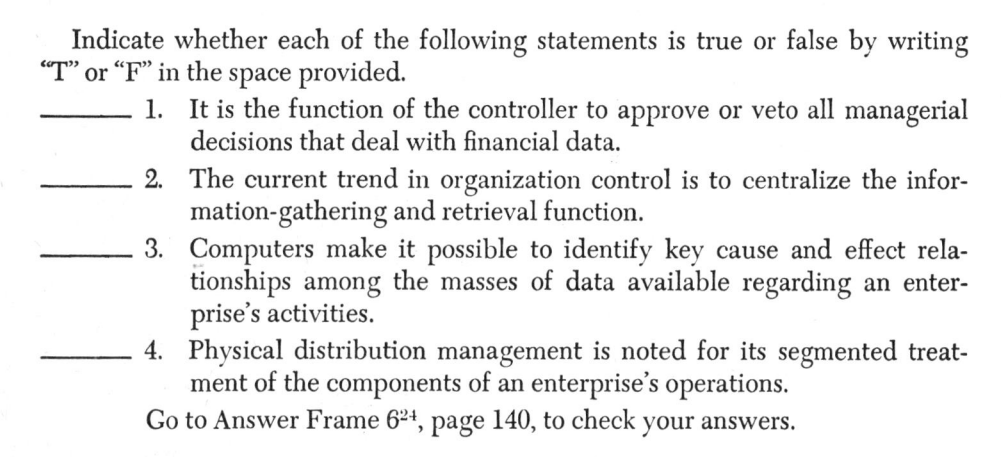

Indicate whether each of the following statements is true or false by writing "T" or "F" in the space provided.

_____ 1. It is the function of the controller to approve or veto all managerial decisions that deal with financial data.

_____ 2. The current trend in organization control is to centralize the information-gathering and retrieval function.

_____ 3. Computers make it possible to identify key cause and effect relationships among the masses of data available regarding an enterprise's activities.

_____ 4. Physical distribution management is noted for its segmented treatment of the components of an enterprise's operations.

Go to Answer Frame 6^{24}, page 140, to check your answers.

Answer frame 6[24]

1. False. The controller supplements the manager's efforts by providing information; the controller does not supervise the manager.
2. True. The establishment of an organization control unit, for the purpose of centralizing information required for control, is gaining favor.
3. True. Computers permit correlation of diverse factors, and thus enable the identification of cause and effect relationships in a company's operations.
4. False. Physical distribution management is an area where computer technology has permitted the adoption of an *integrated* approach to managing an enterprise's operations.

You have completed Chapter 24. Now go to Chapter 25, below.

chapter 25

BUDGETARY AND PERT CONTROL

Frame 1[25]

Budgeting involves both the planning and controlling functions. Strictly speaking, the planning is incorporated in a device called *the budget;* seeing that this planning is followed is the purpose of *budgeting.* More commonly, the term *budgeting,* or *profit planning,* is used to denote both the formulation and the implementation of a budget. Formally stated, *budgetary control is determining performance and comparing it to budget data to determine if corrective action is necessary.* Customarily, the components of the budget are consistent with the organization structure, so that delegation of authority, needed to make the correction, is expedited without loss of control.

Budgeting can commence anywhere in the enterprise and progress until the entire enterprise is covered. For convenience, we will assume that it is to be applied to all activities. A *budget director,* usually the chief accountant, or controller, serves as chief executive for formulating and implementing the budget. This person recommends adjustments when needed and gives official sanction to the budgeting task. A *budget committee* usually provides the means by which the budgeting efforts are implemented. It is made up of managers in charge of major departments, who are thoroughly familiar with their respective units and know the requirements for operating effectively. This committee's chairman is the budget director.

Specific information on objectives, projected

sales, competitive demands, and economic trends is distributed to committee members, who begin the actual compilation of the proposed budget. Past performance is used as a guide but is not inviolate. Each committee member encourages others holding responsibility in his or her department to participate in determining the budget, all in keeping with the general constraints outlined by the director. Also, committee members assist those heading departments who are not committee members in the preparation of their respective proposed targets. In due time, the various budget estimates are submitted to the director, who holds subsequent committee meetings, during which time the estimates are discussed and possible changes indicated. Finally, all departmental estimates are evolved into a final form and submitted to the appropriate top-management member for approval. Some further adjustments are generally suggested. Then the revised figures are returned to the committee members, who further discuss and readjust the estimates. Finally, the reworked data are resubmitted to top management for final approval, the budget is adopted, and it is put to use.

Budgets are prepared for a definite period—usually one, three, six, twelve months. The period selected depends on the budget's purpose, but it should always: (*a*) include the complete normal cycle of activity; (*b*) coincide with the timing of other major controls, such as income statements and control reports; and (*c*) be guided by the extent of available, reasonable forecasts about the activities included. The popular practice is to revise the budget estimates as new developments take place and more information becomes available. This is done by periodically reviewing, say, every month or quarter, the budget for the remainder of the period or for the next six or twelve months. Also, a *moving budget* can be adopted, in which another new month is added to the budget as each current month is completed.

Indicate whether each of the following statements is true or false by writing "T" or "F" in the space provided.

_____ 1. Budgeting, or profit planning, can be carried on only by private profit-seeking enterprises.

_____ 2. A budget committee usually is made up of the chief accountant, the controller, and the chief executive.

_____ 3. Budgeting is nothing more than the summation of a number of unadjusted, independent departmental estimates.

_____ 4. Budgets usually are treated as flexible estimates, subject to revision as more data become available.

Now turn to Answer Frame 1[25], page 142, to check your answers.

Frame 2[25]

The budget director, or whoever is charged with the budgetary control responsibility, compares performance to budgeted data for each activity. Variations are certain to appear, and when viewed as excessive, possible reasons are ascertained and corrective action is taken. Budgeting is designed to help managers manage better; and any correction, decided upon and made, should be the result of joint thought and action by those immediately involved in and affected by the adjustment. Advice, as to what corrective action to take, should be offered. Department heads should be kept fully informed regarding changes and actions being taken. Normally, regular meetings are held between the budget director and the department heads to discuss the current budgeting status, forecast developments, and specific subjects pertinent to the budgeting.

Decisive and vigorous action is usually the best answer when correction is indicated. Doing nothing detracts from the constructive assistance

Answer frame 1²⁵

1. False. Budgeting, or profit planning, can be carried on by all enterprises or entities (*e.g.*, the government); the term *profit planning* merely refers to the fact that most enterprises are profit-oriented.
2. False. The budget committee usually is headed by the chief accountant or controller, and composed of the top managers of the major departments.
3. False. Budgeting depends on the constant *review* and *revision* of individual estimates, in an attempt to obtain an integrated plan for future operations.
4. True. The popular practice is to revise the budget estimates as developments take place and more information becomes available.

Now turn to Frame 2²⁵, page 141, and continue reading.

Frame 2²⁵ continued

otherwise provided by the act of budgeting. For corrections in *nonbudgeted items*, it is best to require specific approval by the person in charge of the work. Thus, the responsibility for these changes is fixed, and the superior management member is made aware of them. From the practical viewpoint, budgetary control requires some flexibility. Achieving work objectives within the cost and time constraints is important, but, in a given case, some variation in the manner of work accomplishment may be justified. These differences are best bridged when all concerned have had a part in the budget formulation, are familiar with the goals sought, and know the preferred means of controlling within the enterprise.

Many types of budgets are available to the manager. Among the more common are: (*a*) sales, (*b*) production, (*c*) purchasing, (*d*) revenue and expense, (*e*) purchasing, (*f*) time and space, (*g*) labor, (*h*) capital expenditures, (*i*) cash, and (*j*) master. The names should be self-explanatory. Most such budgets are expressed in dollars, but some are in terms of physical units. Perhaps the most frequently used are sales, revenue and expense, cash, and master budgets. Sales are basic, and a sales budget is the foundation of budgetary control. Sales supply the principal revenue to support operating expense and to realize net income. Relating expected revenue to expected operating expenses, such as those for cost of goods sold, rent, heat, power, supplies, and so on, is accomplished by means of the revenue and expense budget. A very important need of any enterprise is to have cash available to meet obligations as they fall due. To keep well informed as to the anticipated amount of cash available at various points in time is the purpose of the cash budget. It is helpful in avoiding cash shortages, as well as in revealing any excess cash that could be advantageously invested. The master budget is a principal or supreme budget bringing together, to the extent that this is feasible, the estimates of the other budgets. In the case of the master budget for any particular classification, for example, the master *cash* budget, a consolidation of all the departmental cash budgets would be included. To supply maximum flexibility, consistent with efficiency, *a variable* or *step budget* is used. It is designed to include data at various volumes or steps of operations. It is based on the premise that, at different levels of output, different expenditures will be required for certain activities but will remain constant for other activities. The *budgetary process is a tool of managers;* it should never be identified as management. It must have the backing of top management if it is to contribute its maximum benefits. Encouragement to all management members to make and to defend their budgets and to participate in reviews helps achieve budgetary benefits and makes managers alert. Further, the overall managerial viewpoint, a sense of proportion, and an awareness of the existence and importance of many different activities are encouraged by the budgetary process. Each organization unit is assisted in accomplishing that which is probably best for all units concerned. A positive, balanced viewpoint is promoted.

Indicate whether each of the following statements is true or false by writing "T" or "F" in the space provided.

_____ 1. Corrective action should not be dictated by any one member of the budget committee.

_____ 2. Expenditures not provided for in the budget are clear indications of inefficiency and impropriety.

_____ 3. The preparation of any one type of budget usually is dependent on other budgets.

_____ 4. A *step budget* views all expenditures as being fixed over the entire relevant range of activity.

Now compare your answers with those in Answer Frame 2[25], page 144.

Frame 3[25]

Program evaluation and review technique, PERT, is performed on a set of time-related activities and events which must be accomplished to reach an objective. The evaluation gives the expected completed time and the probability of completing the total work within that time. By means of PERT, it is possible not only to know the exact schedule, but also to control the various activities on a daily basis. Overlapping and related activities are reviewed. PERT is more practical for jobs involving a one-time effort than for repeat jobs. It is a planning-controlling medium designed to: (*a*) focus attention on key components, (*b*) reveal potential problem areas, (*c*) provide a prompt reporting on accomplishments, and (*d*) facilitate decision making.

The time-related activities and events are set forth by means of a PERT network (see Figure 20). In this illustration, the circles represent events that are sequential accomplishment points; the arrows represent activities or the time-consuming elements of the program. In this type of network, an arrow always connects two activities. All of the activities and events must be accomplished before the end objective can be attained. The three numbers shown for each arrow or activity represent its estimated times,

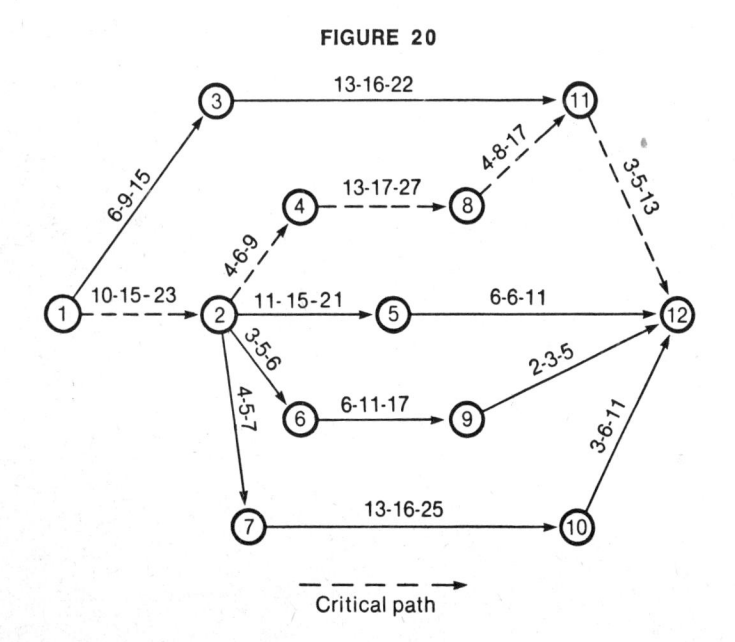

FIGURE 20

Answer frame 2[25]

1. True. Corrective action should be the result of joint thought and action by those managers immediately involved and affected by the adjustment.
2. False. Nonbudgeted items must be reviewed by the manager in charge of that activity to determine their propriety.
3. True. Most types of budgets are interrelated; they depend on the estimates contained in other budgets, *e.g.*, the production budget depends on the sales budget. In fact, most of the budgets are dependent on the sales budget.
4. False. The *step budget,* or *variable budget,* recognizes that, over the entire relevant range of activity, certain expenditures are fixed, whereas others will vary with the level of operations.

Continue with Frame 3[25], on page 143.

Frame 3[25] continued

respectively, for the optimistic, most likely, and pessimistic times. The program starts with event No. 1 and ends with event No. 12. From calculations for the time required for each path from No. 1 to No. 12, it is found that path 1–2–4–8–11–12 requires the *longest time* and, hence, is the *critical path* because it controls the time required to complete the program. Toward it, managers would direct their attention in order to: (*a*) ensure that no breakdowns occur in it; (*b*) better the current times required, if possible; and (*c*) trade off time from the noncritical paths to the critical path, if the net effect is to reduce total time of the critical path.

Indicate whether each of the following statements is true or false by writing "T" or "F" in the space provided.

_____ 1. PERT centers its attention on social constraints.

_____ 2. PERT is best applied to assembly-line operations.

_____ 3. In PERT, the *critical path* is the path that requires the longest time.

_____ 4. In the PERT network, circles represent events and arrows represent activities.

Now turn to Answer Frame 3[25], page 146.

chapter 26

MANAGEMENT IN FOREIGN COUNTRIES

Frame 1[26]

When discussing foreign management, writers and even the ordinary citizen in the United States tend to make comparisons between management abroad and management at home. Insofar as available, statistics on such economic factors as resources, capital goods, production, and income, with few exceptions, overwhelmingly favor the United States as contrasted to foreign countries. The tremendous economic growth of the United States is without parallel, and it is only in recent years that several nations have begun to rival our annual rate of growth. Each year, ours is the highest gross national product per capita. From all this, it is not surprising that we should conclude: (*a*) management in the United States is the best in the world, and (*b*) better management is the principal reason for the economic superiority of the United States.

However, these conclusions are open to question. American management has done a remarkable job in bringing available resources together and in getting people to cooperate effectively in groups so as to achieve objectives. Also, our impressive technological advances have fostered economic growth in the United States; but technology is transferable between countries, and no one nation holds a monopoly on it. Further, foreign countries provided, and still provide, some of the great management innovators; some of the most effective of present-day management techniques are of foreign origin. We find many examples abroad of good management exemplified in accomplishment of stated goals, recognition of social responsibilities, and effective utilization of resources.

To comprehend management in any foreign country, *it is necessary to understand the particular environment created by conditions in that country*. For present purposes, we can divide these conditions into three groups: (*a*) economic, (*b*) social, and (*c*) political.

An extremely important economic consideration is *economic demand*. For example, if a new plant is being considered, management must know whether sufficient purchasing power exists to absorb the output of the plant. Economic demand need not come from within the country's borders, but if it is to come from other countries, there must not be excessive trade restraints and strict control of exports. The *availability of suitable labor* is another highly important economic factor. There must be adequate education to create a labor force with the needed skills. Further, capital is needed, and, unless the prospective manager commands sufficient wealth, it is necessary to secure financial help from others. In countries where borrowing is difficult and high interest rates are charged, the problems of the manager are multiplied. Then, too, the country's utility services, such as electric power, water, and transportation must be adequate. In highly overpopulated countries, an economically suitable site for a plant may not even be available.

Social considerations affecting management in a foreign country are equally significant. Pri-

Answer frame 3[25]

1. False. PERT centers its attention on *time* constraints.
2. False. PERT is more practical for jobs involving a one-time effort than for repeat jobs.
3. True. In PERT, the critical path is the path that requires the *longest* time. If this path can be shortened, the program can be completed in a shorter time period.
4. True. Circles represent events that are sequential accomplishment points, and arrows represent activities or the time-consuming elements for the program.

You have completed Chapter 25. Continue with Chapter 26, on page 145.

Frame 1[26] continued

marily due to custom, a gifted person may be reluctant to participate in a business enterprise. His peers may look down on business as a career lacking in prestige. Business may even be regarded as immoral. In India, for example, some of the religious leaders regard as evil any action leading to the accumulation of wealth. In some countries, management, especially when applied to trade and commerce, is viewed mainly as a means of gaining entry to the most socially esteemed group. Managers are diligent in their managerial efforts mainly because they seek to improve social status and to gain favorable recognition. Also, in many foreign countries, the family is dominant and its objectives are given priority over those of the business. Being a member of a certain family is the main basis for respect, prestige, and status.

Indicate whether each of the following statements is true or false by writing "T" or "F" in the space provided.

_____ 1. It is clear that management talent in the United States is superior to management in other countries.

_____ 2. Management in the United States is greatly influenced by techniques brought from other countries.

_____ 3. A common problem of foreign managers is that they are burdened with an excessive demand for their products.

_____ 4. The social environment of a country is always the greatest stimulus for the development of management skill.

Now refer to Answer Frame 1[26], page 148, to check your answers.

Frame 2[26]

Political and governmental factors in foreign countries are perhaps the most important of all conditions affecting management. A country's politics, operating through the government in power, influences taxes, import-export controls, financial restrictions, regulations regarding operations, and the repatriation of earnings—all of great importance to the manager. The power of taxation is always to be reckoned with by a manager. In same instances, a government may offer tax inducements, and these influence management in important ways. A government can refuse to issue import or export licenses for goods or services it considers nonessential or undesirable in its overall objectives, so that, in essence, the manager is forced to conform to the wishes of the body politic. Furthermore, government can supply needed capital to a manager, or offer a government-sponsored agency by which managers can discuss and plan their affairs. A foreign government can lend encouragement or discouragement to enterprises outside its direct jurisdiction by means of control over the earnings, by granting special favors and considerations, or, in contrast, by setting up repatriation requirements.

Some of these conditions may be referred to as *cultural factors*—particularly skills and abilities, the desire for products and services, and general customs and beliefs within a foreign country. In addition, the economic and political considerations of labor regulation, fiscal policy, and restrictions on trade establish a climate in which managers can achieve progress by designing and utilizing techniques to take these various factors into account. The fact that cultural differences exist has led some to conclude that the framework of management knowledge, as it exists in the United States, is applicable only in societies similar to that existing in the United States. People who hold that management cannot effectively be exported from one country to another point to the difficulties cultural differences create in interpersonal relationships, including those between managers and nonmanagers; and between managers and vendors, customers, owners, government, and competitors. On the other hand, one can truthfully state that there are instances where managerial knowledge has been transferred from the United States to foreign countries, even in the face of differences in cultural and political factors. True, managers may be skeptical in the beginning and may be slow in adapting response to unfamiliar customs, but once full indoctrination is gained, these customs become the accepted way of doing things.

This leads to a basic statement: *The framework of management knowledge should be considered separate from its application to a given situation.* Management knowledge is universal, in that the structure of concepts and principles is valid regardless of physical location, even though the approach and techniques employed in applying the concepts and principles will vary in different cultures. In other words, the theory and concepts around which management knowledge and principles are organized represent fundamental truths that are useful in describing and predicting the results of certain variables in a given situation. How these management truths are applied—the techniques followed—may be identical or may differ in different cultures.

What works successfully in one society may fail in another, or what is successful in one may succeed in others with very few, if any, changes. That is, the manager, designing a technique for a different culture, ascertains the extent of change necessary to meet the existing differences. Furthermore, the differences in society are not confined to countries. There are different social variations within the same country, and these are of importance to the manager.

Of special interest is decision making in foreign countries. The trend is toward more participation whereby the individual, groups, work committees, work councils, or similar bodies are involved in activity participating and sharing in what is decided in matters concerning them. It is not merely advising or suggesting. No longer does the manager alone decide how the work is allocated, the working hours, or what cost-cutting measures will be followed.

The techniques followed in participative decision making differ widely around the world. Similarities and dissimilarities exist within a given country. *Ringisei* practiced in Japan is of special interest. Literally the term means "reverential inquiry about superior's intention." To a Japanese manager knowing how a subordinate feels about a given issue is vital, for without this knowledge, it is extremely difficult to make decisions that maintain the peace, harmony, and cooperation of the work group. The technique followed begins with an employee at a low organization level outlining an idea or suggested solution to a problem along with an explanation of how to implement the recommendation. The contribution is circulated among all affected by the suggestion and subsequently is circulated to the various superiors in succession. The purpose is to reach a concensus among not only the group members, but also the managers affected by the decision. After considerable discussion a decision is reached. The decision is considered a commitment by all parties involved in the discussions.

Although centuries old, from the U.S. viewpoint the Japanese decision-making approach features modern managerial techniques. Among its advantages are (1) initiative from a low level upward is strengthened, (2) managerial experience and judgment are utilized, (3) wide at-

Answer frame 1²⁶

1. False. Differences in the environment make it difficult to meaningfully compare managers in the United States with those in foreign countries.
2. True. Some of the most effective techniques used in present-day management were derived from foreign innovation.
3. False. Many foreign managers are plagued by a lack of demand for their products. Some countries have excessive trade restraints and strictly control exports.
4. False. The social environment of a country may impede the development of management talent. In some countries, the accumulation of wealth is considered to be immoral.

Now turn to Frame 2²⁶, page 146, and continue.

Frame 2²⁶ continued

tention is given to an employee's desires, interests, and welfare, and (4) the manager is a facilitator of decision making, not an arbitrary issuer of orders. On the other hand, it should be observed that the use of *ringisei* takes much time, the approach may be limited for most emergency situations, participants (especially those at the lower levels) do not always possess the desired overall comprehension of the total enterprise, and responsibility is not fixed—the decision is a composite or group-mix variety.

Indicate whether each of the following statements is true or false by writing "T" or "F" in the space provided.

_____ 1. A government can affect the application of management techniques through the passage of legislation.

_____ 2. Managerial knowledge can only be transferred between similar societies.

_____ 3. Although the application of management principles may differ from culture to culture, the principles themselves are still valid.

_____ 4. Cultural differences can affect the application of management principles between different regions of the same country.

_____ 5. *Ringisei* is an example of authoritarian decision making.

Now turn to Answer Frame 2²⁶, page 150, to check your answers.

Frame 3²⁶

A major task of management *in any society is the achievement of stated enterprise goals.* This gives rise to imponderables, including the identifying of goals, the degree to which these goals represent optimization and suboptimization with the available facilities, and the mobility of labor and capital, which in most foreign countries cannot always be shifted from less profitable to more profitable alternatives. Nevertheless, certain definite economic measurements regarding a foreign country do exist; among them are: (*a*) gross national product per capita—both as to the level and to the rate of growth, (*b*) the level of competition or the incentive to be competitive, and (*c*) the degree of utilization of land, labor, and capital. Reducing these measurements to the viewpoint of the individual enteprise, we find these indicators: (*a*) return on investment, (*b*) output per employee, (*c*) degree of success in competing in export markets, and (*d*) cost and price levels as compared to those of another enterprise in the same country.

Competent managers and potential managerial talent exist in every country. The managers may have limited and narrow experience, and the potential talent must be located and developed before full competency can be attained. It is in the nature of things for innate human intellectual qualities to be dispersed among a group of persons. Differences in effectiveness as managers will exist owing to education, environment, and tradition. Also, some of a country's ablest people may not aspire to managerial careers.

What predominant characteristics distinguish the members of the managerial class in a foreign country? The answer: (*a*) *achievement motivation*, and (*b*) *independence of social pressures or disapproval.* They have deep concern with achievement, enjoy problem recognition and problem solving, are usually highly self-reliant, can work effectively under pressure, and generally will act in spite of risks when they know their efforts will influence the outcome. They readily assume responsibility, and have the ability to accurately assess future possibilities.

The manager in many foreign countries must be independent enough in thought to go against prevailing practices and values—to be a social deviant or maverick. This is most apt to be true in the less highly developed countries. The businessperson in many of these countries is not completely accepted by the ruling groups. To persist in a business career, therefore, requires a good deal of independence. In a sense, these business managers are not fully integrated into the culture in which they live. Yet, they are in a position to bring about changes that may alter basic values. Some are expert in pioneering special skills and in introducing certain knowhow. Many operate, under conditions dissimilar to those existing in the United States, within a particular system of producing, marketing, and financing that usually has deeply ingrained attitude values and modes of behavior that do not quickly or easily erode.

Indicate whether each of the following statements is true or false by writing "T" or "F" in the space provided.

_____ 1. Management in a foreign country differs from management in the United States in that foreign managers are not held to any stated goals.

_____ 2. An important area of management in foreign countries is the development of competent managers.

_____ 3. One of the main characteristics of managers is that they are concerned with personal or group achievement.

_____ 4. Social deviants are precluded from being managers, because they are not accepted by the society in which they live, much less by an enterprise within that society.

Now check your answers by referring to Answering Frame 3[26], page 150.

Answer frame 2[26]

1. True. The political environment of a country significantly affects the actions of managers.
2. False. Managerial knowledge has been transferred from the United States to foreign countries where differences in cultural and political factors exist.
3. True. Management principles are universally valid; however, the application of these principles must accommodate the different cultures.
4. True. There are different social variations in the same country and these are of importance to management.
5. False. *Ringisei* is the Japanese decision-making approach which is participative in nature and has been practiced for centuries.

Now turn to Frame 3[26], page 148, and continue reading.

Answer frame 3[26]

1. False. In any society, management is responsible for achieving the stated goals of the enterprise.
2. True. In any country, potential management talent must be located and developed before full competency is attained.
3. True. One of the predominant characteristics of the managerial class is their concern with achievement.
4. False. Social deviants or mavericks are not committed to maintaining the status quo and, therefore, can be very effective managers, especially in underdeveloped countries.

You have now completed Chapter 26. Continue with Chapter 27, page 151.

chapter 27

MANAGEMENT IN THE FUTURE

Frame 1[27]

Management is growing, developing, and becoming more and more important. New managerial techniques are evolving rapidly. The stimulus for change comes not only from within management, but also from without, including every field of human activity—social, economical, and technological. In all these areas, the pace of change has been rapid, and the accumulation of new knowledge has been tremendous. As a result, *the manager's role is expanding in every kind of enterprise and at every level.* New knowledge and techniques stimulate further innovation, creating environments where work can be accomplished with efficiency and human satisfaction never before thought possible.

With all these changes will come new theories of management. Dynamic management thought will continue because of the importance of management and the fundamental issues with which it deals. Scholars and practitioners will continue to blend efforts toward improvement in areas of management. Their contributions will benefit all people. *Currently we find ourselves in the position of having too much knowledge to manage arbitrarily and not enough knowledge to manage with certainty.*

The future manager is likely to operate in a disorderly environment. Change will make it so. This means that the future manager will have to be flexible and speedy in reacting to change in every segment of his or her managerial efforts.

In this dynamic state of affairs, *the manager is compelled to take advantage of the improvements in management science and art.* Society and increased competition make this inevitable. This means that to the manager *the danger of becoming obsolete will keep on becoming greater.* The use of old practices and trial and error methods is inadequate for the practice of modern management, and will be increasingly so in the future. New structures of management thought and new findings in management, inadequate as they may be, are supplying the approaches and means for achieving managerial excellence in the future.

A prominent characteristic of management in the future will be *the consideration of problems from an overall or inclusive viewpoint.* For example, the constraints of a difficulty in production will not be confined to that area alone but will include a much broader scope because, in fact, the difficulty will increasingly be seen to affect areas outside the immediate production activity. An enterprise will be looked upon for what it really is—an integrated unit and not a grouping of many divisive activities each one of which acts more or less autonomously. Again, it is becoming more and more clear that an organization is a single entity in which various elements are contributing toward common goals.

In this inclusive approach, two factors are prominent or, in fact, have made the approach feasible. They include: (*a*) the systems approach, and (*b*) the computer. As pointed out in Chapter 1, management can be viewed as a system of variables, parameters, and constraints. It encompasses subsystems and these, in turn, subsubsystems. For example, within the system of government is a social system; within the social system is an industrial system; within the industrial system is an enterprise system; within the enterprise system is a sales system; and so forth. Systems serve as vehicles of thought to expedite the inclusive approach. However, of equal importance is the availability of the computer, which has made it possible to process masses of data representing a multitude of variables, and to reveal complex relationships, an understanding of which is vital to the manager. The computer has given reality to the utilization of the systems approach and to the inclusive concept in management. Both the systems approach and the computer will play an increasingly important role in management in the future.

More emphasis will be given information in the future. This follows because the future manager will have to meet problems of change in a dynamic environment of economic, social, and political forces. Taking advantage of these changes, being competive, and maintaining managerial flexibility depends on having adequate information at the time and place where it can be of maximum assistance. *The extent of a manager's influence is conditioned largely by the information the manager has and is able to use.* In the years ahead, this will become increasingly important. The information must be relevant to the manager's particular task, be designed to assist in evaluating actions, and show how and where goals are not being attained. Managers will have increasing need for regularly collected and analyzed data concerning the external environment and internal operations.

Indicate whether each of the following statements is true or false.

_____ 1. Management has reached a plateau in its development and usefulness.

_____ 2. Managers of the future will be forced to rely exclusively on their intuition in the analysis of problems.

_____ 3. Managers of the future will rely heavily on the use of computers.

_____ 4. Managers of the future will deal exclusively with data concerning internal operations.

Now turn to Answer Frame 1[27], page 154, to check your response.

Frame 2[27]

The computer has contributed enormously to this informational need in that it processes data into a usable form that we identify as information. A great expansion of the quantity of management information is expected in the immediate future. Existing gaps are being identified, and efforts are under way to make basic information available concerning such items as product cost, technological developments, and quantitative goal accomplishment. But *one of the big needs is improved design of information,* so that relevant information is supplied in a form most useful for the decision maker. Like raw materials of industry, information must be converted into a useful form, and in management this means relating it to a problem for which it has relevance. Much progress in this area will be made in the future.

Management members are giving more attention to determining the kinds of information that will help them and the information formats that will expedite their work. The trend is away from utilizing reports and projections that are duplicates, in format, of old manual reports. Information is being updated to meet new managerial requirements. Some large companies have established a "management analyses and services" unit, to suggest and design information suited for special use at all levels and in all activities of management. However, doubt exists whether a single unit is the best organizational arrangement; some suggest several units to provide the more responsive service that appears necessary.

The probability appears to be high that *much more knowledge of human behavior will become available,* and the manager of the future will possess more factual information on how to cope with human behavior. Already it is claimed that accurate and reliable quantitative measurements of the human element in the decision-making process are possible. Some believe it possible to measure the efficiency and adequacy of communication, the amount of anxiety and stress felt by members within an organization, the loyalty of a member toward the organization of which that member is a part, and the degree of confidence existing among the members of an organization. Some have suggested that, by the turn of the century, psychological theories as accurate and successful as theories in chemistry will be available. With better and more quantitative measurements to come, the avenues will be opened toward maximizing the quality of human assets. The importance of the human being will take on even higher recognition and importance, which is as it should be, because nothing is as important as human beings, and there is no substitute for them. Computers cannot think. Their performance is only as good as the programming done for them by humans. Furthermore, management is performed for the benefit of human beings; its ultimate aim is to serve and satisfy them better. This is its most meaningful justification.

The future appears to hold the *innovation and development of many new inventions, such as techniques, charts, concepts, and designs* that will be *helpful to managers in performing their work*. The need for creative talent in management is slowly but surely being recognized. As management knowledge and skill increases and the need for better tools becomes more widely recognized, it is reasonably certain that the challenges in these areas will be accepted and eventually solved. The current level of research effort and support in management is relatively low compared to that in other areas, especially the physical sciences. True, management research is both difficult and expensive. Facts and proven relationships are difficult to attain. Controlled laboratory experimentation cannot be employed in many managerial studies unless dangerous simplifications are made. With the upsurge in management, these difficulties will be met and, in the forthcoming decades, management research will occupy the high position and status that it merits.

The manager of the future will be better educated than those of today, primarily *because: (a) formal management education has increased and will continue to increase (b) managers have a will to learn, and (c) the sophistication of new management concepts and techniques will require periodic updating and redeveloping of managers*. A larger part of the population will be better educated, and it is now recognized that a body of management knowledge exists and instruction in it can be given. A person active in an area as dynamic as management simply has to be open-minded and willing to learn how to effectively perform managerial work. Most managers have, and will continue to have, a propensity toward learning. Last, there will be increasing acceptance that there is no terminal degree for management education. Because of its dynamic nature, the manager of the future will find that periodic updating sessions will become the accepted custom.

Finally, during the years ahead more and more acceptance will be given the concept that *management is the important resource basic to most achievement*. Management is purposive, deals with obtaining results, and is the effective medium to apply and coordinate knowledge of many disciplines and sciences. Management is the means toward accomplishment and is basic in all our efforts to progress. Management knowledge and skill are vital resources of our nation.

Answer frame 1[27]

1. False. Management is growing, developing, and becoming more and more important.
2. False. In the future, managers will be compelled to be familiar with and to use the improvements in management science and art.
3. True. The computer will aid the development and implementation of new management techniques.
4. False. Managers of the future will require not only data on internal operations, but also data on the external environment in which the enterprise operates.

Now turn to Frame 2[27], page 152, and continue reading.

Frame 2[27] continued

Indicate whether each of the following statements is true or false by writing "T" or "F" in the space provided.

_____ 1. The only requirement of information is that it be timely.

_____ 2. Information regarding human behavior will be of more importance in the future than it is currently.

_____ 3. In the future, the most valuable resource of an enterprise will be its computer.

_____ 4. The current level of research effort in management is low compared to that in other areas.

Now check your answers with those in Answer Frame 2[27], page 156.

Answer frame 2²⁷

1. False. For information to be useful, it must be timely, pertinent, and in a form that is suited to its users.
2. True. Information regarding human behavior will hold a prominent position in future management development.
3. False. The most valuable resource of a company is, and will continue to be, its human resources.
4. True. The level of research in management is low compared to that in other areas. Controlled laboratory experimentation cannot be employed as readily, and proven relationships are difficult to attain.

This concludes Chapter 27. Now work the examination on page 165, which covers Chapters 20–27. Then, you may want to review the Index-Glossary beginning with page 173, to further test your understanding of the concepts in this study guide.

Examination 1: chapters 1–10

Directions: Write your answer True (T) or False (F); *a, b, c*; or the necessary words on the appropriate numbered lines in the margins. Check your answers by turning to page 169. Review and study the questions you missed.

1. To manage effectively a manager must have:
   a. A great interest in people.
   b. Knowledge of current laws affecting business.
   c. Belief in a good life for all.
   d. A philosophy of management.
2. Questions relative to international trade exemplify a social environment factor important to many managers.
3. Today's manager sees to it that all members of the work group have values similar to those the manager holds.
4. Management practice can be considered an art utilizing a science.
5. Match the approaches to management thought shown in the left column with the proper descriptions shown in the right column.

   a. Human behavior.
   b. Systems.
   c. Quantitative.

   1. Uses mathematical models and processes quantifying variables and relationships resulting in decision or answer to problem.
   2. Features inter- and intrapersonal relationships among employees and their affect on management.
   3. Views the many activities as related and provides a framework and a means for identifying the critical variables and constraints important in a managerial situation.
6. Management is one of the newest and most helpful fields of study to which humanity has devoted efforts.
7. The eagerly sought-for, unified approach to the study of management is just about to break through.
8. Managerial controlling can be defined as _____
   _____.
9. Every member of management performs the managerial functions.
10. Coordinating is considered by many to mean the same as managing, in that coordinating is performed to achieve a unified action toward a stated goal.

158   Programmed learning aid for principles of management

_____ 11. Most managers have:
   a. No objectives.
   b. Multiple objectives.
   c. A single objective.
   d. None of these.

_____ 12. "Satisficing" an objective means:
   a. Accomplishing the targeted work within time and cost allowed.
   b. Having an objective that the manager finds easy to attain.
   c. Maintaining present competitive and profit positions.

_____ 13. In quantitative decision making, the same mathematics is used for either maximization or minimization.

14. The advantages of using strategic planning include:
   (a) _____ (b) _____
   _____ (c) _____

_____ 15. A decision trees is an interesting decision making aid. It can:
   a. Reveal issues of greatest controversy so that preparation to resolve them is enhanced.
   b. Identify what will most probably emerge from the decision required.
   c. Provide the best sequence of decision making steps to be taken in a given situation
   d. All of these.
   e. None of these.

_____ 16. Value systems are:
   a. Relatively simple.
   b. Rational.
   c. Relatively complex.
   d. Consistent.

_____ 17. Probability is the degree or extent of an individual's belief in the truth of a declared statement, expressed as a percentage.

_____ 18. Arranging the data in a matrix form is most characteristic of:
   a. Monte Carlo.
   b. Linear programming.
   c. Simulation.
   d. All of these.
   e. None of these.

19. In managerial decision making, both tangible and intangible factors are considered; examples of the former are (a) _____ and (b) _____ and of the latter are (c) _____ and (d) _____.

_____ 20. For decision making to take place, there must always be present:
   a. No alternative.
   b. Two or more alternatives.
   c. None of these.

_____ 21. Group decision making gives what some managers call patterned decisions.

22. Match each of the techniques (left column) with its proper description (right column).
_____   a. Simulation.   1. Find the best combination of several variables
_____   b. Queueing.   to satisfy the objective.

_____   c. Linear programming.

2. Substitute representation of communication flows.
3. Numerical significance of random occurrences.
4. Balance the cost of bottlenecks against idle capacity.
5. Systematic trial-and-error approach to complex problems.

23. Arrange the following steps of quantitative decision making into their proper sequence.
   a. Test the mathematical model.
   b. Construct the mathematical model.
   c. Formulate the objective.
   d. Quantify the variables.
   e. Derive a solution from the mathematical model.
   f. Identify the variables.
   g. Adjust mathematical model.
   h. Put solution into effect.

_____ 24. Usually the planner finds it better to work forward to the objective.

_____ 25. Within an enterprise, existent plans do not:
   a. Need to be considered interdependent.
   b. Tend to beget plans.
   c. Apply to simple, repetitive work.
   d. All of these.
   e. None of these.

26. Dynamic planning is _____.

_____ 27. Too much or too little information can hamper planning, yet all information is useful to the planner.

28. Match the type of plan (left column) with its proper definition (right column).
_____   a. Method.
_____   b. Policy.
_____   c. Budget.
_____   d. Procedure.
_____   e. Program.

1. Chronological sequence of specific tasks required to achieve the work.
2. Comprehensive and variable in makeup.
3. The details of how the work is to be done by each employee.
4. General understanding that guides thinking in decision making of subordinates.
5. A numerical plan showing expectancies for a stated period and also accomplishments.

29. A planning premise is _____.

_____ 30. An outstanding characteristic of managerial planning is that it is:
   a. Made up of variable components only.
   b. A tentative process.
   c. Impervious to the influence of the human element.

_____ 31. The fundamental functions of management are normally performed in a particular and prescribed sequence.

_____ 32. The so-called "hierarchy of objectives" exists only in profit-making enterprises.

_____ 33. For effective management, the following statement of objective is preferable:
   a. To make more profits.
   b. To supply greater service.

        c. To reduce costs 7 percent.
        d. To expand facilities.

_____ 34. In the systems approach to management thought, management is viewed as a system of cultural interrelationships.

_____ 35. Every management member has planning to perform within a particular area of activities.

_____ 36. The chief informational needs required for effective planning are:
        a. Objectives, personnel, and political.
        b. Environmental, competitive, and of the individual enterprise.
        c. Environmental, political, and price levels.
        d. None of these.

_____ 37. Decision making based on analysis eliminates the uncertainty of the decision.

_____ 38. Emergency situations requiring a decision are typically decided by the individual instance.

_____ 39. "What if" questions are answered by managerial staffing.

40. A procedure can be defined as _____.

Examination 2: chapters 11–19

Directions: Write your answer True (T) or False (F); *a, b, c;* or the necessary words on the appropriate numbered lines in the margins. Check your answers by turning to page 169. Review and study the questions you missed.

_____ 1. Nonformal behavior within an organization is usually undesirable.
_____ 2. The illusion of communication is best described as
   a. What is expressed by the sender of a communication is not always understood by the receiver.
   b. Messages are transmitted, meanings are not.
   c. Perceptions of people communicating are not alike.
   d. All of these.
   e. None of these.
_____ 3. There is a tendency for an individual to behave as others expect that individual to behave.
_____ 4. It is a truism in management that effective directing can best be carried out by one person for one group.
_____ 5. An acceptable definition of an instruction as used in management directing is _____
_____ 6. Job satisfaction comes from and is the result of performance; it is not the reverse, i.e., performance leads to job satisfaction.
_____ 7. An accurate and up-to-date organization chart ensures an effective organization.
_____ 8. Foremost in importance in managerial organizing is (are):
   a. Cost.
   b. Time.
   c. Tasks.
   d. People.
_____ 9. Inflexibility is a characteristic of most formal organizations.
_____ 10. Departmentation by managerial function is a widely accepted practice.
_____ 11. Committees are not well suited for work pertaining to:
   a. Review of past activities.
   b. Innovations for improved control.
   c. Evaluation of working conditions.
12. Match the type of departmentation (left column) with the appropriate description (right column).
_____ *a.* Process.   1. Sales representatives.
_____ *b.* Product.   2. Work group members having all the knowl-
_____ *c.* Task team.   edge and ability to accomplish the work.

161

_____ d. Territory.

3. Operative production personnel, where product moves through a single channel to completion, such as an assembly line.
4. Bank employees performing commercial loan work.

13. Responsibility is _____
_____

_____ 14. Delegation of authority is always subject to recovery by the delegator.

_____ 15. An astute manager will take all necessary measures to eradicate a clique detected within the organization.

_____ 16. Dysfunctions are best defined as:
   a. Informal organization characteristics that permit nonformal behavior to exist.
   b. Formal organization characteristics that permit nonformal behavior to exist.
   c. Formal organization characteristics that permit formal behavior to exist.
   d. Informal organization characteristics that permit formal behavior to exist.

_____ 17. The fusion theory of organization deals with combining measurable work with the formal arrangement of functions in order to obtain an effective organization.

_____ 18. Among the common approaches to departmentation are:
   a. Top–down and derivative.
   b. Bottom–up and integrative.
   c. Top–down and bottom–up.
   d. Derivative and integrative.
   e. None of these.

19. Four important types of staff authority include: (a) _____, (b) _____, (c) _____, (d) _____.

_____ 20. Within an organization, members with common social interests normally band together to form:
   a. Dysfunctional groups.
   b. Informal groups.
   c. Role status groups.
   d. None of these.

_____ 21. In the normal growth pattern of an organization, growth follows vertical growth.

_____ 22. The use of motivation starts with the manager, not with motivating others.

_____ 23. The subordinate-acceptance approach to authority is based on:
   a. The nonmanager recognizing someone must make decisions.
   b. The opportunity to contribute to group's efforts.
   c. The manager winning support.
   d. All of these.
   e. None of these.

_____ 24. It is generally agreed that the most important activity of the board of directors is:
   a. Trusteeship.
   b. Assisting in public relations.
   c. Selection of executives.
   d. None of these.

25. Most executive selection includes appraisals in: (a) _____, (b) _____, (c) _____.

_____ 26. Participation has motivating effects, because it gives the individual:
   a. Interesting work to do.
   b. Efficient leadership.
   c. Accomplishment of useful work.
   d. Adequate knowledge to contribute to progress.
   e. All of these.
   f. None of these.

_____ 27. Requiring a manager to listen to or to read proposals from the staff manager is called:
   a. The requirement doctrine of authority.
   b. The centralized authority span.
   c. The responsibility request.
   d. The decentralized delegation.
   e. None of these.

_____ 28. Psychological tests for executive selection are helpful, but have a serious limitation, which is:
   a. Cost in terms of time and of interpretative grading.
   b. Lack of agreement on what traits should be included.
   c. Dislike of many competent managerial candidates in being subjected to them.

29. The need for self-esteem represents: (a) _____ wants, that for protection from possible harm (b) _____ wants, and that for group relatedness (c) _____ wants.
   (1) Social.
   (2) Safety.
   (3) Ego.

_____ 30. In modern management, the belief is common that including the "reason why" in an order is a waste of time and effort.

_____ 31. One of the major reasons for obtaining a manager from outside an enterprise is:
   a. To obtain fresh ideas and new applications of management.
   b. To enhance the public image of the enterprise being a good place to work.
   c. To avoid a morale problem among old employees.
   d. None of these.

_____ 32. Providing information needed for effective action by an employee is normally advocated for:
   a. New employees only.
   b. Long-tenured employees only.
   c. Employees below production standards.
   d. None of these.
   e. All of these.

_____ 33. To rescind an order is a mark of poor management.

_____ 34. There is no such thing as overcommunication; a manager needs all the information he or she can get.

_____ 35. The study of group dynamics shows that when group members select their fellow employees the result is:
   a. Job satisfaction increases.
   b. Productivity decreases.
   c. Wants satisfaction increases.
   d. Productivity increases.
   e. a,b.

     f. c,d.
     g. a,d.
     h. b,c.
    36. The so-called communication gap is _____.
_____ 37. Orders requiring a subordinate to act in a certain manner in a given circumstance are employed by all managers.
_____ 38. Communicating is a fundamental function of management.
_____ 39. The fact that a manager influences greatly the behavior of the group promotes the concept that she or he is apart from the group.
_____ 40. Because the grapevine can carry rumors and does not have official information sources, it is not utilized to benefit managers.

Examination 3: chapters 20–27

Directions: Write your answer True (T) or False (F); *a, b, c;* or the necessary words on the appropriate numbered lines in the margins. Check your answers by turning to page 170. Review and study the questions you missed.

_____ 1. The work-centered style of leadership focuses on task performance and gives excellent results in many cases.

_____ 2. The trend in management is toward greater acceptance of the statement that management is the important resource basic to most achievement.

_____ 3. Ringisei as practiced in Japanese management features:
   a. The superior listening to and discussing possible decisions with nonmanagement members to be affected by the decision.
   b. Ideas and suggestions for improvement originating at the lower organizational level.
   c. Concensus among the management and nonmanagement members affected by a particular decision.
   d. All of these.
   e. None of these.

_____ 4. A leader typically:
   a. Seeks to understand problems of followers.
   b. Puts plans into action and generates enthusiasm for them.
   c. Motivates others to accomplish the required work.
   d. All of these.
   e. None of these.

_____ 5. Appraising of management members consists of one step only, namely, evaluating the incumbent on a number of selected factors.

_____ 6. Neither the style of personal-behavior leadership nor that of personal leadership makes use of work-centered decisions.

7. The three dimensions for measuring leadership effectiveness stated by Fiedler are (*a*) _____ (*b*) _____ (*c*) _____

8. Match the type of leadership (left column) with its proper characteristic (right column).

_____ *a.* Indigenous leadership.   1. Features close relationship between leader and non-leader, and commonly person-to-person contact.
_____ *b.* Personal leadership.
_____ *c.* Democratic leadership.   2. Originates from informal organization.
                                             3. Emphasizes the group's interest and initiative.

_____ 9. For the best management, controlling should be:
   a. Profit-oriented.
   b. Cost-oriented.
   c. Objective-oriented.
   d. Person-oriented.

_____ 10. Leadership is best described as being:
   a. Creative and continuous.
   b. Dynamic and continuous.
   c. Decisive and dynamic.

_____ 11. The control process is basically the same for quality, morale, and finance.

_____ 12. Current trends in management development programs include:
   a. Shaping them to serve as adjunct programs by lightening the management load during the development period.
   b. Making the manager a finder, not a giver of answers.
   c. Using formal and well-planned programs more extensively.

13. For a leader to have skill in practicing empathy means _____
_____.

_____ 14. In controlling, a common means for determining performance is by means of:
   a. Reports.
   b. Personal objectives.
   c. Standards.
   d. Key cases.

15. For appraising managers, the basis on which selected factors are chosen include the basis of: (a) _____, and (b) _____.

_____ 16. Customer orders received and shipments are illustrative of:
   a. The INPUT and the controlling within an enterprise.
   b. The close relationship between planning and controlling.
   c. The key points for controlling.
   d. The exceptional cases of controlling.

17. Controlling, a fundamental function of management, is the _____
_____
_____.

_____ 18. Included in the category of overall controls are:
   a. Sales budgets, strategic points, and organization pattern.
   b. Ratios, break-even analysis, and return on investment.
   c Authority, standards, and PERT.
   d None of these.

_____ 19. For cost-controlling purposes, an effective approach is PPBS, which stands for:
   a. Public planning budget spending.
   b. Private productive base system.
   c. Payout planning budget system.
   d. None of these.

_____ 20. Adequate consideration of the use value is important in a zero defect program.

21. Exceptional cases in controlling are _____
_____.

_____ 22. The best controlling corrects undesirable deviations after they occur.

_____ 23. An income statement for each department is the most effective and feasible overall control to adopt.

_____ 24. A common expression for measuring and comparing sales for control purposes is:
  a. Profit per unit.
  b. Number of sales.
  c. Return on sales calls.
  d. None of these.

_____ 25. To a great extent, overall controls are financial.

_____ 26. One hundred percent inspection is preventive as well as remedial.

_____ 27. The period selected for a budget should:
  a. Coincide with the period used for the profit and loss statements.
  b. Include the complete cycle of activity being budgeted.
  c. Be guided by the limits of the forecasts about the activities.
  d. All of these.
  e. None of these.

_____ 28. For superior management, controlling should be viewed as an isolated and independent activity.

_____ 29. Representative of a ratio for overall control is:
  a. Break-even point.
  b. Company sales to total sales in industry.
  c. Input to machine ratio.
  d. All of these.
  e. None of these.

_____ 30. By use of the return-on-manager-time criterion, emphasis is given to:
  a. Making necessary decisions.
  b. Reducing waste.
  c. Increasing quantity flow.

_____ 31. When the deviation found from the control process is within the expected range, it is commonly termed standard deviation.

_____ 32. Of major significance in comprehending management in foreign countries is:
  a. Economic environment.
  b. Social environment.
  c. Political environment.
  d. All of these.
  e. None of these.

_____ 33. Many effective techniques used in present-day management were developed from foreign innovation.

_____ 34. Overlapping and related activities are eliminated by PERT.

_____ 35. Obsolescence among managers will no doubt become greater in the future.

_____ 36. The utilization of land, labor, and capital is a common measurement for evaluating the quality of management operating within a foreign country.

_____ 37. The role of the manager is narrowing.

_____ 38. Illustrative of a social consideration affecting management in a foreign country is the purchasing power of the population to absorb the output of the plant.

_____ 39. The overall or inclusive viewpoint of management has been made feasible by:
   a. Techniques developed by managers in foreign countries.
   b. Improved design of information for the manager.
   c. The systems approach and the computer.

_____ 40. The manager of the future will probably enjoy the availability of measurement about human behavior.

Answers to examinations

Examination 1: chapters 1–10
1. (d)
2. (F) International trade is an economic environmental factor.
3. (F)
4. (T) Management is both an art and a science.
5. (a2, b3, c1).
6. (F) Management is as old as civilization.
7. (F) There are currently many different approaches to management study.
8. The follow-up to see that events conform to plans. It is accomplished by evaluating performance and correcting for undesirable deviations.
9. (T) The functions of the management process identify what a management member does.
10. (T) Coordinating is the synchronization of individual efforts, with respect to amount, time, and direction, to achieve unity of effort toward a stated goal.
11. (b) A manager strives to make progress toward several objectives simultaneously.
12. (c) A satisficing objective is one of maintaining the status quo.
13. (T) The maximum or minimum is when the rate of change of the variable is equal to zero.
14. Any three of: (a) present mistakes and weak areas can be corrected, (b) assistance in making decisions about the right things at the right time are provided, (c) being able to cope better with future contingencies is gained, (d) possible future actions to take are indentified.
15. (e)
16. (c)
17. (F)
18. (b) Linear programming; but this approach can also be graphic or algebraic, wherein the matrix form is not used.
19. (a and b) Profits, dollars, labor-hours, machine-hours (any two of these).
    (c and d) Inventories, strike possibility, future tax situation (any two of these).
20. (b) For decision making to exist, there must always be two or more alternatives.
21. (F) Patterned decisions result from a follow-the-leader practice.
22. (a5, b4, c1).
23. (c, f, d, b, e, a, g, h).
24. (F) Better to work backwards from the objective.
25. (e)
26. Planning whereby the decision of what to do is made at each stage of a multistage planning project. Reevaluation of each remaining phase is done as advancement along the plan takes place.
27. (F) The planner must select what appears relevant to the task at hand.
28. (a3, b4, c5, d1, e2).
29. An assumption providing a background against which estimated events affecting the planning will take place.
30. (b) Planning is a trial-and-error, would-this-work type of activity.
31. (F) Performed as individual need seems to require.
32. (F) The hierarchy exists in all enterprises.
33. (c) Quantify objectives wherever possible to do so.
34. (F) The social system approach views management in this light.
35. (T) Planning is a fundamental function of management.
36. (b)
37. (F) All decisions have uncertainty about them, because they apply to the future.
38. (T) Speed is of the essence.
39. (F) "What if" questions are answered by planning.
40. A plan prescribing the exact chronological sequence of specific tasks required to achieve designated work.

Examination 2: chapters 11–19
1. (F) Much nonformal behavior contributes to efficiency and satisfaction of employees in unique ways.

2. (d)
3. (T)
4. (T)
5. The medium that serves to supply the how-to-do-it aspect for performing a particular task.
6. (T)
7. (F) The chief advantage is in thinking about organization as the chart is drawn. It shows the formal arrangement of activities, their relationships, and who performs what activities.
8. (d) In organizing, people are foremost in importance and interest.
9. (T) The structure is set and usually is not easily changed.
10. (F) The enterprise functions—producing, selling, and financing—are common.
11. (b)
12. (a3, b4, c2, d1).
13. The obligation of an individual to perform assigned activities to the best of one's ability.
14. (T) A manager delegating authority is not permanently released from that authority.
15. (F) Some cliques have desirable objectives from the viewpoint of the manager.
16. (b)
17. (F) The fusion theory deals with the individual using the organization to achieve personal goals and, in turn, the organization using the individual to further its goals.
18. (c) Common approaches include top–down, bottom–up, and following-the-work plans.
19. Any four of: (a) advisory staff, (b) service staff, (c) control staff, (d) functional staff, (e) assistant to, (f) general staff.
20. (b)
21. (T) Created by the superior getting helpers.
22. (T)
23. (d)
24. (a)
25. (a) Ability, (b) Personality, (c) Social.
26. (f) Participation gives recognition to the individual desire to feel important and to contribute to progress.
27. (e) It is called compulsory staff advice.
28. (b)
29. (a) 3, (b) 2, (c) 1.
30. (F) Adding the "reason why" adds to the order's believability.
31. (a)
32. (e) Adequate directing is appropriate for all employees.
33. (F) The manager should see that an order is carried out, or rescind it if not needed.
34. (F) Excess is common when the subject holds only casual interest to the receiver.
35. (g)
36. The difference between what the communicator believes has been communicated and what the receiver feels has been received.
37. (T)
38. (F)
39. (T)
40. (F) The believability of the grapevine is great, and it can be used advantageously by the manager.

Examination 3: chapters 20–27

1. (T)
2. (T)
3. (d)
4. (d)
5. (F) It also includes interviewing to discuss the evaluation with the incumbent.
6. (F)
7. (a) the leader-led relationship or confidence of followers in their leader, (b) the degree to which followers' jobs are task structured, and (c) the extent to which power is inherent in the leadership position.
8. (a2, b1, c3).
9. (c) Controlling is a means to an end, which is the objective.
10. (b)
11. (T)
12. (b)
13. The leader can project oneself mentally and emotionally into the position of the employee.
14. (a)
15. (a) Accomplishment, (b) Behavior.
16. (c)
17. Evaluating of performance and, if necessary, correcting what is being done to assure attainment of results according to plans.
18. (b)
19. (d) PPBS is planning, programming, budgeting system.
20. (F) Use value is important in value analysis.
21. Those cases in which the comparisons show deviations much greater than what can be considered normal.
22. (F) It corrects them before, such as in statistical quality control.
23. (F) Requires excessive paperwork.
24. (b)
25. (T)
26. (F) Statistical quality control is preventive as well as remedial.
27. (d)

Answers to examinations

28. (F) Controlling is interrelated to the other fundamental functions of management, especially planning.
29. (e)
30. (a)
31. (F) Standard deviation is a statistical term.
32. (d)
33. (T)
34. (F)
35. (T) Due primarily to the increasing knowledge availability and changes taking place.
36. (T)
37. (F) It is increasing and widening.
38. (F) This is an economic consideration.
39. (c)
40. (T) Judged on the progress being made and on predictions by behavioral scientists.

GLOSSARY-INDEX OF MANAGEMENT TERMS

This glossary-index provides assistance in the study of management and the use of this book. The numbers given refer to page numbers. Terms in common usage are defined. Also defined are terms without numbers where it is believed such terms will prove helpful to the student of management.

Differences of opinion exist regarding definitions of management terms. The definitions given here reflect the most prevalent views.

A

Accountability, the holding of a subordinate directly responsible for results, good or bad.

Actuating, starting and continuing action, called for by planning and organizing, by means of stimulating group members to perform their required tasks, 7

Administration, commonly used as a synonym for *management,* especially at the higher levels.

Advisory staff authority, 75

Appraising, a formal system of evaluating a manager's performance periodically and discussing the evaluation with him, 115
    basis for, 115
    and interviewing, 115
    properties of, 115

Art, the know-how to accomplish a desired result.

Assistant to, a title indicating that its possessor has been given functional staff authority, usually with limited duties and no major supervisory responsibilities, 75

Audit
    external, 135
    internal, 135
    management, 135

Authority, the power to exact action by others.
    centralized, 72
    computer, 76
    decentralized, 72
    delegation of, 70
    limits of, 73
    line, 74
    source of, 69
    span of, 71
    staff, 74
        types of, 75
    types of, 69

Automation, processing of work in which the transfer is made from one operation to another without human intervention.

B

Bayesian Formula, a mathematical theorem developed by Thomas Bayes to determine the probability of an event occurring, 27

Behavior
    formal, 55
    group, 61
    individual, 60
    informal, 63
    and leading, 109
    and motivating, 91
    nonformal, 55
    and organizing, 55
    and wants, 91, 93

Behavior sciences, sciences dealing with human behavior, especially psychology, sociology, and anthropology.

Bell-shaped curve, 126

Board of directors, a group elected by stockholders in order to supply general guidance for a corporation, 68

Break-even analysis, 134

Break-even point, the amount of sales by an enterprise that will produce just enough revenue to cover all costs but with no profit, 134

Budget, a plan in which data, arranged logically, represent expectancies for a stated period, 140
    committee, 140
    director of, 140
    formulation of, 140
    moving, 141
    summaries, 133
    time of, 141
    types of, 142

Buyer trading area, 125

C

Capital, working, the difference between current assets and current liabilities.

Cash flow, the amount of cash flowing in and out of a business in a given period.

Centralized authority, 72
Change in organization, 52, 85
Civil Rights Act of 1964, forbids in employment discrimination on account of sex, race, color, religion, or national origin, 82
Clique, in organization, 63
Coaching, 118
Command, the giving of orders.
Committees, 68
Communication
 classification of, 105
 defensiveness in, 104
 and gap in, 103
 and the grapevine, 105
 illusion of, 103
 meaning of, 103
 meeting for, 105
 and messages, 103
 and motivation, 104
 perceptions and, 103
 suggestions for effective, 105
 two-way, 104
 types of, 105
  illusion of, 103
  and understanding, 103
Completed staff work doctrine, 76
Compulsory staff advice, 75
Computers and controlling, 138
Control staff authority, 76
Controller, 138
Controlling, the evaluating of performance and, if necessary, correcting what is being done to assure attainment of results according to plan, 7, 119
 and audits, 135
 and break-even analysis, 134
 budgetary, 133, 140
 characteristics of, 122
 and computers, 138
 and the controller, 138
 of cost, 122, 129
  approaches in, 129
  classifications of, 129
  standard of, 129
 defined, 7, 119
 and distribution logistics, 139
 and exceptional cases, 121
 guides for, 122
 and human relations, 122
 and key areas, in overall, 137
 and key points, 121
 and organizational unit for, 138
 overall, 131
  media of, 132
 and PERT, 143
 and planning, 119
 and PPBS (planning, programming, budgeting system), 130
 and problems in management, 123
 process of, 119
 and profit and loss statement, 132
 of quality, 122, 125
  inspection, 125
   100% inspection, 125

Controlling—*Cont.*
  sample inspection, 125
  statistical quality control, 125
 of quantity, 122, 124
  of sales, 124
  units of, 124
 and ratios, 133
 and reports, 121, 133
 and return on investments, 133
 and rhochrematics, 139
 steps in, 119
 of time-use, 122, 127
  approaches in, 127
 and value analysis, 130
 and zero-base budgeting, 130
 and zero defect program, 130
Coordinating, synchronizing individual efforts with respect to their amount, time, and direction in order to obtain unified action toward a goal, 8
Cost
 factory, expenses incurred in manufacturing a product. Includes direct labor, direct material, and factory overhead costs, 129
 fixed, cost that tends to remain constant as total sales increase or decrease within reasonable limits, 134
 labor, wages and fringe benefits, 129
 standard, the normal or predetermined cost of a unit of production by calculation of the normal amount of expenditures for labor, material, and overhead costs, 129
 types of, 129
 unit, the cost of a single unit of a product, 129
 variable, cost that tends to vary with total sales increase or decrease, 134
Counseling, 118
Critical, path of PERT network, 144
Cultures, 11, 59

D

Decentralized authority, 72
Decision making, selecting an alternative from two or more alternatives to determine an opinion or course of action, 19
 and bases for, 21
  analysis, 21
  experience, 21
  experimentation, 21
  follow-the-leader, 21
  intuition, 21
  marginal analysis, 21
  psychology theory, 21
 decision tree and, 27
 defined, 19
 experience and, 21
 and experimentation, 21
 and follow-the-leader, 21
 group, 22
 individual, 22
 intangible factors in, 20
 intuition in, 21
 and marginal analysis, 21
 and probability, 27
 and psychological theory, 21

Glossary-index of management terms

Decision making—*Cont.*
  quantitative, 25–29
    gaming, 28
    linear programming, 29
    minimization in, 26
    model in, 26
    Monte Carlo, 28
    optimization in, 26
    queueing, 28
    simulation, 27
  Ringisei and, 147
  tangible factors in, 20
Decision tree, a diagrammatic chart showing the estimated outcomes of each decision in measurable terms, usually dollars, 27
Defensiveness, self-concept of preservation by the processor for his or her perceptions against those held by others, 104
Delegation of authority, the conferring of authority from one manager to another or from one organization unit to another in order to accomplish specific assignments, 70
Departmentation
  advantages of, 66
  approaches to, 64
  means of, 64
  suggestions for, 67
Developing managers, 115; *see also* Manager development
Direct cost, 129
Directing, getting members of a group to accomplish their tasks by integrating their efforts in the interest of individual and group objectives, 7, 97
  of group, 101
    dynamics of, 61
  and habit, 97
  and implementing, 98
  and information necessary for, 98
  and the order, 99
  and organizing, 99
  tools of, 100
Directors, board of, 68
Distribution logistics, 139
Dynamic programming, planning in which the effect of each decision at each stage in the plan is reevaluated so that improvement, if possible, takes place along the prescribed pathway, 47
Dynamics of organizing, 85
Dysfunction, condition bringing use of nonformal behavior to meet a situation. Exemplified by structure, work process specifications, and differentiation of decision making by different employees. Brings about modified behavior existing within formal organization, 55

E

Earthquake approach in reorganization, 88
Ego wants, 93
Empathy and leadership, 113
Environment of management
  economic influence of, 13
  external, 13

Environment of management—*Cont.*
  in foreign countries, 145
  government influence and, 13
  internal, 13
  social influence and, 13
  technological influence and, 13
Equal Employment Opportunity Commission (EEOC), a federal government agency which receives and initiates charges alleging violations of Title VII of Civil Rights Act of 1964, 82
Equity, commonly used with financing with reference to the sale of stock or its ownership.
Exceptional case, in controlling, the case where comparison between respective expectancy and performance shows a deviation much greater than what can be considered normal, 121

F

Feedback, the arrangement whereby the results of communication may be easily ascertained by those who issued it. Also used in reference to a machine sensing and correcting its own mistakes, 120
Fiedler, Dr. Fred
  dimensions of leadership, 110
  leadership theory, 110
Float, extra time available for a job in a PERT network because work cannot proceed further until another job requiring longer time is completed, 143
Foreign countries
  management in, 145
    cultural factors of, 147
    economical considerations of, 145
    evaluation of, 149
    political considerations of, 146
    Ringisei in, 147
    social considerations of, 145
    talent of, 149
  managers operating in, 149
    characteristics of, 149
Formal behavior, 55
Formal organization, the organization resulting from use of prescribed communication channels, standardized methods, clearly defined jobs, and stated chains of command, 55
Fringe benefits, insurance plans, pensions, vacations, and similar benefits.
Functional staff authority, 76
Fundamental functions of management, the activities that make up the process of management, 5
Fusion theory of organization, 52
Future and management, 151; *see also* Management, of the future

G

Gaming, a technique emphasizing competition and measurable data in which objectives are sought amid the counter-moves by competitive players, 28
General staff authority, 77
Grapevine, in communication, 105

Group
  behavior, 61
    and organization, 62
  dynamics, the interactions among a group's members, 61
  manager coping with, 62
  needs, satisfied by leader, 61
Growth of organization, 86

H

Herzberg, Dr. Frederick, 93
Hierarchy of objectives, the integrated pattern of objectives existing within an enterprise from the top to the bottom level, 18
Horizontal growth of organization, 86
Human behavior approach to management, 3
Human relations
  and management of future, 152
  and role playing, 117

I

Illusion of communication, believing that mutual understanding has taken place because one person has spoken or written to another, 103
Image, company, the public's general impression of a company.
In-basket exercises, 117
Indirect cost, 129
Infiltration approach to organization change, 88
Informal groups, 63
  clique, 63
Informal organization, an organization of members with common social interests, not prescribed by formal organization, and existing as an addition to the formal organization, 63
Information
  for directing, 98
  and management of future, 152
  Innovating, developing new ideas or combining new thoughts with old ones for products or processes. Also used to designate the stimulation of others to develop and apply new ideas in their work, 8
    as function of management, 8
    and management of the future, 153
Instructions and directing, 100
Interaction, reciprocal reactions of people in a group to variables in a situation or to each other.
Inventory, stocks on hand including any one or all of the following: raw materials, work in process, and finished goods.

J

Job content, 93
Job context, 93
Job description, the objectives, authority and responsibility, and relationships with others required by the person occupying a specific position, 79
Job enlargement, 66
Job enrichment, 94

Job evaluation, a systematic determination of the proper relationships among wages paid for various jobs within an enterprise.
Job rotation, 117
Junior boards, 117

K

Key areas, in overall controlling, 137
Key points, in controlling, 121

L

Labor cost, 129
Leadership
  action of, 108
  defined, 108
  dimensions of, 110
  Fiedler's theory of, 110
  and followers, 111
  qualifications for, 112
  research on, 112
  skills for, 109
  types of, 110
  work-centered, 111
  worker-centered, 111
Leverage, concerns the advantage of a manager operating with a significant ratio of liabilities to gross assets.
Linear programming, a mathematical technique for determining either optimization or minimization for problems where the variables are related linearly, i.e., in straight-line relationships, 29

M

McGregor, Professor, 93
Make-or-buy decision, choice between producing a part or product by use of the company's own plant or buying it from an outside supplier.
Management
  actuating, 7
  age of, 2
  approaches, 3
  art, 1
  attributes, 1
  audit, 135
  as basic resource, 153
  controlling, 7
  coordinating, 8
  development, 115; *see also* **Manager,** development
  directing, 7, 97
  and environment, 13
  functions, 5
    interrelation of, 9
  of the future
    characteristics of, 151
    and human relations, 152
    and information, 152
    and innovation, 153
    and manager's education, 153
    and obsolescence of managers, 151
  to a group, 1
  innovating, 8
  meaning of, 1

Glossary-index of management terms

Management—*Cont.*
  motivating, 7
  by objective, 18, 95
  organizing, 7
  philosophy, 11
  planning, 5
  process, 3, 9
    advantages of, 9
  representing, 8
  science, 1
  staffing, 7, 78
  thought; *see* Schools of management thought
  values, 11

Management prerogative, the right of a manager to decide certain issues if he is to manage effectively.

Manager
  appraisals of, 115
  future education of, 153
  and group, 61
  job description for job of, 79
  and multiplier, 95
  obsolescence, 151
  qualifications of, 81
  recruitment of, 82
  selection of, 83
  sources for, 83
  specifications for, 81

Manager development
  characteristics of, 116
  importance of, 115
  measurement of, 118
  media of, 117
  objectives of, 116
  trends in, 116

Manning the organization, 78

Marginal analysis, the determination of the point at which the cost of an extra unit of input will exactly pay for itself, 21

Marketing trading area, 125

Material cost, 129

Matrix, departmentation, 65

Measurement of management development, 118

Merit rating, formal periodic evaluating of employee's performance of his job.

Method, a plan prescribing the details of how a specific task is to be done, 43

Minimization, the attainment of the least quantity possible under the existent relationships of variables, objectives, and constraints of a problem, 26

Model, mathematical, an abstraction in which the relationships existing among the variables and the objective are expressed in mathematical terms, 26

Monte Carlo, a quantitative technique used for predicting the timing or frequency of events within a specific period, 28

Motion study, analysis of motions performed and determination of improvements so that work can be accomplished more efficiently, 43

Motivation
  and achievement, 95
  approaches to, 91
  and communication, 104

Motivation—*Cont.*
  defined, 91
  and group behavior, 92
  group influence in, 92
  and growth, 95
  and job content, 93
  and job context, 93
  and management by objectives, 18, 95
  means to, 91
  and multiplier manager, 95
  and participation, 95
  and recognition, 95
  and responsibility, 95
  and supervision, 95
  and wants, 93

Multiplier manager, 95

N

Neoclassical theory of organization, 52

Nonformal behavior, behavior that is not formally intended, but exists *out of,* not in addition to (informal behavior), the formal behavior prescribed by formal organization, 55

Nonlinear programming, a mathematical technique used when some of the variables in the mathematical model are not linear, i.e., mathematically are of squared power (X^2) or higher.

Numerical control, direction of machine by tape or punched card.

O

Objectives
  characteristics, 15
  defined, 15
  determined by, 16
  harmonized, 17
  hierarchy of, 18
  importance, 15
  long-range, 15
  management by, 18
  multi-, 16
  quantified, 15
  and profits, 15
  satisficing, 17
  types of, 17

Obsolescence of managers, 151

On-the-job satisfaction, 58

One hundred per cent inspection, 125

Operational approach to management, 3

Optimization, the attainment of the greatest quantity possible under the existent relationships of variables, objectives, and constraints of the problem, 26

Order and directing, 99

Organization, formal, the official relationships of positions or of people occupying them shown by the organization chart and embodied in the formal job descriptions, 55

Organization, informal, the interpersonal relationships of an organization which are not shown by the formal organization and may or may not be consistent with it, 63

178 Glossary-index of management terms

Organization control unit, 138

Organizing, the grouping of component activities, assigning each grouping to a manager, and establishing authority relationships among the groupings, 7
and authority, 69; *see also* **Authority**
behavior from, 55
and board of directors, 68
and change, 52, 85
   growth, 86
   steps in, 88
   when to make, 78
chart, 56
and clique, 63
and committees, 68
components of, 53
and departmentation, 64
and dynamics, 85
   growth, 86
and dysfunctions, 55
and formal organization, 55
and fusion theory, 52
and informal
   groups, 63
   organization, 63
manuals, 56
and neoclassical theory, 52
and nonformal organization, 55
and personal implication, 58
and project, 65
and quantitative theory, 52
and role in, 60
and social influences, 59
and staffing the organization, 78
and structure, 55
   flat, 71
   steep, 72
and synergism, 51
and systems theory, 52
and task teams, 65
theories, 52
and work units, 53

Overall controls, 131
media of, 132

Overhead cost, 129

P

Participation, and motivation, 95

Payout period, the time required for an investment of a new machine or piece of equipment to pay for itself, 41

Performance appraisal, formal periodic evaluating of employee's performance of his job.

PERT
critical path of, 144
defined, 143
network, 143

Philosophy of management, 11
advantages of having, 11
meaning of, 11
and values, 12

Planning, determining what work must be done to accomplish stated goals, 5, 30
and achievement, 32
advantages of, 33
and constraints, 35
and controlling, 119
defined, 30
department of, 48
disadvantages of, 33
and dynamic programming, 47
and forecasting, 35
goals of, 30
implementation of, 45
importance of, 30
and information, 37
organization for, 48
participation in, 48
performance of, 30, 48
phases of, 31
and premises, 35
for profit, 40
programming, budget system (PPBS), 130
steps in, 46
strategic, 38
   goals of, 38
   topics of, 38
and strategies, 38
tactical, 39
timing of, 31
and types of plans, 40, 42
   budget, 43
   method, 43
   objective, 42
   policy, 42
   procedure, 43
   program, 43
   standard, 43
   techno-factor, 43
and "what if" questions, 33

Policy, statement setting forth elastic and comprehensive boundaries within which managerial action will take place, 42

PPBS (planning, programming, budgeting system), 130

Probability
meaning, 27
use in decision making, 27

Procedure, a type of plan prescribing the exact chronological sequence of specific tasks required to achieve designated work, 43

Process of management, 3, 5

Productivity, output per man-hour.

Profit and loss statement, 132

Profit planning, 40

Program, a comprehensive plan, frequently inclusive of future uses of different resources of an enterprise, expressed in an integrated format, 43

Programmed instructions, 117

Project organization, 65

Protestant ethic, the viewpoint that hard work, individual effort, and thrift are qualities to be admired.

Psychological wants, 93

Q

Quality control, 125
  statistical, 126
    bell-shaped curve, 126
    quality control chart, 126
    standard deviation in, 126
Quantitative approach to management, 3, 25–29
Quantitative theory of organization, 52
Quantity control, 124
Queueing, the quantitative approach to determine the facilities to be provided when the need for them varies at random, 28

R

Ratio analysis, means of evaluating performance of an enterprise by examining the relationships between various figures such as net sales to working capital, 133
Ratios, for overall control, 133
Recruitment of managers, 82
Reorganization, 88
  steps in, 88
  when to, 88
Representing, serving officially an enterprise in its dealings with outside groups, 8
Responsibility, the obligation of an individual to perform assigned duties to the best of his ability, 70
Return on investment, 133
Return-on-manager time criterion, 127
Rhochrematics, 139
Ringisei, "reverential inquiry about superior's intention"
  advantages, 147
  application of, 147
  disadvantages, 148
  practiced in Japanese management, 147
Role, in organizing, 60
Role playing, acting or assuming a role of a situation, frequently for purposes of human relations training, 117

S

Safety wants, 93
Sales potential, 125
Sample inspection, 125
Satisfactions
  off the job, 58
  on the job, 58
Satisficing objective, one that points out a goal good enough from all viewpoints, rather than seeking a better objective, 17
Science, organized body of knowledge.
Schools of management thought, 3
  human behavior, 3
  operational, 3
  process, 3
  quantitative, 3
  social systems, 3
  systems, 3

Selection of manager, 83
Self-fulfillment wants, 93
Selling cost, 129
Seniority, length of service.
Service staff authority, 76
Simulation, the trying out of various alternatives and values of variables to determine what results they bring about. A model is used and work is expedited by a computer, 27
Social deviant, one who goes contrary to the mores of those surrounding him, 149
Social ethic, the concept that man is primarily a group member and should subordinate his individuality to the group mores, 51
Social implications of organizing, 61
Social responsibilities of management, those managerial responsibilities to employees, the local community the state, the nation, and the human race, 3, 13
Social systems approach to management, 3
Social wants, 93
Span of authority, the number of subordinates that report to a manager, 71
Staff authority, types of, 74
Staff work, completed, 76
Staffing, recruiting, selecting, promoting, transferring, and retiring of management members, 7, 78
Standard, a norm or expectancy used to evaluate performance, 43
Standard cost, 129
Standard deviation, 126
Statistical quality control, 125
Strategic planning, answers the question, "Where should we (managers of an enterprise) be going?" 38
  advantages of, 38
  goals of, 38
Strategy, the choice of means by which the enterprise's resources may be employed to reach best the intended goals, 38
  examples, 38
Supervision, and motivation, 95
Synergism, the action of separate but related parts producing a sum greater than its components. It is sought for in organizing, 51
System, assemblage of two or more functions related in some way so that an action in one brings about reaction in the other or others, 3
Systems approach to management, 3
Systems theory of organization, 52

T

Task-teams, 65
Techno-factor, 43
Theory X, 93
Theory Y, 93
Time study, the determination of the time necessary to perform a task. Several different methods are available.

180 Glossary-index of management terms

U

Unit cost, 129

V

Value analysis, efforts to improve the relationship of present worth to product cost, 130
Values in management
  defined, 11
  importance in management, 11
  use of, 12
Vertical growth of organization, 86

W

Wants of managers, 93
Work center leadership, 111
Worker centered leadership, 111
Working capital, the difference between current assets and current liabilities.

Z

Zero-base budgeting, 130
Zero defect program, planned efforts emphasizing the importance and self-will of personnel to give high quality performance, 130